GIFTED YOUNG CHILDREN

A guide for teachers and parents

2nd edition

Dedication

*For Murray (1931–1998)
who, like many of the gifted,
did not recognise his multiple special talents.*

GIFTED YOUNG CHILDREN

A guide for teachers and parents

2nd edition

Louise Porter

Open University Press

Open University Press
McGraw-Hill Education
McGraw-Hill House
Shoppenhangers Road
Maidenhead
Berkshire
England
SL6 2QL

email: enquiries@openup.co.uk
world wide web: www.openup.co.uk

and Two Penn Plaza, New York, NY 10121-2289, USA

First published 2005

A catalogue record of this book is available from the British Library

ISBN 0335217729 (pb)

Library of Congress Cataloguing-in-Publication Data
CIP data applied for

ABOUT THE AUTHOR

Dr Louise Porter PhD, MA(Hons), M. Gifted Ed, Dip. Ed is a child psychologist and trained teacher with 25 years' experience working with young children, their parents and educators. She is an adjunct senior lecturer in Education at Flinders University, South Australia, and author and editor of several books including *Educating Young Children with Special Needs* and *Behaviour in Schools*.

CONTENTS

About the author   v
Figures, tables and boxes   xi

Part I   Understanding giftedness

1   **Signs of gifted development in young children**   3
    Introduction   3
    Definition of giftedness and talent   4
    Difficulty of identifying giftedness in young children   4
    Common signs of advanced development in young children   5
    Exceptionally gifted children   23
    Prodigies   25
    Conclusion   26
    Suggested further reading   26

2   **Transforming giftedness into talent**   27
    Introduction   27
    The nature of giftedness   28
    Transformation of giftedness into talent: A developmental model   38
    Conclusion   43
    Suggested further reading   44

Part II   Emotional needs of gifted children

3   **Emotional issues for gifted children**   47
    The emotional adjustment of gifted children   47
    Reasons for the persistence of myths about gifted children's
    emotional status   55
    A model of emotional needs   60

Conclusion 62
Suggested further reading 63

4 **Self-esteem** **64**
Introduction 64
The nature of self-esteem 64
Self-esteem issues for gifted children 66
Causes of low self-esteem 72
Routes to healthy self-esteem 73
Conclusion 77
Suggested further reading 77

5 **Social needs** **78**
Introduction 78
Friendships 78
Social issues for gifted children 79
Factors influencing gifted children's social adjustment 84
Methods to promote social adjustment 86
Conclusion 90
Suggested further reading 90

6 **Autonomy** **91**
Introduction 91
Autonomy issues for gifted children 92
Ways to promote autonomy 95
Conclusion 102
Suggested further reading 103

Part III Educational provisions

7 **A rationale for gifted education** **107**
Attitudes to giftedness 107
A rationale for gifted education for the young 114
The range of gifted education provisions 115
Conclusion 119
Suggested further reading 119

8 **Assessing developmental advances in young children** **121**
Introduction 121
Some key terms 122
Principles of assessment 122
The assessment process 126
Assessment measures 128
Reasons for discrepancies between assessments 134
Testing for exceptional levels of giftedness 139

Conclusion 140
Suggested further reading 140

9 Meeting gifted young children's learning needs 141
Introduction 141
Aims of early childhood programs 142
Educational challenges for gifted young children 143
Curriculum differentiation 145
Parent collaboration 161
Conclusion 163
Suggested further reading 164

10 Disadvantaged gifted children 165
Introduction 165
Gender and giftedness 165
Gifted children from minority cultures 169
Children in poverty 175
Rural children 177
Conclusion 178
Suggested further reading 179

11 Gifted children with learning disabilities 180
Introduction 180
Specific learning disabilities 180
Central auditory processing disorder 184
Sensory integration difficulties 185
The autism spectrum disorders 186
The attention deficit disorders 186
Gifted underachievers 190
Programming for gifted children with learning difficulties 193
Conclusion 197
Suggested further reading 197

12 Formulating a policy about gifted learners 199
Introduction 199
Benefits of formal policies 199
Components of a policy 200
Conclusion 204
Suggested further reading 205

13 Parenting gifted children 206
Introduction 206
Personal implications for parents 206
Parenting issues 208

Schooling options   214
Advocating for gifted children within educational settings   217
Information required by gifted children   219
Conclusion   222
Suggested further reading   223

Bibliography   224

Index   263

FIGURES, TABLES AND BOXES

Figures

2.1 Correlation between ability levels and performance quality 29
2.2 A hierarchy of intellectual skills 35
2.3 A model of the transformation of giftedness into talent 39
3.1 Hypothesised curvilinear relationship between IQ and emotional adjustment 59
3.2 A model of individuals' needs 61
4.1 Self-esteem as the overlap between the self-concept and ideal self 65
8.1 An assessment-by-provision model for the recognition of advanced development in young children 127
8.2 The distribution of abilities within a population 136
13.1 Emotional maturity of gifted children 210

Tables

1.1 Levels of giftedness 24
6.1 Common dysfunctional thinking patterns of children 98
9.1 Young children's modes of learning and corresponding modes of teaching 156
9.2 Common and differentiated features of curricula for young children 162

Boxes

1.1 Summary of common indicators of advanced development in young children 8

3.1   Positive and dysfunctional expressions of some
       common emotional characteristics of gifted children   58
4.1   Characteristics of individuals with low versus healthy
       self-esteem   66
8.1   Advantages and disadvantages of IQ tests for gifted learners 135
8.2   Some interpretive statistics   137
9.1   Criteria for early entry to school or grade skipping   154
10.1   Gender-based life patterns   170
10.2   Measures to encourage high achievement in girls and boys   171
11.1   Characteristics of gifted children with specific learning
       disabilities   183
11.2   Distinctions between giftedness and ADHD   187

UNDERSTANDING
GIFTEDNESS

Part I

SIGNS OF GIFTED DEVELOPMENT
IN YOUNG CHILDREN one

The gifts of nature are infinite in their variety, and mind differs from mind almost as much as body from body. (Quintilian, in Laycock 1979: 59)

Introduction

Let's say that you are a preschool teacher with a four-year-old student who has been attending your centre for two months. Even after this length of time, she still seems unable to separate comfortably from her mother, even with your patient guidance. She becomes distressed and clingy and, long after her mother leaves, remains unsettled and forlorn. When she does play, you observe the child hanging back during activities, either not becoming engaged or flitting from one activity to another without becoming engrossed in any. She does not make friends with any of the other children. She avoids drawing and painting activities and does not appear to enjoy sand play or many other activities. If permitted, she will accompany the adults at preschool, talking with them incessantly. Their suggestions to play with the other children go unheeded, and sometimes they almost have to be rude to get her to leave them to their other duties. In your conversations with her mother, she reports that her daughter used to dress herself independently at the age of two, but that it is a running battle most mornings to get her to cooperate with dressing now.

You could be forgiven for thinking that a child such as this has delayed development. That is certainly a possibility. But it is also possible that the child is gifted. This chapter will describe how this pattern of behaviour can emerge with gifted children.

Definition of giftedness and talent

In the past, there was a hierarchical view of giftedness and talent which upheld that *giftedness* referred to academic skills while *talent* referred to non-academic abilities—for example, in the fine arts. But this hierarchy cannot stand up to scrutiny: our abilities define who we are as people, so artistic expression is as central to the artist's personhood as academic achievement is to the intellectual. It is hoped that both will be a means for self-fulfilment, so one talent simply cannot be of less value than the other.

Another way of seeing giftedness has been as a general or pervasive trait, whereas talent is in a specific field. This too seems inadequate. So instead—and at the risk of over-simplification—I adopt Gagne's (1995, 2003) distinction between giftedness as exceptional innate ability (the potential to excel) and talent as the expression of that potential (that is, exceptional performances in any field or fields). The advantage of this distinction is that it allows us to include within the gifted population those whose circumstances disadvantage them educationally, and so who do not display exceptional skills in everyday settings. This can include gifted learners who also have a disability; those living in poverty; children for whom English is a second language; and boys or girls who, for reasons of their gender, are held back from achieving.

Difficulty of identifying giftedness in young children

Many parents and professionals are unwilling to label children—and young children in particular—as gifted. Even when they *are* willing to identify gifted-ness in very young children, accurate assessment remains a difficult task. Some young children are not identified as being gifted for the following reasons.

- Children can be gifted in a range of domains, and our ability to identify giftedness is likely to be better in some areas than in others (Robinson 1987). For instance, a verbally talented child can be more obvious than a child with advanced mathematical or creative abilities.
- The detailed knowledge of child development which is the hallmark of early childhood care and education can unwittingly set a ceiling on our expectations of children, with the result that we do not offer sufficient challenge either to keep gifted children stimulated or to allow them to demonstrate their advanced skills (Shaklee 1992).
- Some have not yet had experiences in the domain in which they might later develop special talents (Fatouros 1986).
- Some young children's advanced skills are hidden by their as yet immature social or emotional behaviours (Kitano 1990a) or their in-ability to direct their own learning: they might not concentrate for long enough to display their talents, for example (White 1985).

- The behaviour of young children often changes markedly in various environments, giving observers in different settings an inconsistent view of their skills (Fatouros 1986).
- Although it is crucial that teachers and caregivers be aware that talent can occur in any domain, there is a risk of overdifferentiation — that is, adults may not expect children who are talented in one domain (such as verbal skills) to be talented in another domain (e.g. the arts) as well, and so might fail to identify a child's multiple talents (Guskin et al. 1988).

The variation in the outward behaviours of young gifted children makes it difficult to discriminate giftedness from other conditions. However, guided by the maxim gleaned from the child protection literature — that 'I wouldn't have seen it if I hadn't believed it' — once aware of the characteristics associated with advanced development, parents and educators will be more able to recognise gifted learners.

Common signs of advanced development in young children

In this section, I describe a range of characteristics that children with advanced development might display during their early childhood years. Such lists are a mixed blessing, however. They can sensitise adults to the possibility of advanced development; but, at the same time, they can give a false impression that all gifted children are the same. This is as patently untrue for gifted children as it is for any group of children, as the 'gifted' label spans a broad range of ability from mild to exceptional giftedness, and because advancement can occur in any domain of human endeavour. Even two intellectually gifted children with similar IQs (for want of a better measure) will differ in their stronger and weaker skill domains, in how evenly their talents are spread across domains and in the extent to which their environment adequately meets their needs, with resulting implications for their emotional and social behaviours.

Also, what we know about the characteristics of gifted children could be inaccurate, because research into gifted children is plagued by a problem of the selection of subjects. This comes about because, in order to study gifted students, researchers have to be able to locate them. The most sound way to do so would be to test huge numbers of students on a group IQ measure and then include in a study those who achieved at high levels on the test. However, only 3–5 per cent of the student population will achieve at significantly higher levels; so 95–97 per cent of students have been tested unnecessarily — at some disruption to their own lives, and at great cost to the investigators.

Therefore, the more common methods for locating gifted subjects are to involve students who have already been identified as gifted, or simply to go to gifted programs, where these students are in attendance. The first method could taint your subject group in that children are often identified as gifted only in response to parental or teacher concerns about their performance at school, or some emotional or social difficulties that they are experiencing. This group might not be typical of all gifted children: others may be equally gifted but are overlooked because they do not present with problems. The upshot is that the researchers arrive at a group of subjects who are not typical of the entire gifted population.

The alternative method—researching those who attend gifted programs—could result in a group that has more than the usual problems (which, as with the group above, caused the children to be identified as gifted in the first place); or fewer than the usual problems, because the gifted program is meeting their academic, emotional and social needs. Furthermore, attendance at such programs tends to rely on teacher nominations of gifted children, leading to a disproportionately strong representation of middle-class children and to the inclusion of only those children who are academically well adjusted while under-representing children who are experiencing school-based difficulties (Gross 2004; Hastorf 1997; Roedell et al. 1980).

This fundamental difficulty of sampling is compounded when the children about whom we read are those who have consulted psychologists, as *all* of these will have problems at the time. So statements from clinical psychologists about the needs of their clients are not about the needs of gifted children in general: we have no way of knowing how many gifted children never need to see psychologists.

Therefore, we must be cautious about descriptions of gifted children. It is also important to reiterate that children who are gifted can be so in one developmental domain, or across many. Few will be gifted at everything. Each section in this chapter, then, will describe the characteristics of children who are advanced in that particular domain; self-evidently, those who are gifted in more than one area will display traits from each.

Intellectual giftedness

When children are intellectually gifted, their advanced cognitive skills can be evident even from birth, when many are already keen observers of their environment. Even as babies, they play an active role in eliciting stimulation from their physical and social environments (Damiani 1997; Morelock & Morrison 1996).

The defining characteristic of giftedness is that the children acquire developmental skills at least one-third earlier than their age mates. However, some will acquire their first milestones at the same age as average learners, but thereafter will progress more quickly than usual and achieve each subsequent milestone sooner.

Early intellectual skills are facilitated by increased input from the environment and also provoke more input. When the children are mobile early, acquire reading early or can converse readily, they can access knowledge which is not typically available to children of their age.

They can benefit from environmental stimulation partly because of an efficient memory. It appears that gifted learners store *more* information in their memory; *organise* it well, ensuring that they 'park' a memory near other related information, which makes it easier to retrieve later; and can *access* a wide range of relevant information efficiently (Borkowski & Peck 1986; Haensly & Reynolds 1989; Perleth et al. 1993; Rabinowitz & Glaser 1985). Having accessed many related facts, they can hold these in the forefront of their mind—that is, manipulate many facts within their working memory. They can also *scan* their memory efficiently to search for relevant information and possible solutions (Borkowski & Peck 1986; Carr et al. 1996; Risemberg & Zimmerman 1992). This function is called *metamemory* and may be a better predictor of achievement than IQ (Carr & Borkowski 1987). As a result of their proficiency with metacognitive skills, gifted learners characteristically have quick and accurate recall, allowing them to show competence in a skill they were taught some time ago.

Nevertheless, while a good memory is necessary for advanced development, on its own it is not sufficient to produce giftedness. *That* level of performance also requires superior metacognitive skills, which are the strategies we use to monitor our own thinking, rather like the conductor regulating the performance of the orchestra. These metacognitive skills comprise three aspects: *awareness* of our thinking processes; *knowledge* about our abilities, how to use learning strategies, and when and why to use them; and *control* over the planning, monitoring and evaluation processes used to regulate our thinking (Schraw & Graham 1997).

Gifted learners have superior metacognitive knowledge and tend to employ metacognitive strategies earlier than average learners (Hannah & Shore 1995; Schwanenflugel et al. 1997). These skills are listed in Box 1.1. Their superior metacognitive skills are displayed mainly when the children are interested in a task, however (Kanevsky 1992). Fatigue can also influence their use of metacognitive skills and can set in more noticeably in young, high-ability children, owing to the fact that they have invested so much energy in the task.

Intellectually gifted children's facility with memory and metacognitive control permit quick learning, complex problem solving and the abilities to monitor the effects of their actions and adjust their actions as necessary (Rabinowitz & Glaser 1985; Shore & Dover 1987). This is especially crucial when tasks are new and challenging (Carr et al. 1996): it leaves processing capacity available for carrying out higher-order tasks, such as comprehending the meaning of a passage in a book rather than simply deciphering the words (Jackson & Butterfield 1986).

The outcome is that gifted learners develop wider and deeper knowledge than average learners (Kitano 1985) and can often apply this information to abstract or complex concepts—such as death or time—much earlier than their age mates. However, they cannot necessarily cope emotionally with the degree of information which they crave intellectually.

Box 1.1 Summary of common indicators of advanced development in young children

Cognitive (thinking) skills

Children who are intellectually gifted display many of the following features:

- early achievement of developmental milestones (at least one-third sooner);
- quick learning;
- keen observation of the environment;
- active in eliciting stimulation from the environment;
- quick and accurate recall;
- recall of skills and information introduced some time ago;
- deeper knowledge than other children;
- understanding of abstract concepts (e.g. death or time).

Academic giftedness

Children who are intellectually *and* academically gifted might:

- read, write or use numbers in advanced ways;
- write words other than their own name prior to school entry;
- show advanced preferences for books and films (unless too sensitive to older themes).

Learning style

Many gifted children not only achieve more than average, they also approach tasks with a sophisticated style. However, their application to tasks is responsive to fatigue, discouragement (immediate or long term) and the degree of challenge. Nevertheless, when highly achieving, they display:

- alertness;
- responsivity to novel stimuli;
- speed and efficiency of information processing;
- willingness to reflect when necessary in order to maintain accuracy;
- preference for challenge and complexity;
- openness to new ideas and experiences;
- motivation and curiosity in a search for understanding;
- wide-ranging interests;

- an intense focus on, or the ability to immerse themselves in, an area of interest in order to achieve a depth of understanding;
- longer than usual concentration span on challenging topics of interest (but may 'flit' from one activity to another if activities are not challenging enough);
- early use of metacognitive skills to manage their own thinking processes;
- internal locus of control;
- independence at challenging, non-routine tasks;
- willingness to take risks;
- perseverance in the face of obstacles;
- tolerance of ambiguity.

Creative thinking style

Children who are intellectually *and* creatively gifted might display the following learning styles, applying these across domains or in a single domain in which they excel:

- imagination;
- creative problem solving;
- use of intuition (that is, allowing some of their thinking to occur at a preconscious level);
- fluency, which reflects an ability to employ a range or quantity of ideas;
- flexibility, which refers both to the quality of ideas brought to bear on the problem and to skill at adapting their learning style to the task demands and goals;
- being nonconforming and rejecting limits.

Auditory-sequential style

Children who learn by listening and ordering ideas often:

- learn sequentially, one idea at a time;
- are analytical—that is, able to break problems down into their parts;
- attend well to details;
- learn well from verbal instructions;
- are able to carry out instructions to do several things in succession;
- think logically;
- have good planning skills;
- are organised;
- are less impulsive than age mates;
- have a clear understanding of cause and effect;
- use rehearsal to remember;

- once in school, achieve reasonably consistent grades across all subject areas.

Visual-spatial (or holistic) style

Children who learn by forming visual images of concepts may be later than others to excel, but nevertheless:

- learn concepts all at once;
- synthesise ideas—that is, put them together;
- see the big picture and, correspondingly, may miss details;
- learn intuitively;
- have what can only be termed 'quirky' organisational systems;
- learn instantly and so do not benefit from rehearsal or repetition;
- once in school, obtain uneven grades across subject areas.

Speech and language skills

Intellectually gifted children with advanced verbal skills often show:

- early comprehension;
- advanced speech in terms of vocabulary, grammar and clear articulation;
- use of metaphors and analogies;
- ability to make up songs or stories spontaneously;
- ability to modify language for less mature children;
- use of language for a real exchange of ideas and information at an early age;
- a sophisticated sense of humour.

Motor abilities

Many intellectually gifted children have fine motor skills that lag behind their intellectual level. On the other hand, those who are gifted in the motor domain can show a range of the following characteristics:

- early motor development, particularly in skills that are under cognitive control such as balance;
- ability to locate themselves within the environment;
- early awareness of left and right;
- facility at putting together new or difficult puzzles;
- ability to take apart and reassemble objects with unusual skill;
- ability to make interesting shapes or patterns with objects;
- advanced drawing or handwriting;
- high levels of physical energy.

Artistic expression

Although most young children may not yet have been exposed to the arts in any formal way and so may not be showing artistic talent, some display early signs of instinctive art skill, such as:

- superior visual memory;
- engaging with an imaginary playmate in elaborate conversations and games;
- assigning elaborate characters to dolls or teddies;
- creating and performing in plays;
- enjoyment of drama, role playing;
- advanced skill at drawing, painting or other artistic modalities.

Musical skills

Musical giftedness may be among the earliest to emerge—by the age of one year—although very young children's motor ability can block their musical performance. Musically gifted children:

- are enthralled by musical sounds;
- have a deep appreciation and understanding of music (with or without musical performance);
- are sensitive to musical structure—tonality, key, harmony and rhythm;
- appreciate the expressive properties of music—timbre, loudness, articulation and phrasing;
- have a strong musical memory that permits them to recall music and play it back later either by singing or through an instrument.

Social skills

Intellectually and verbally advanced young children typically are also advanced in their social skills, showing some of the following characteristics:

- highly developed empathy for others;
- less egocentricity: they can deduce the cause of others' emotions;
- advanced play interests;
- early ability to play games with rules;
- early ability to form close friendships;
- seeking out older children or adults for companionship;
- withdrawing to solitary play if intellectual peers are not available;
- often being sought out by other children for their play ideas and sense of fairness;
- leadership skills;

- early development of moral reasoning and judgment;
- early interest in social issues involving injustices.

Emotional and behavioural characteristics

Some intellectually gifted children are emotionally gifted as well. These children might display:

- emotional sensitivity, intensity and responsiveness;
- for some, early existential awareness;
- early development of fears;
- early development of self-concept and awareness of being different;
- self-confidence in their strong domains;
- perfectionism, in the sense of having high standards;
- over-sensitivity to criticism;
- frustration, which can lead to emotional or behavioural outbursts;
- acceptance of responsibility usually given only to older children;
- nonconformity.

Sources: Amabile 1990; Anderson 1992; Baska 1989; Borkowski & Peck 1986; Chamrad & Robinson 1986; Chan 1996; Cheng 1993; Clark 2002; Damiani 1997; Davis & Rimm 2004; Delisle 1992; Ebert 1994; Gallagher & Gallagher 1994; Gross 2004; Haensly & Reynolds 1989; Haensly et al. 1986; Hodge 2004; Jackson 1992; Jackson & Butterfield 1986; Kanevsky 1992; Kitano 1985, 1990a; Klein 1992; Knight 1995; Lewis & Louis 1991; Lovecky 1994a, 1994b; McClelland et al. 1991; Mares 1991; Maxwell 1998; Meador 1996; Mendaglio 1994; Miller et al. 1994; Moltzen 2004a; Morelock 1996; Morelock & Morrison 1996; Moss 1990, 1992; Parker & Adkins 1995; Parker & Mills 1996; Perleth et al. 1993; Piirto 1999; Rabinowitz & Glaser 1985; Renzulli 1986; Roedell et al. 1980; Runco 1993; Shore & Dover 1987; Silverman 1993b, 2002; Smutny et al. 1989; Sternberg 1988; Sternberg & Lubart 1991, 1992; Tannenbaum 1983, 1992, 2003; Tardif & Sternberg 1988; Whitmore 1980; Winner 1996; Winner & Martino 2000, 2003.

Academic giftedness

Intellectually gifted children are not necessarily academically gifted. Few are early readers (Perleth et al. 1993; Robinson 1993): if young children are reading prior to school age without structured teaching, this usually means that they are exceptionally gifted (Gross 1999, 2004). Similarly, although some will relate to numbers in an advanced way, many do not. And their drawing and handwriting skills can be average.

This lack of advancement in academic domains is understandable when we recognise that there are many ways to be intellectually bright other than in reading, writing and maths skills: while some intellectually gifted children will be both intellectually and academically gifted, others will perform at average levels academically. This accounts for some instances of disagreement between parents and teachers about whether a child is or is not gifted, as discussed in Chapter 8.

If reading early, young gifted children can have advanced preferences for books and films, although their emotional sensitivity causes many to avoid the themes in books or videos intended for older children. At the same time, some children who are reading early disguise this at school. Some might think that they are reading wrongly and so copy the halting style of their classmates; some do not want to draw attention to themselves by reading in their normal fluent style; and some do not want to embarrass their classmates. So the teacher does not hear their advanced skills and is unaware that, at home, their reading is sophisticated. Audiotaping their reading at home and bringing the tape to the teacher is one way to overcome this misperception.

Learning style

Not only are intellectually gifted children able to learn more, but *how* they learn is typically more sophisticated than for average learners (Sternberg & Grigorenko 1993). They have a tendency to be more reflective, less impulsive in their thinking and more methodical in their approach to tasks. On the other hand, they can respond quickly when warranted.

Motivation

When presented with a challenging and exciting environment, young gifted children are intensely curious: they seek to know and understand from an early age. Gifted individuals appear to have a strong, intrinsic drive to apply their skills meaningfully and to use their resources well (Gruber 1986; Sternberg & Lubart 1991). They seek to master new skills, which may be due to their neurological need for heightened stimulation (Morelock & Morrison 1996). Given sufficient challenge, they are willing to invest energy in and give attention to tasks in order to develop competence (Baska 1989; Csikszentmihályi 1991; Renzulli 1986; Runco 1993; Sternberg & Lubart 1991; Vallerand et al. 1994).

Attention skills

The picture of gifted children's attention skills is mixed, partly because of a multitude of types of attention. These forms have been described by Zentall (1989). The first type of attention is maintaining a level of *arousal* or *alertness* in order to attend. On this dimension, gifted children are often described as being more alert than less advanced children (Morelock & Morrison 1996; Tannenbaum 1992), which is sometimes said to be associated with a poor sleeping pattern, although there is little evidence of this (Freeman 1983, 1991; Moltzen 1996a; Perleth et al. 1993).

The second type of attention is *coming to attention* to focus on an activity. From a few months of age, gifted children show a preference for novel stimuli and a tendency to habituate (that is, lose attention) to stimuli which are repeated (Lewis & Louis 1991; Perleth et al. 1993; Slater 1995; Tannenbaum 1992). In short, gifted children's focus on an activity will depend on how intellectually stimulating it is.

The third type of attention is *maintaining attention over time*—that is, concentration span. Young gifted children may show intense absorption (a long concentration span) when engaged in a topic of interest; however, when an activity is not challenging, they might 'flit' from one activity to another without really becoming absorbed in any. They can be particularly impatient and inattentive with repetition of activities that they already understand (Clark 2002; Kitano 1990a). Meanwhile, those who are intrinsically motivated—which is a positive thing—will not be convinced to apply themselves to tedious tasks even by the promise of external rewards (Kolb & Jussim 1994). Their apparently brief concentration span can sometimes raise queries about Attention Deficit Hyperactivity Disorder (ADHD), but this condition does not mean an inability to sustain attention but rather an inability to give a task the attention it requires; if bright children are not concentrating, it can be that the task is so easy that there is no need for them to apply themselves to it (Kaufmann & Castellanos 2000).

The fourth type of attention is *selective attention*. This involves scanning a range of stimuli to see which aspects of each are the most important and which can be ignored.

Finally, there is *alternating* or *divided* attention. This is a crucial skill for beginning school, as children need to be able to listen to the next directive while completing an earlier task, which involves dividing their attention between what they are doing and the next instruction. Given their advanced metacognitive control, gifted learners are likely to be adept at these last two forms of attention control.

Locus of control

An important belief that children learn through experience is whether they themselves can control outcomes (which is termed having an *internal* locus of control), or whether luck, fate or other people control what happens to them (which is called having an *external* locus of control). There is some evidence that highly-achieving gifted children develop an internal locus of control earlier than less advanced children (Brody & Benbow 1986; Clark 2002; Kammer 1986; McClelland et al. 1991). It is thought that their strong belief in personal control underpins their enhanced self-management and motivates them to use their problem-solving strategies effectively (Chan 1996).

Independence

Gifted children's drive for independence can be paradoxical in early childhood. Many prefer to work independently, perhaps because of the discrepancies between their skill levels and those of their age mates. Others seek a lot of stimulation and, as infants, might have learned to rely on adults to supply this; they continue to do so even after they are capable of generating input themselves. Still others might fiercely insist on doing things (e.g. getting dressed) for themselves but, once they have mastered the task intellectually and it holds no further interest for them, will then refuse to do it at all.

Creative thinking style

Gifted children's problem-finding and problem-solving skills are often creative, allowing them to see an issue from a range of perspectives, sometimes yielding original insights (Shore & Kanevsky 1993). Their divergent or flexible thinking is enabled by their proficiency at metacognitive control (Carr & Borkowski 1987) and possession of a large body of information and ideas to manipulate.

Auditory-sequential learning style

The majority of individuals—according to Silverman (2002), perhaps as many as two-thirds—learn most efficiently by listening. Because with language one word is delivered before another, these people also tend to be competent at sequencing ideas. Their characteristic learning style (as listed in Box 1.1) is compatible with most teaching methods in schools, so these gifted children often cope well with school and are academically gifted.

Visual spatial (or holistic) learning style

Meanwhile, the remaining one-third of learners use images to learn. They gravitate towards activities involving the building, creating or manipulation of objects, including art, building, cooking, design, drawing, inventing, and the assembly and disassembly of objects (Lubinski 2003).

These children see a whole pattern all at once, so have no need to break it down into its component parts in order to understand it. This means that they often find sequential tasks frustrating, as these require a one-step-at-a-time approach, whereas they prefer to do things as a whole. Their learning style is often at odds with the more usual auditory teaching style in schools and their nonconformity can be misinterpreted as a learning difficulty rather than a strength. It can show itself as:

- an apparent difficulty with following more than one instruction in a sequence;

- irritation at having to show workings with such things as arithmetic equations;
- the ability to read words as a whole, rather than phonetically—and teaching reading phonetically only confuses them;
- having difficulty with tasks that, to auditory-sequential learners, seem easy (as they contain few steps) while being very able at tasks that, to others, seem difficult because they demand abstract reasoning. As a result, visual-spatial learners can fail or appear not to be applying themselves to routine tasks—which, in turn, can mean that they are not given the challenge of more stimulating tasks (at which they are likely to be very successful);
- being more than usually intolerant of rehearsal and repetition as, once you have seen a complete picture, rehearsal does not improve that image (whereas rehearsal does improve the recall of auditory-sequential learners);
- being inflexible when adults' instructions differ from the plan they imagine in their head, such that they will negotiate with adults rather than conform to their instructions; and/or
- tuning out auditory information (appearing to daydream or withdrawing physically from auditory stimulation), especially when exposed to visual stimulation, such as when they are watching TV and are unable to hear their parents.

Speech and language skills

Many intellectually gifted children speak much earlier than is typical, resulting in a wider and more complex vocabulary and sentence structure from an early age (Lewis & Louis 1991; Moltzen 2004a; Perleth et al. 1993). Even more important than speech is the children's precocious comprehension of language, which from an early age is a robust indicator of intellectual ability (Freeman 1993; Guilford et al. 1981; Moltzen 2004a; Perleth et al. 1993; Robinson 1993; Smutny et al. 1989).

Gifted children's advanced facility with language has three effects: first, it allows them to express their needs from an earlier age. Their logical thinking can lead to constant questions to which they demand detailed, in-depth answers. Their resulting constant talk can lead either to indulgence or to being ignored (Bromfield 1994). Meanwhile, their advanced language—being such an obvious sign of intellectual giftedness—can deceive adults into expecting too much of them in other spheres.

Second, their facility with language allows them to understand information supplied by adults. Verbally gifted young children can comprehend adult conversations earlier than usual, with a resulting increase in the amount of information that is available to them, but also an early interest in 'adult business'. Their advanced conversation can make them interesting companions but there is an associated risk that parents will confide too much in them, resulting in their children becoming worried about adult issues.

Third, their language skills permit the use of self-talk (metacognitive skills) to govern their own learning and behaviour. These three aspects of language further infants' development at the time, and represent an advantage that lasts (Freeman 2000).

In addition to their wide vocabulary, advanced verbal reasoning skills, accurate grammar and early comprehension, some specific signs of young gifted children's advanced language skills are listed in Box 1.1. Perhaps an unexpected manifestation of their advanced cognitive and language abilities is gifted children's early appreciation of humour. This comes about because their cognitive and language skills allow them to know what is typical and so they appreciate the humour in exceptions or incongruities.

When watching a cricket match on TV, a five-year-old enjoyed the duck that walked across the screen when a batsman was dismissed without scoring—that is, was 'out for a duck'. A few weeks later, at the beginning of a match, a utility van with the sponsor's advertisement scrolled across the bottom of the screen and she announced with amusement: 'He's out for a truck!'

Motor abilities

As with all other areas of development, children with advanced learning capabilities often acquire motor skills early—particularly skills that rely on cognitive control such as balance, in contrast with those that rely only on strength or endurance (Robinson 1993; Roedell et al. 1980). This can show up extremely early, such as when newborns develop head control and integrate the innate reflexes early, permitting (for example) asymmetrical hand use at a younger than usual age. Later, they learn new physical movements with ease and can locate themselves in the environment. Their superior coordination, environmental perception and advanced planning skills contribute to a lowered rate of childhood accidents. These skills can also lead to early awareness of left and right.

Nevertheless, intellectually gifted children's fine motor skills (hand–eye coordination) might not proceed earlier than the norm (Tannenbaum 1983), and their slower development of these skills can stand in the way of their other accomplishments.

In contrast, children who are gifted in their fine motor skills can be competent at putting together new or difficult puzzles, taking apart and reassembling objects with unusual skill, or making interesting shapes or patterns with objects.

Artistic skills

Children who are gifted in drawing typically become proficient at the artistic style that is dominant in their culture; in the West, this leads to representational drawings at a young age, with detail and perspective (Winner & Martino 2003). Gifted child artists draw complex images, as if trying to understand how objects are structured. By the middle primary school years, they might repeat drawings of particular objects or might repeatedly draw the same story or theme, with each picture a rendition of an 'episode' in the story (Winner & Martino 2003). It is common for the aesthetic qualities of their artwork to diminish during the school years: those who were mimics only will not progress beyond this level, whereas those destined to develop artistic creativity will acquire their own style from adolescence onwards.

Musical skills

As with children who are gifted in other domains, the musically gifted learn quickly and display a 'rage to master' and intuitive understanding of their skill domain (Winner & Martino 2000). They show deep appreciation and understanding of music from a very young age—perhaps as young as one or two years (Winner & Martino 2000). As infants, musically gifted children have a deep interest in environmental sounds and music. They are sensitive to the structure of music and have excellent musical memories; they are therefore able to play music back vocally or with an instrument, displaying great accuracy, matching of pitch and precise timing. They are also sensitive to the emotional or expressive qualities of music, which is the basis of musicality (in contrast to mere reproduction).

As a result, musical giftedness first emerges in performance rather than composition, which might not appear until late childhood (Winner & Martino 2000). Whereas many young children generate their own songs during their preschool years, by school age they are often concerned with correctly reproducing known songs; the reverse is the case for musically gifted children who improvise and transpose tunes into different keys (Winner & Martino 2000).

Social skills

Gifted children can display a range of social aptitudes from early childhood onwards.

Empathy

Many gifted children are less egocentric than their age peers (Shore & Kanevsky 1993). Egocentricity does not refer to selfishness, but to the ability to notice others' emotions and deduce their cause, using awareness that others' feelings might be different from one's own. Thus children with elements of emotional giftedness are more sensitive to the needs or feelings of other people than their age mates may be.

A child was told that her friend, Sophie could not come to her upcoming third birthday party because Sophie's grandmother had died suddenly, requiring Sophie to travel interstate for the funeral. Much later in the day, the almost-three-year-old was eating a sandwich with quiet tears rolling down her face. Her mother asked her what was the matter, thinking that she was disappointed that her friend could not come to her party. The reply was: 'I'm sad for Sophie. She didn't get to say good-bye to her Nanna before she died.' The child then burst into piteous and prolonged crying.

Play

Young gifted children often learn to play games with rules earlier than other children and incorporate academic and literacy activities spontaneously into their play (Kitano 1985). They have advanced play interests and behaviours (Robinson 1993), and so may attempt to structure the play of a group of age mates in too complex a way (Webb 1993). When the less able children lose interest and wander off, gifted children sometimes interpret this apparent lack of interest as a rejection of them, rather than attributing it to the fact that the other children cannot yet play at more sophisticated levels.

Friendships

Because of their ability to empathise with others and the scarcity of intellectual peers, young gifted children will often form strong attachments to one or two friends (Baska 1989). Whereas young children usually regard as friends the children with whom they play the most, gifted children tend to be able to develop true reciprocal friendships far earlier.

This pattern is apparent, however, only when gifted children can find true (intellectual) peers. To do this, many seek out older children and adults for companionship, or seek to be alone (Clark 2002; Davis & Rimm 2004; Lewis & Louis 1991). In order to meet their need for company, many have an imaginary playmate, although this is common also with highly imaginative children (who may not be gifted).

Educators cannot expect gifted children to display appropriate peer skills when they lack peers. This highlights that social skills rely on the social context, as shown by the fact that gifted children's social difficulties usually diminish when they find intellectual peers (Morelock & Morrison 1996).

Leadership

Young gifted children often show early leadership abilities, such as being willing to accept responsibility, use of clear communication, adaptability, flexibility, preference for directing rather than following activities, ability to synthesise group members' ideas to formulate a plan, and self-confidence around others (Moltzen 2004a). They are often looked to by other children for their ideas and decisions. Their verbal and reasoning skills allow them to handle conflict non-aggressively by suggesting a number of solutions to social dilemmas (Morelock & Morrison 1996). They have the verbal abilities to influence other children's behaviour, although they might also use their skills manipulatively.

Moral judgment

Being less egocentric and more empathic than is usual at their age, gifted children typically have an advanced sense of justice (Baska 1989; Clark 2002; Davis & Rimm 2004; LeVine & Tucker 1986). This is expressed in their ability to make complex moral judgments earlier than their age mates (Gross 2004), although they are not necessarily any more capable of enacting moral decisions in real life (Freeman 1993; Moltzen 1996a; Robinson 1993).

This advanced value system can present some problems for gifted children. First, it can intensify their feelings of being different (Gross 2004). When other children do something which is developmentally normal but which they know to be 'wrong', gifted children can be offended and confused.

Second, their moral values can drive their personal interests, leading at times to a disdain for popular activities (e.g. sport) which have no 'meaning'.

Third, boys' altruism and compassion may be in conflict with the stereo-types of boys as 'tough guys' and so can lead to peer rejection or can cause them to behave in ways that contradict their values, just so that they can fit in (Lovecky 1994b).

Fourth, gifted children's interest in social issues—especially those involving a violation of justice—sometimes exceeds their emotional maturity and ability to cope, and can clash with their need to focus on their own growth (Baska 1989).

Finally, their sense of morality and intolerance of hypocrisy can mean that they are reluctant to tell those 'white' (social) lies that often oil the wheels of social interactions: their brutal honesty sometimes disturbs other people (Gross 2004).

Emotional characteristics

Children can be gifted in the intellectual domain alone, or gifted both intel-lectually and in the social-emotional sphere. It is probably the latter group to whom Silverman and others refer when they describe many gifted children as being more emotionally sensitive, intense and responsive than average learners (Miller et al. 1994; Morelock 1996; Piechowski 2003; Silverman 1993b). In my clinical practice I too find many intellectually gifted children who, in contrast to the myth about the poorly adapted bright child, are indeed more emotionally aware, intuitive, insightful, perceptive and caring. This is often reflected in others' descriptions of these children: grandmothers often comment that a newborn has 'been here before'; others speak of the child as having been born wise; the Irish call this being fey; some say the child is 'an old soul'. All this sounds fanciful but, language aside, such comments are referring to children's emotional awareness, to the fact that they are tuned into themselves and others and that, without explanation, they can understand others' emotions and use their own feelings to guide insightful decisions.

Emotional intelligence entails both emotional self-awareness, whereby individuals observe, recognise and understand their own emotions and their source; and self-regulation, whereby they can manage their emotional responses, with the result that emotional perception facilitates thinking, and reasoning takes emotions into account (Maree & Ebersöhn 2002; Mayer et al. 2001; Pfeiffer 2001). In this way, emotions and thinking processes are inte-grated, resulting in better adjustment to life's demands, heightened awareness of one's own and others' feelings, and improved ability to manage relationships.

At the same time, the ability to be emotionally tuned in to oneself and others can come at some cost to its owner. For example, the deeper and broader knowledge base of gifted learners can propel them into examining abstract issues before they have the emotional maturity to cope (Roeper 1977). These emotional traits can produce the appearance of social or emotional immaturity, as the children become intensely upset about issues that can seem trivial to others. Meanwhile, as already mentioned, sensitive boys can be rejected by their peers for not being 'macho' enough (Lovecky 1994b). So emotional giftedness can be both a blessing and a challenge.

Early development of fears

One result of the combination of advanced cognitive and social awareness with heightened sensitivity is that gifted children sometimes develop fears earlier than other children (Derevensky & Coleman 1989; LeVine & Tucker 1986; Robinson 1993), when they might be too young emotionally to cope with their precocious imagination (Chamrad & Robinson 1986). Another consequence of cognitive and social advances is that gifted children lose their innocence and their belief in magical thinking earlier (Roeper 1977).

Self-esteem

Gifted children's self-concept develops early (Delisle 1992), which in turn hastens their recognition that they are different from other children (Clark

2002; Harrison 2003). Although this awareness can lead them to assume that there is something 'wrong' with them, on the whole most gifted children are confident of their skills, particularly in their gifted domain.

Perfectionism

Despite a paucity of evidence, gifted children are often described as setting high standards for their own performance and as demanding far more of themselves than do their parents or teachers. This trait is commonly called perfectionism. It is not unique to gifted learners, of course, nor necessarily detrimental personally (as will be discussed in Chapters 3 and 4). However, when punishing standards are applied to other children, this can result in their rejection by others and thus in social isolation.

Existential awareness

Sometimes called 'spiritual intelligence', existential awareness refers to children's investigation of intellectual questions such as the meaning of life and the emotional search for personal signficance or value, for interconnections or a communication between themselves and others (Zohar & Marshall 2000). Such existential issues occupy many gifted children at an earlier age and with more intensity than is typical of their peers (Lovecky 1998; Sisk 2002). From their earliest years, many perceive the big picture or context in their world and begin a life-long quest for balance in life itself and a richly meaningful path in life.

Sensitivity

Having high standards for themselves and being perceptive to others can make gifted children overly sensitive, especially to criticism (Mendaglio 1994, 1995b). It is possible that, while they are more perceptive to other people's signals, their limited life experience causes them to misinterpret these messages (Freeman 1983; Mendaglio 1994).

Frustration

While extremely gifted preschoolers tend to be precocious across all developmental domains, those with mildly advanced intellectual development achieve only slightly better than average in gross and fine motor skills (Tannenbaum 1992). The result is dissonant development between the various developmental domains, which can lead to frustration. The children might be able to conceptualise what they want to do, but cannot achieve it because of their age-appropriate manual dexterity (Chamrad & Robinson 1986; Freeman 1983; Kitano 1986; Roedell et al. 1980; Webb 1993; Whitmore 1980).

Maturity

On the one hand, gifted children often accept responsibilities that are usually given only to older children; on the other, they can have emotional or behavioural outbursts that seem very immature (Robinson 1993).

Behavioral nonconformity

Because of their independence, gifted children tend to resist attempts by adults to control their behaviour (Delisle 1992; Kitano 1990a) (an issue I discuss again in Chapter 6). Although their intellectual risk taking is often reflected in advanced learning, it can result in breaking 'rules' in unusual and unanticipated ways, and so can appear to be 'mischief-making' (Mares 1991). Whilst not necessarily conforming to expectations themselves, young gifted children often want others to obey the rules (Kitano 1985).

Exceptionally gifted children

Just as degrees of hearing impairment have significant implications for whether children will learn aurally or by signing, so too degrees of giftedness have significant implications for children's learning needs. When describing the characteristics and needs of gifted children, we need to be aware of the level of giftedness to which we are referring, as information about mildly or moderately gifted children might not be relevant to those who are exceptionally gifted, while descriptions of the exceptionally gifted can inflate our concept of giftedness and cause us to overlook it in its milder forms.

Although IQ scores are not a perfect measure of intellectual giftedness, and although individuals can be gifted in domains other than the intellectual, levels of giftedness are often denoted by their IQ scores. For reasons discussed in Chapter 2, I adopt a conservative definition of giftedness that encompasses only the top 3–5 per cent of the population, yielding the categories of intellectual giftedness outlined in Table 1.1. The prevalence figures in this table are uncertain, however: for unknown reasons, there are more people in the exceptionally gifted range than would be expected (Gross 2004). But even if we double the figures given in the table, children with exceptional and profound levels of giftedness are extremely rare. This makes them difficult to recognise, as most teachers will go through their whole careers without ever meeting one.

Exceptionally gifted children are generally extremely advanced across most developmental domains, extremely early (Gross 1999, 2004; Lovecky 1994a). As with other gifted children, they might acquire talking, walking and reading skills early but, compounding this, then advance so quickly that some developmental stages are virtually imperceptible. They might go from walking with assistance to walking alone in one month instead of the usual

Table 1.1 Levels of giftedness

Level IQ[1]	Wechsler Binet IQ[2]	Stanford- prevalence[3]	Expected
Mild	130–144	132–148	2 in 100
Moderate	145–159	149–164	1 in 1000
Exceptional	160–174	165–180	3 in 100 000
Profound	175+	181+	3 in 10 million

[1] The WPPSI-III and WISC-IV do not actually measure above 160 IQ points (Wechsler 2002, 2003).
[2] The Stanford-Binet Fifth Edition does not measure above 164 IQ points.
[3] Source for prevalence figures: Sattler (2001)

3.5 months, and will link words into phrases within a few months of their first word (Gross 1999, 2004; Gross & Start 1990). Their numeracy skills are typically advanced, while their spelling can appear to be careless but in fact errors are due to their use of a sophisticated vocabulary (Gross 2004). Early reading reliably differentiates between mild and high degrees of giftedness, with many exceptionally gifted children learning to read prior to entering school despite little instruction and continuing to regard reading as their favourite form of recreation throughout childhood (Gross 1993a, 1999, 2004; Gross & Start 1990).

Socially, with the exception of a lack of interest in competitive sport, their hobbies, interests and friendship choices typically resemble those of children four or five years older (Gross 2004). The wider discrepancy between their skill levels and those of age mates means that their social isolation is more pronounced than for children with lesser degrees of giftedness (Gross 1993a, 2004; Gross & Start 1990).

In terms of their learning style, the exceptionally gifted have been described as possessing a strong—even stubborn—goal orientation, being intensely driven to utilise their skills, with a 'rage' or vital urge to master (Gross 2004; Maxwell 1998).

Exceptionally gifted children also often make the simple complex, seeing intricacies and exceptions in things others take for granted (Lovecky 1994a). Lovecky reports that this characteristic can be coupled with the need for extreme precision in order for the world to make sense, and so can result in extensive arguments or debates with others.

A reverse characteristic is that exceptionally gifted children make the complex simple (Lovecky 1994a) because they master concepts as a whole and are proficient at both verbal-sequential and visual-spatial skills. This makes it difficult for these children to explain a concept's components parts, which is why many exceptionally gifted children have trouble with peer tutoring. The same phenomenon is found with reading: once the children no longer need to sound out words, it is frustrating and difficult for them to be required to do so (Gross 2004).

In order to fit in socially, these children may spontaneously stop reading when they begin school, having observed that other school entrants cannot read (Gross 2004). They might also modify their complex vocabulary when away from home. Thus many exceptionally gifted learners are not detected by their teachers, although their classmates often notice their exceptional skills (Gross 1999, 2004; Gross & Start 1990). And, because of unfamiliarity with giftedness—particularly in its extreme form—teachers might not know to offer very advanced learning experiences. This makes it crucial for parents to document their children's skills and for assessment to include IQ tests, as teacher nomination is likely to overlook the children's extraordinary skills, particularly if they hang back in activities or are nonconformists (Gross 1999, 2004; Hodge 2004).

Prodigies

Child prodigies demonstrate adult-level performances in demanding fields at an extremely early age (Feldman 1993). Their skills are usually in specific domains such as chess and music, probably because these do not require much prior learning (Montgomery 1996). Not only do prodigies learn skills *earlier* (i.e. more quickly), but they achieve a *higher* level of competence than others, even those with the best training and most extensive practice. In contrast with savants, whose general abilities are usually below average, prodigies are usually very able intellectually, although not exceptionally so; like exceptionally gifted children, prodigies have a fierce determination to develop their talents (Feldman 1993).

Prodigies appear not to be a product of genetics (as their parents and siblings are seldom prodigies), but neither are they a product of their environment, as these very young children have not been alive long enough to benefit from even the most enriched environment (Tannenbaum 1992). On the other hand, they do require environmental exposure in their area of special ability: in order to play the violin like a virtuoso, they obviously need to have been introduced to the instrument (Tannenbaum 1992).

There appears to be higher than usual hostility to the special needs of prodigies within the education system, resulting in many parents choosing home schooling (Feldman 1993). At the same time, there is a fascination with prodigies which, in my view, unintentionally ill-serves other gifted children. The frequent mention of prodigies in the media and literature (vastly out of proportion to the prevalence of prodigious children) can create an inflated view of giftedness, and so blind educators to the more common forms that giftedness can take.

Conclusion

Remember the scenario presented at the beginning of this chapter? The description of gifted children's skills outlined here allows us to understand how a child who relies on her parent to translate the world to her and to translate her to the world can then have difficulty separating from that parent. This chapter has also explained that gifted children—particularly at young ages—have few intellectual peers and so rely even more heavily on adults for company when older children are not available to them. This means that they have a depth of attachment to a few key individuals, but not necessarily a breadth. They have age peers but no age mate who is interested in the same ideas and activities as themselves, and so they naturally gravitate towards adults. Moreover, when the intellectual curriculum does not meet their needs, they are not induced to separate from the parent on whom they rely so keenly.

Next, to the child's dressing skills. She was interested in dressing herself when she was aged two and it was an intellectual challenge, but now that it is mundane and offers no new challenge, she is not interested in doing it. She can—but no longer finds it fascinating.

Finally, the characteristics listed in this chapter explain the child's lack of engagement and apparent brief concentration span. She has already achieved—perhaps a year ago—the tasks on offer at preschool and so has little interest in engaging with them now. When she does engage, she achieves the tasks the first time so has no need to repeat or practise them. So her attention span—while appearing delayed—is actually the result of an unchallenging program.

So while the child's behavioural pattern signals atypical development, it is up to educators and parents collaboratively to piece these observations together with assessment of the child's developmental skills across settings in order to determine the direction of that atypicality. The signs of gifted-ness described here can at least alert us to the possibility of advanced development.

Suggested further reading

For more detail on the characteristics and needs of exceptionally gifted children, I recommend:

Gross, M.U.M. 2004 *Exceptionally gifted children* 2nd edn, RoutledgeFalmer, London.

TRANSFORMING GIFTEDNESS
INTO TALENT
two

It takes no more than plain common sense to realize that it takes much more than extraordinary brainpower for a person to become demonstrably gifted . . . Making the leap from promise to its fulfillment requires not only ability, but also ancillary personal attributes, along with enriching and opportunistic life experiences, all of them reinforcing each other in a rare and subtle combination. (Tannenbaum 1991: 27)

Introduction

Two stories illustrate the need to examine what giftedness is and how it is expressed. The first anecdote is that of a couple who consulted me for an IQ test for their daughter. They had been aware that many of her skills were advanced, but assumed that this was because she was an only child and they spent a good deal of time with her: they thought the cause was her environment, rather than lying within her. However, while you can download a sophisticated software program on to your computer, it will grind to a halt if the hardware is not powerful enough to utilise the program. So it is with giftedness: children cannot surpass their genetic capacity (although, of course, they can achieve below it). This means that if they are showing advances, this is due to both their genetic endowment *and* the fact that their environment is stimulating: the cause cannot be environmental alone.

The second comment came from a school principal with whom I was negotiating early school entry for a young gifted child. The principal dismissed the concept of giftedness by saying that, even when children begin school with advanced skills, by the end of their junior primary (elementary) years, their skills have 'come back to the pack'. Like the parents just described, this principal's argument was that the children had been hothoused while in the care of their parents. (Of course, the opposite could be true: that the children were displaying their innate abilities prior to school but that the school environment was so stultifying that it repressed their skills.)

In light of such misconceptions, this chapter has two purposes: first, to define giftedness; and, second, to examine what factors allow children's talents to be expressed.

The nature of giftedness

In the last chapter, I defined giftedness as the *potential* for significantly advanced development and talent as *displays* of advanced skills. However, this practical definition needs some refinement. To achieve this, we can turn to the literature on giftedness. However, it yields some definitions which differ on at least four dimensions: first, whether they are liberal or conservative; second, whether they regard ability as a single entity or in multidimensional terms; third, whether gifted and average learners possess qualitatively or merely quantitatively different abilities; and fourth, how culture-specific the definitions are.

Conservative versus liberal definitions

Taking the liberal or conservative debate first, liberals argue that there is little difference in productivity between the top 5 per cent of the population and the 5 per cent just below them, so they advocate for the inclusion of up to 10–20 per cent of the population in the gifted category (Reis & Renzulli 1982; Renzulli 1982). However, conservatives point out that differences in performance can never be statistically demonstrated within a narrow range of abilities because, within a restricted band, the correlation between ability and performance is actually zero, as depicted in Figure 2.1. Conservatives agree that, although it is important not to overlook individuals who truly are exceptional, to include such a large proportion within the gifted category renders it meaningless and shifts the educational focus away from those with most need.

As a clinician, I would add to this argument the statistic that, whereas only 3–5 per cent of children fall above an IQ level of 130, 13.56 per cent fall in the IQ range of 115–130 (see Figure 8.2). In that case, these young people have access to numerous peers who match their abilities; moreover, they are able learners and are therefore often well adjusted to schooling. Thus they have few clinical needs arising from their ability profiles, whereas those falling within the gifted range as defined by the conservatives can be more isolated from peers and be receiving an educational program that is not routinely meeting their learning needs. I and others therefore contend that

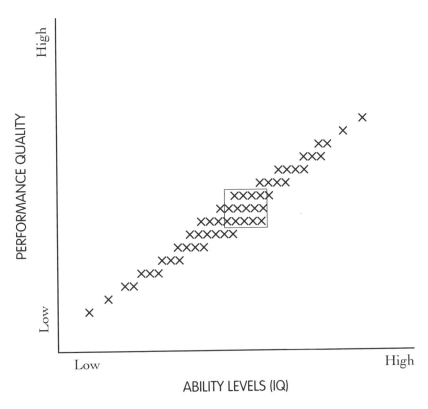

Figure 2.1 Correlation between ability levels and performance quality
Note that, although across the continuum of abilities there is a strong correlation between ability and performance quality, there is no correlation within a narrow range of ability levels.

the gifted category should encompass only the top 3–5 per cent, with levels of giftedness as classified in Table 1.1.

Single versus multiple capacities

The debate about whether ability is governed by a single characteristic or many, relatively separate, skills has persisted since the beginning of the twentieth century. Two theories believe in a single entity which they name either 'high intelligence' or 'creativity'; three leading theorists argue for separate subskills.

The high intelligence definition

Since the beginning of the twentieth century, two separate schools have debated the nature of intelligence. On one side of the Atlantic, the British community of scholars under Charles Spearman (1927) believed that a single capacity underlies all cognitive processes and that possession of more of that capacity distinguishes giftedness from average achievements. This capacity has been called 'general ability', 'g' or intelligence, and is thought to be a global, stable, unchangeable trait.

Early attempts to measure intelligence occurred in the absence of any scientific understanding of it (Khatena 1992; Kline 1991). Definitions continue to proliferate and agreement is unlikely; for simplicity, therefore, I draw on David Wechsler's (1958) definition to define intelligence as 'the ability to harness one's thinking skills and emotional awareness to produce behaviours that deal effectively with one's environment'. This simply means that the word *intelligence* could best be used to refer to *products* (thoughts or actions) that are well suited to the circumstances, arrived at through the *processes* of thinking and feeling. Some thinking gives rise to intelligent behaviour; some does not.

Thinking skills that enable individuals to produce adaptive (that is, wise, successful or 'intelligent') behaviours include the abilities to apprehend, comprehend and integrate intellectual and emotional knowledge to solve problems—or in colloquial terms, 'the ability to catch on, make sense of things and figure out what to do' (Gottfredson 2003: 26).

According to the high intelligence definition, giftedness, then, is made possible by the especially proficient use of these skills. In turn, this comes about because of efficient transmission between brain cells, which allows gifted individuals to process information very accurately—that is, with few errors (Eysenck 1986). As a result, they learn quickly. This suggests that accuracy (and thus speed) of information processing is not only *related* to advanced abilities, but may actually be the *cause* of giftedness (Borkowski & Peck 1986; Kail 2000).

Like many human characteristics, intelligence—that is, the ability to produce intelligent or adaptive behaviours—is thought to be 'normally' distributed. A 'normal' distribution means that the mode (the most common measurement) is also the average, and that half of the population falls above and half below the average. However, while half of the population has above-average abilities, we do not classify these people as gifted until their skills are 'significantly' advanced. The point at which we determine this advancement to be significant is both arbitrary and historical. In the cognitive domain, we have defined this point as being around an IQ of 130 points (when the average IQ is 100). This then includes 3–5 per cent of the population. Although this applies to intellectual giftedness, the same proportion of the population can be defined as gifted in any domain of human endeavour.

The debate about the high IQ definition of intelligence has been contaminated by the debate about the limitations of IQ tests, with the key theme being that these tests offer a truncated definition of intelligence. However, even those who believe that intelligence underpins all other cognitive functions accept that high intelligence and high IQs are not the same thing. To paraphrase Albert Einstein, not everything that counts can be counted. Thus it is possible to believe in a single general ability called intelligence, while recognising that our tools for measuring it are imperfect.

Creativity

Rather than seeing *intelligence* as the defining characteristic of giftedness, some researchers believe that, beyond a certain threshold of intellectual ability, there is an additional skill called *creativity*. According to these writers, creativity is fundamental to distinguishing mere precociousness from successful giftedness, or conservers of knowledge from producers of ideas (Albert & Runco 1986; Khatena 1992; Moore & Sawyers 1987; Renzulli 1986; Runco 1993; Sternberg 2003; Sternberg & Grigorenko 2002). Arguments against this point to the fact that scores on intelligence and creativity tests correlate so highly that both must be tapping similar skills (Khatena 1992).

As with intelligence, there is little agreement on what the term 'creativity' means. Many align it particularly with divergent thinking, and also with planning and improvisation; however, although these skills are clearly necessary, they are not sufficient to produce creative outcomes (Cropley 2000; Han & Marvin 2002; Naglieri & Kaufman 2001). Alternatively, creativity is often aligned with the processes of fluent, flexible, original and elaborate thinking (Wallace 1986b). However, these processes may not be entirely separate: flexibility (the production of *alternative* ideas) and originality (the production of *unique* ideas) must, by definition, be closely related to the ability to produce *many* ideas (Borland 1986). In turn, this fluency is closely related to general ability or intelligence (Borland 1986), suggesting once again a close link between creativity and intelligence.

An assessment that an idea or individual is creative requires a judgment—one which is in the eye of the beholder (Cropley 2000). Creative products can be assessed in two ways. The first measure is social acclaim for the product's originality and uniqueness: no one else has ever produced it before. However, the social judgment of the worth of a product may not accurately reflect the creativity of the thought processes involved in its discovery or invention, but may simply reflect the product's timeliness. Therefore Cropley (1997) and Runco (1997) reject evaluating creativity by its product, yielding the paradox that creativity implies producing something new and yet creativity cannot be judged with reference to that product.

The second way to assess a product (such as an idea) is to establish whether it is novel to the person thinking it. By this measure, *all* thinking is creative: if you have never had a particular thought before, thinking it for the first time is creative—at least for you (Ebert 1994). However, this is not a perfect resolution, because if an individual knows nothing, any new thought will be creative—but it is difficult to accept that ignorance is a valid source of creativity (Cropley 1997; Runco 1997).

In the early childhood years, notions that equate creativity with gifted-ness face the difficulty that very young children do not yet have an extensive enough knowledge base to manipulate ideas and facts creatively—certainly not in the 'social acclaim' sense (Sternberg & Lubart 1991, 1992). It is also apparent that creativity is not simply a function of individuals' abilities, but requires a conducive environment (Cropley 1997). Children who are in an environment that discourages experimentation might fail to display creativ-ity and so, by the creative definition, would not be identified as gifted.

The debate about creativity is complex and will be ongoing for some time. In the meantime, I have reached three interim conclusions. Drawing on my earlier definition of intelligence as the capacity to adapt to the environment or the task, my first conclusion is that creativity is not necessarily superior to convergent thinking because sometimes it will be most adaptive to be creative and sometimes it will not. If you wish to exit a room, the most intelligent thing to do is the most orthodox: use the door. But if a fire is blocking that exit, the most intelligent thing to do is find a new or creative solution for leaving the room. Creativity (divergent thinking) and convergent thinking will each be more intelligent (or adaptive) in one situation or another.

My second interim conclusion is that simply because there are separate tests for intelligence and creativity does not mean that they actually *are* two separate skills. Perhaps the omission from IQ tests of divergent thinking has contributed to an artificial schism between the concepts of intelligence and creativity (Carr & Borkowski 1987).

Finally, creativity—previously considered a general capacity in the same way that intelligence has commonly been—might after all be domain-specific: individuals will use different creative skills in different domains (Han & Marvin 2002). This implies that creativity cannot be taught out of con text, but must be fostered within children's particular talent domains (Han & Marvin 2002).

Multiple capacities

In contrast with the originally British view of a single capacity, on the other side of the Atlantic the U.S. view has held that intelligence comprises a small set of distinct mental skills which are relatively independent of each other and which come into play in different tasks. Three main theorists have advanced this view.

The first was Thurstone (1938). He contended that, rather than a single global capacity, intelligence comprised seven separate abilities: verbal comprehension; word fluency; numerical fluency; spatial visualisation; asso-ciative memory; perceptual speed; and reasoning.

Next came Guilford's (1959) structure-of-intellect model, updated in 1977 and again in 1988, which proposed that six separate intellectual opera-tions could be applied to five content areas to produce six types of product, thus yielding 180 separate functions. These are:

- *intellectual operations*: evaluation, convergent production, divergent production, memory retention, memory recording and cognition;
- *content areas*: visual, auditory, symbolic, semantic and behavioural;
- *products*: units, classes, relations, systems, transformations and implications (Guilford 1988).

Third was Gardner (1983), whose review of evidence from psychology and other disciplines caused him to conclude that there are several relatively autonomous multiple 'intelligences' which are potentials that can be activated in many adaptive ways by individuals and cultures. His original list (Gardner 1983) comprised seven of these intelligences; he has subsequently added an eighth (Gardner 1999; Kelly & Moon 1998; Vialle 1997).

- *Linguistic intelligence* involves sensitivity to language in spoken, written or signed forms and the ability to use language to accomplish goals.
- *Logical-mathematical skills* entail analytic and systematic problem-solving skills, including scientific investigation and the ability to recognise patterns and manipulate objects or symbols.
- *Musical intelligence* involves skills in discriminating sounds, performing, composing and appreciating music, and the ability to express or gain meaning from ideas or emotions in music.
- *Bodily-kinaesthetic skills* comprise the physical coordination skills necessary for using one's body.
- *Spatial skills* involve being able to interpret information in two or three dimensions, such as when appreciating art, reading maps or completing jigsaw puzzles.
- *Interpersonal intelligence* refers to the capacity to understand the intentions, motivations and desires of other people and enacting this social awareness and knowledge to produce effective social behaviour.
- *Intrapersonal skills* involve the capacity to understand yourself and to use this emotional perceptiveness to inform your thinking, and to make choices that will promote personal growth.
- The eighth and most recent intelligence to be identified by Gardner is *naturalistic intelligence*, described as expertise in recognising and classifying species and being attuned to the natural environment. However, I see the first aspect as classification, which is an applied aspect of language skills and the second as part of interpersonal intelligence, albeit a communion with non-human species.

Gardner believes that each of these skill areas has its own characteristic cognitive style and that individuals' potential is unevenly distributed across them (Morgan 1996; Smerechansky-Metzger 1995). Mostly, however, the intelligences work in harmony (or co-mingle), and so 'their autonomy may be invisible' (Gardner 1983: 9).

In the definition of intelligence already given, intelligence is a *behaviour* (act or thought) that is well adapted to the demands of the task or environment. In other words, it is an *outcome* of thinking *processes*. Given that Gardner uses the term to denote neither intellectual processing skills nor intelligent outcomes, I and others (Anderson 1992; Morgan 1996) believe that the title 'intelligences' could be misleading, and instead his list might better be regarded as domains of human functioning. (See Gardner (1999), however, for his contrary argument.)

Conclusion: The single versus multiple capacities debate

Statistical tests themselves are too limited to settle the issue of single versus multiple intelligences, and the competing conclusions of the unitary versus the multiple camps can be equally right and equally wrong, depending on the way the statistical analysis and subsequent interpretation are carried out (Gould 1981). Whether statistical tests yield a single factor or many depends on how the analysis is conducted, and this in turn depends on the orientation of the researcher.

It could be that a single factor emerges because IQ tests tap a narrow range of related skills; perhaps if divergent and other forms of thinking were included in the tests, multiple factors would emerge (Sternberg et al. 1996). Or it could be that a general ability does exist, given that Thurstone's and Guilford's various factors correlate so highly with each other that a general ability factor appears to underpin them all (Clarizio & Mehrens 1985; Grinder 1985; McNemar 1964).

The theoretical contribution of the multiple capacity models is to remind us not to overlook children whose talents lie in non-academic domains such as emotional and social skills. On the other hand, in purely practical terms, although the multiple models raise the possibility of many types of giftedness, it is not yet possible to test reliably for each and, even if it were, differential scores across subtests still cannot predict achievement any better than can a single IQ score (Fasko 2001; McNemar 1964). At the same time, no intellectual tasks can be achieved by using a single discrete skill but instead require the blending of aptitudes; therefore, one could argue, the separation of intelligence into its subskills is more theoretical than practical given that, in real life, the skills are used in unison anyway.

Two simple facts argue for a general mental ability. First, no mental test has yet been found that does *not* load on to a general factor (Gottfredson 2003); second, virtually all measures of intellectual functioning correlate with each other: 50–70 per cent of the score on one measure can be accounted for by general ability (Brody 2000; Gridley 2002). (This means, of course, that as much as 50 per cent of the performance is specific to the task.) Gottfredson concludes that multiple 'intelligences' are like different flavours of ice-cream: deliciously different from one another, but all made from the same basic ingredient.

This is illustrated in a hierarchical model, as depicted in Figure 2.2— which is a simplified version of Gottredson's (2003) model. This upholds that a general ability factor (perhaps efficiency of neurological communication) contributes to all mental functioning, with task performance calling both on this general factor and on skills or knowledge specific to a particular domain. Below these are information processing skills such as attention; the ability to retrieve stored information from memory; sequencing, simultaneous or holistic thinking; and the use of metacognitive skills such as planning and self-instruction—all of which are employed to varying degrees in the various domains. Whether we then measure general or domain-specific abilities will depend on which questions we are trying to answer: if trying to identify intellectual skills, an IQ test would be adequate; if trying to identify skills in other domains, other measures would be needed.

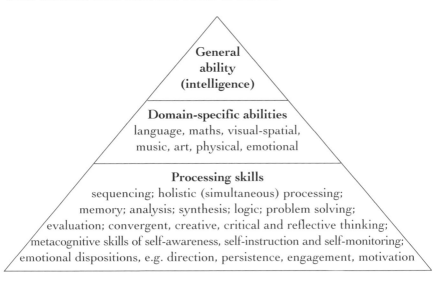

General ability (intelligence)

Domain-specific abilities
language, maths, visual-spatial, music, art, physical, emotional

Processing skills
sequencing; holistic (simultaneous) processing; memory; analysis; synthesis; logic; problem solving; evaluation; convergent, creative, critical and reflective thinking; metacognitive skills of self-awareness, self-instruction and self-monitoring; emotional dispositions, e.g. direction, persistence, engagement, motivation

Figure 2.2 A hierarchy of intellectual skills

The qualitative debate

The third debate about the nature of giftedness is whether the disparities between gifted and average learners are due to differences in the quality or merely the quantity of their thinking and emotional skills.

With respect to their thinking skills, it is clear that advanced learners can produce high-quality products. However, these products can be achieved by simply using *more* of a relevant skill than someone else. This argument is advanced by Laycock (1979), who asserts that gifted children's talented per-formances come from 'awesome combinations' of otherwise ordinary mental powers—that is, that the difference between gifted and average achievers is a quantitative rather than a qualitative one (Feldman 1984; Pendarvis & Howley 1996). This contention is supported by findings that gifted children use the same intellectual processing skills as older average learners, which suggests a quantitative difference (Jackson & Butterfield 1986).

Gallagher (1996) offers a dissenting conclusion, using the analogy that changes in temperature (a *quantitative* measure) can produce *qualitatively* different outcomes when water turns to ice or steam; in the same way, gifted children can combine their advanced skills to produce qualitatively different thinking. The information about gifted learners' thinking skills in Chapter 1 suggests that they can manipulate and juxtapose ideas in such sophisticated ways that it is probably safe to conclude that their thinking is both quantitatively and qualitatively distinguishable from that of average learners.

There is also a second element to this debate: namely, the claim that there are qualitative differences in the emotional makeup of gifted learners. The Columbus group believes that gifted individuals' highly attuned nervous systems (their brains) contribute both to advanced learning and to an increase in their emotional sensitivity, intensity and responsiveness (Miller et al. 1994; Piechowski 1997; Morelock 1996). The Columbus group's working definition (1991, in Silverman 1993b: 3) is:

> Giftedness is *asynchronous development* in which advanced cognitive abilities and heightened intensity combine to create inner experiences and awareness that are qualitatively different from the norm.

These writers argue that these emotional differences are overlooked in definitions that focus only on high intelligence or thinking skills and, in turn, this results in a loss of important information about the emotional needs of gifted children (Morelock 1996; Porath 1996).

Four points need to be made about this qualitative definition, however. First, evidence about gifted individuals' heightened emotionality is weak. (This issue is debated in Chapter 3.) Second, if individual children have only advanced cognitive development but not heightened sensitivity, it would surely be absurd to define them as 'not gifted' on the basis of their emotional status (Gagné 1997). Third, the definition arises from the Columbus group's interest in the exceptionally gifted, who comprise one in 3000 of the gifted population; their description may not apply to all gifted children (Gagné 1997). Fourth, even if heightened emotionality is found to characterise gifted children, this could be due to their unresponsive environment rather than to their inherent makeup.

The cultural debate

A fourth debate about giftedness relates to its cultural context. Although the notion of giftedness and its basic elements are universal, the way in which talent is manifested will vary with a child's cultural and historical context

(Passow & Frasier 1996). If intelligent behaviour entails being well adapted to one's environment, different skills will be intelligent in different settings. Bevan-Brown (1999, 2004) reports that traditional New Zealand Māori peoples value a broad range of qualities in the spiritual, affective, aesthetic, intuitive, creative, leadership and cultural domains in addition to Western culture's intellectual emphasis. The Māori emphasis is holistic and group-oriented. It is expected that individuals who excel in any domain will use their special abilities in the service of others.

Similarly, Harslett (1996: 100) reports that traditional Australian Aboriginal peoples value talents in areas such as 'healing, lore, story telling, religion, music, crafts, hunting and tracking'. Individuals who are talented in these domains are expected to be humble and, although recognised for their talent, are not accorded higher status because of it (Harslett 1996).

Because giftedness is a dynamic concept which reflects changes in societies' needs and priorities, some discrepancy in definitions is inevitable. Indeed, according to Borland (1990: 166): 'giftedness *should* be defined differently in different settings, but in the manner that is logical and consistent with the realities that obtain in each of those settings'. Therefore, any definition needs to be liberal enough to recognise those talents that the child's particular culture considers valuable (Gibson 1998; Harslett 1996).

Conclusion: the nature of giftedness

It is probably fair to say that intelligence, creativity and giftedness have each been defined in so many ways that the terms are now almost devoid of meaning. For practical purposes, this clearly is an unsatisfactory state of affairs. In theoretical terms, however, Cohen and colleagues (1988) defend the ambiguity on the grounds that most constructs have vague definitions with no sharp boundary between them and related concepts. Defining 'health', for instance, would be difficult: there is no clear demarcation between being in perfect health and being ill—having cancer, for example, is clearly unhealthy, but good health encompasses more than lacking cancer.

It is not possible to establish empirically whether definitions are the 'whole truth' because descriptions cannot be testable as valid or invalid: they can only be more or less useful educationally (Gallagher 1996; Nevo 1994; Sternberg & Davidson 1986). Nevertheless, some working definition is necessary so that practices that arise from it are coherent. Therefore, I propose the following definitions:

> Gifted young children are those who have the capacity to learn at a pace and level of complexity that is significantly in advance of their age peers in any domain or domains that are valued in and promoted by their sociocultural group.

Some gifted children will be recognisable by their talented behaviours. Others will be hidden and may not display their talents in everyday situations. Therefore, part two of my definition for children is:

Talented behaviours are performances that are quantitatively or qualitatively exceptional compared with those of age mates.

These definitions are liberal in the sense that they incorporate many domains of human endeavour rather than intellectual skills alone, and permit the inclusion in the gifted category of individuals who do not display talents because of their gender, disadvantaging circumstances or accompanying disabilities. The definitions are also culturally grounded in that they accept as valued skills those that are well suited to children's social and cultural context. On the other hand, the definitions are relatively conservative because I argue for inclusion within the gifted category only the top 5 per cent of the population on the grounds that the preponderance of people achieving just below this level (13 per cent) makes them less rare and thus more likely to have their educational or social needs met naturally.

Transformation of giftedness into talent: A developmental model

Theories abound about how giftedness (the potential to excel) becomes actualised in the form of talented performances. Drawing on many of the major theories, I have proposed a model (see Figure 2.3) that describes many dynamic influences. The theoretical aspects of this model are described elsewhere (Porter 1997, 2002c); here I shall focus on its practical implications.

Overview of the model

For gifted potential to flourish into talented performances, individuals need a supportive environment, stimulating tasks, a brain (hardware) that can profit from these, sophisticated information processing skills (software), and the ability to draw on previous experience. Their subsequent performance will then be judged by themselves and others, with criteria for excellence being modified in light of their age, experience and obstacles to achievement.

The model describing the translation of gifts into talents is based on three fundamental premises: first, that talent is fostered by a rare and complex convergence of many factors (Haensly & Reynolds 1989; Sternberg & Lubart 1991; Tannenbaum 2003); second, that the specific factors which best facilitate learning may differ at various stages of children's development

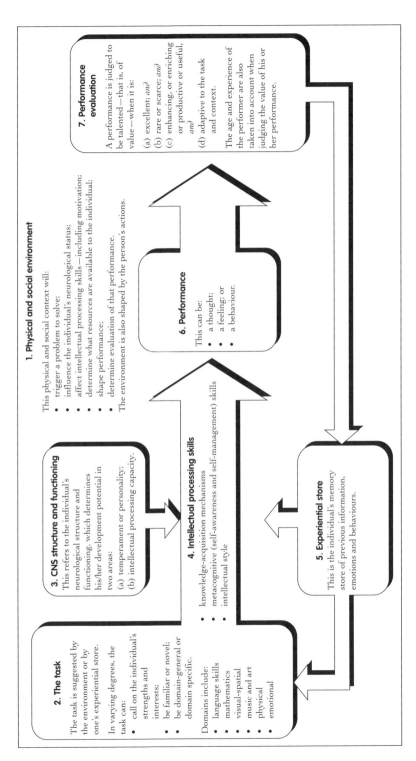

Figure 2.3 A model of the transformation of giftedness into talent

Source: Porter (1997c: 39, adapted from Gagné 1995).

(Horowitz 1992); and third, that the environment needs to provide *optimal* rather than perfect conditions, which implies that one can have too much of a good thing. For example, although group acceptance is usually considered necessary for optimal personal growth, feeling out of step with others or with the current state of knowledge is usually a necessary catalyst to the gifted person's search for a creative solution (Sternberg & Lubart 1991).

The model is an attempt to describe the influences on performances, regardless of a child's developmental potential. It can equally well apply to children with intellectual disabilities as to advanced learners. This obviates the need to generate a separate model for giftedness and so allows us, when relevant, to transfer into the gifted field knowledge that is well recognised in other disciplines and fields of special education.

Component 1: The environment

The environment encompasses both the physical and social context. It determines what catalysts and resources are available to support individuals' use of their personal skills, both in the short term and ultimately. It will make children either resilient or vulnerable to the quality of the stimulation they receive, such that when their environments facilitate optimal development, both resilient and vulnerable children will prosper, whereas when their environments are not conducive to optimal development, resilient children will still prosper but the functioning of vulnerable children will be impaired.

It is clear that, more than at any other age, young children are particularly reliant on the quality of the environment provided to them because, compared with later ages, they are less able independently to seek out an environment that meets their needs. For giftedness to flourish, children need an environment that is emotionally nurturing, offers educational opportunities that cultivate learning, fosters friendships with peers, and encourages exploration while not castigating mistakes. These features are detailed further in Chapter 9.

Component 2: The task

The second trigger for skill development is the task itself. For giftedness to express itself, tasks must offer sufficient challenge to entice children to engage and develop mastery. Tasks designed on the basis of age norms rather than children's actual developmental capacity might do neither for gifted children. Moreover, this challenge must be offered across many skill domains, rather than concentrating only on the academic. It is only by challenging children in non-traditional domains that we will allow their talents in these to emerge.

There are probably many ways of classifying these domains but, notwithstanding my criticism of the title 'intelligences' for Gardner's (1983) domains, I consider Gardner's original list to have at least face validity, so I adopt them in this component of my model with the exception that I blend interpersonal and intrapersonal domains into a single category of emotional skills because I cannot imagine how one could be tuned into others' emotions without also understanding one's own, and because interpersonal skills seem closely related to linguistic abilities (Gridley 2002) so may not be a discrete set of skills.

Component 3: Central nervous system

Children cannot profit from a supportive environment and stimulating activities unless they have a robust nervous system—rather like the hardware of a computer. Their neurological functioning is set down genetically, but is also influenced by external factors such as trauma, prenatal insults (e.g. maternal alcohol abuse leading to fetal alcohol syndrome) and environmental stimulation. Whereas parents will have little control over the genes that they pass on to their children, in many cases they will be able to avoid damage from such traumas.

Not only does individuals' genetic endowment shape the fitness of their brain, it also influences how their environment is shaped around them—for example, bright children read and think more, so contribute to their own enrichment (Plomin & Price 2003).

Thus both genetic and environmental influences affect individuals' intellectual functioning, as explained by the following sequence of ideas (Gottfredson 2003; Patrick 2000; Plomin & Price 2003; Segal 2000; Thompson & Plomin 2000).

- Parents provide environments for themselves that meet their own genetically prescribed needs.
- Their children share their genes, so environments that suit parents generally also match their children's genetic needs.
- Young children are not in command of their environments, so their abilities at young ages are determined both genetically and environmentally; however, by late adolescence they can actively select, modify and even create environments that foster the development of their genetic proclivities. By this age, their performance levels thus result from *genetic* rather than environmental influences. This seems counter-intuitive, as adolescents and adults have experienced more diverse environments and life events than earlier in life, so it could be expected that the environment would have increasing influence throughout life, but the opposite is verified by the fact that unrelated (e.g. adopted) siblings growing up in the same family have similar IQs in early childhood but by late adolescence resemble each other no more than if they were strangers.
- Thus environmental influences are more potent in the early years of development (Freeman 2000). This creates an imperative to optimise the environmental stimulation of young children.

These statements apply only to adequate levels of environmental stimu-lation; if the environment is suboptimal, its influence is greater, although gifted individuals seem to be able to extract more benefits from whatever environment they face (Freeman 2000). Individuals' genetic endowment sets the ceiling on their abilities, while their environment dictates how closely they approach that ceiling, so an impoverished environment will cause indi-viduals to achieve below their genetic potential, but even an enriching environment cannot allow them to surpass their potential.

Component 4: Information processing skills

The next influence on the worth of individuals' performances is the quality of their thinking. Information processing is not a passive process: individu-als must actively select which aspects of a task to attend to and store, and what information from previous experience to retrieve from memory to apply to the task being undertaken.

Because their learning typically happens quickly and automatically, gifted children might not be aware of the information-processing skills that they use to be successful at tasks. Therefore, it can be useful for adults to give them specific feedback about their thinking processes (some of which were listed in Figure 2.2 and are further detailed in Chapter 9).

As with environmental influences, individuals will need *optimal* levels of these dispositions in order to produce high-quality performances (Sternberg & Lubart 1991). For example, while perseverance is usually a useful quality, it is inefficient to persevere past the point where a solution is possible.

Component 5: Experiential (memory) store

Children will need to draw on their experience if they are to solve a task successfully. From past experience, remembered information or knowledge and emotional memories will tell them about their preferences and values, and thus guide them to select wisely from their repertoire of potential responses (Goleman 1994).

One way to harness their experience is for adults to describe how the present task resembles something that the children have achieved in the past. Adults can also detail the problem-solving skills and dispositions (such as planning or persisting) that they have employed previously, and which would be useful on the present task.

Component 6: Performance

The final outcome of all the previous influences is the production of a thought, feeling or behaviour. Performances or products do not have to be inventions or works of art, nor even be in a public domain, but can also entail acts of altruism, leadership, nurturing of one's family or community, or self-fulfilment (Noble et al. 1999). And, according to Sternberg (2003), they can be measured as successful according to whether they satisfy personal rather than external standards. On the understanding that individuals need to find fulfil-ment in what they do (see Chapter 3), their achievements should not have to meet external standards of fame or status, but instead should be evaluated according to whether they satisfy their own inner agenda or life script. Nevertheless this self-actualisation is not self-centred: humans are understood to be fulfilled only with reference to both themselves and others (Grant & Piechowski 1999).

Component 7: Evaluation of a performance

Individuals will evaluate their own performance using standards learned from their social environment. Meanwhile, the outside world will judge their performances and, if they are considered excellent, the performer may be labelled as gifted. When it comes to external acclaim, adults' performances are typically judged to be exceptional when they are *excellent* (that is, of high quality); *rare*; of *value* (that is, they enrich or enhance life in some way or are useful in that they make life easier, safer, healthier, more intelligible or more enjoyable); and are *appropriate to the time and place* (Ebert 1994; Feldhusen 1986; Gruber 1986; Haensly & Reynolds 1989; Renzulli 1986; Shore & Dover 1987; Sternberg & Lubart 1991; Sternberg & Zhang 1995; Tannenbaum 1983). With children, judgments of talent also have to be tempered by awareness of their age, experience and obstacles to achieve-ment. With this in mind, young children can be considered gifted even though they are not yet in a position to contribute in the public sphere.

Conclusion

Giftedness is not an entity with which some individuals are blessed, but is incremental: it blossoms into talent when an optimal environment facilitates children's growth.

Returning to the anecdotes at the beginning of this chapter, it is clear that children's internal makeup has to be able to profit from the input that their environment provides, which means that they cannot be induced to perform at advanced levels simply through hot-housing. Thus individuals' achievements are a result of both makeup *and* their environment. Beyond a threshold level of environmental stimulation, their makeup has most influ-ence on the quality of their performances but, in a suboptimal environment that provides inadequate stimulation and learning opportunities, the envi-ronment has most influence on outcomes. This implies a strong imperative to offer all children, and the young in particular, an environment that will foster their development and well-being.

Suggested further reading

For an academic discussion about intelligence:
Sternberg, R.J. (ed.) 2000 *Handbook of intelligence* Cambridge University Press, Cambridge.

For detailed academic reading about the various conceptions of giftedness, I suggest:
Sternberg, R.J. and Davidson, J.E. (eds) 1986 *Conceptions of giftedness* Cambridge University Press, Cambridge.

For a less technical discussion of various models of giftedness:
Colangelo, N. and Davis, G.A. (eds) 2003 *Handbook of gifted education* 3rd edn, Allyn & Bacon, Boston, MA.

Or, for less detailed information, see:
Montgomery, D. 1996 *Educating the able* Cassell, London.

EMOTIONAL NEEDS OF
GIFTED CHILDREN
Part II

EMOTIONAL ISSUES FOR
GIFTED CHILDREN three

> *We want more for our children than healthy bodies. We want our children to*
> *have lives filled with friendship and love and high deeds. We want them to be*
> *eager to learn and be willing to confront challenges ... We want them to grow*
> *up with confidence in the future, a love of adventure, a sense of justice, and*
> *courage enough to act on that sense of justice. We want them to be resilient in*
> *the face of the setbacks and failures that growing up always brings.*
> *(Seligman 1995: 6)*

The emotional adjustment of gifted children

Since Terman's finding (Terman et al. 1947) that gifted individuals are well
adjusted was compared with Hollingworth's conclusion that highly gifted
children are emotionally and socially vulnerable, there has been an ongoing
debate about the emotional well-being of gifted individuals. On one side of
the debate is an impressive body of writers who contend, first, that gifted
children have unique emotional characteristics compared with average
learners and, second, that these emotional traits undermine their emotional
stability.

These writers believe that gifted individuals' highly attuned nervous
systems (their brains) contribute both to advanced learning and to an
increase in their emotional sensitivity, intensity and responsiveness (Geake
1997; Lovecky 1992; Miller et al. 1994; Morelock 1996; Piechowski 2003).
In other words, giftedness and emotional intensity are biologically linked,
with Geake attributing this to more efficient communication between gifted
individuals' limbic systems (the seat of emotions in the brain) and their
prefrontal lobes, which are responsible for the executive functions or
metacognitive abilities that oversee our learning. Therefore, when children

demonstrate advanced learning capacities—which (among other things) involve superior use of metacognitive skills—it is likely that they also have more ready access to their emotional stores.

The specific emotional vulnerabilities said to characterise the gifted population include: emotional sensitivity and intensity (or 'overexcitability'); low self-esteem; perfectionism; anxiety about having to meet high expectations; depression; increased suicide ideation and attempts; behavioural difficulties, including delinquency and elevated rates of high school drop-out; social difficulties; and psychiatric disorders including mood disturbances and eating disorders. Such an extensive list calls for examination of the evidence about each.

'Overexcitability'

Looking back on the lives of eminent adults, Dabrowski identified five areas in which the gifted can be 'overexcitable': the intellectual, emotional, imagination, psychomotor and sensual domains. To many, the term 'overexcitability' might have negative connotations of neurosis, but in fact is taken by Dabrowski and his adherents to mean an abundance of psychic energy which provides 'positive potential for further growth' (Tucker & Hafenstein 1997).

This view has attracted many gifted education commentators, and may in the future prove to be true; however, the present state of evidence has not yet made its case. The first source of apparent support comes from a study which found that gifted doctoral students did characterise themselves as being more intense intellectually and emotionally, and that these intensities both enriched their lives and provided positive potential for their personal growth (Lewis et al. 1992). Nevertheless, this pattern might simply apply to doctoral students rather than to gifted people in general.

Another study, which offered at least partial support for Dabrowski's characterisation of gifted individuals as intense, found no relationship between preschool children's high scores on IQ and creativity tests and displays of 'overexcitability', although parents did report that their children in the highest IQ brackets were more intense intellectually than less gifted children (Kitano 1990b). This 'intensity' does not signify emotional difficulties, although it could be hypothesised that thwarting an intense need could bring about a stronger than usual reaction (Freeman 1983), in which case it is not the intensity as such, but instead inappropriate responses from others, that can create difficulties for gifted children.

Shaywitz and colleagues (2001) found that highly (but not moderately) gifted boys were active in exploring and experimenting, yielding a restless behaviour pattern that was not pathological but nevertheless was demanding on teachers and parents. Ackerman (1997) found evidence of psychomotor, intellectual and emotional excitabilities (in that order) in gifted adolescents. She hypothesised that motor intensity supplies the necessary energy to achieve, particularly for the twelve- to fourteen-year age group which she studied. On the other hand, fully one-third of the 'nongifted' children resembled the gifted children in their pattern of excitabilities, while a quarter of the gifted students matched the 'nongifted' ones. Ackerman took this to mean that these children had been mislabelled, although it could equally mean that the excitable emotional profile is neither unique nor essential to giftedness.

A further source of evidence comes from a study by LeVine and Tucker (1986). These researchers found that gifted six- to eight-year-olds showed greater awareness of others' feelings, and had more sophisticated moral reasoning and a more internal locus of control than average learners. These characteristics, of course, could simply be aspects of intellectual sophistication rather than signs of emotional sensitivity. On the other hand, when combined with limited life experience, precocious perceptiveness can cause children to misinterpret events and this, in turn, could lead to emotional difficulties (Freeman 1983).

A further study claims to strengthen the case for 'overexcitability'. Tucker and Hafenstein (1997) asked teachers to nominate a child (aged four to six years) who fitted the description of each of Dabrowski's five types of 'overexcitability'. Next, the researchers gathered assessment data about each child, questionnaire information from parents and observations of the children in class. The researchers concluded that the nominated children did indeed display the characteristics of intellectual, imaginational and emotional 'overexcitability'. However, this research method is akin to volunteering smokers for a study and then discovering that they all smoke! The results tell us nothing of how typical the pattern of 'overexcitability' is for gifted children in general.

A more recent study claims to find higher levels of various overexcitabilities in college (university) students who had attended gifted programs in their school years compared with those who had not (Bouchet & Falk 2001). However, many of those not selected for gifted programs could nevertheless still be gifted, in which case the comparison group is tainted. Furthermore, correlations are meaningless within a narrow range of abilities as represented by college students (as illustrated in Figure 2.1).

Together, then, these studies tell us little: some gifted children are 'overexcitable' in the sense of being super-stimulated; however, many are not, and some average learners are also 'overexcitable'. Only time will tell whether the prediction that gifted children are *more* 'overexcitable' than average is accurate, and whether it proves useful in understanding and meeting their needs.

Low self-esteem

Gifted children typically have high self-esteem when it comes to their area of talent (Chapman & McAlpine 1988; Hoge & Renzulli 1993; Sekowski 1995;

van Boxtel & Mönks 1992), although as many as 20 per cent seriously underestimate their abilities (Phillips 1984, 1987), while some will have lower self-esteem in other domains such as physical and social skills.

The children's educational placement affects research findings about their self-esteem. It seems that attendance at gifted programs lowers the children's academic self-esteem (but still to above-average levels), while raising their social self-esteem (Chan 1988; Coleman & Fults 1982; Craven & Marsh 1997; Gross 1997, 1998; Hoge & Renzulli 1993; Marsh et al. 1995; Olszewski et al. 1987; Schneider et al. 1989; Wright & Leroux 1997). There is more about this topic in Chapter 4.

Perfectionism

Gifted children have often been accused of perfectionism, with the assumption that this is a bad thing. However, perfectionism comes in many forms: a healthy striving for excellence; a neurotic or dysfunctional form in which individuals are never satisfied with their performances, no matter what their quality; and organisational perfectionism where individuals try to exert control over all aspects of their lives.

This issue is discussed in Chapter 4, but suffice it to say here that there is little evidence that gifted children are more prone to the dysfunctional form of perfectionism, although it is probably true that they are perfectionists in a positive sense, in that they strive for high achievement because they know they are capable of it (LoCicero & Ashby 2000; Parker & Adkins 1995; Parker 1996; Siegle & Schuler 2000; Wood & Care 2002). Their perfectionism is the engine that drives them to achieve, and so acts as a positive influence in their lives, rather than contributing to emotional difficulties (Silverman 1994).

Anxiety and stress

Strictly speaking, *stress* is a physical reaction to feeling out of control, particularly of negative events in life, while *worries* are negative thoughts and *anxiety* is the emotional aspect of distress. However, in common usage, the word 'stress' is usually a shorthand way of referring to all three elements.

A stress reaction can arise from major life upheavals or an accumulation of everyday strains. Gifted children are said to be exposed to higher levels of stress because of high expectations of their achievement, particularly for those in gifted programs. But some research has found the opposite: that gifted learners are less anxious about their academic skills and feel more in command of their learning (Davis & Connell 1985). The evidence suggests that, generally, both students in gifted programs and those in regular education do not differ from average learners in their anxiety levels, although a rise in gifted adolescents' anxiety in the late high school years is possible (Baker 1996; Neihart 1999).

Moreover, even if gifted children have higher demands placed on them, this does not mean that they will actually develop a stress reaction. Challenging life events (stressors) lead to stress only if individuals believe that the challenge exceeds their coping resources. Given that gifted children have excellent problem-solving skills, it is likely that these would allow them to cope even with elevated stressors.

Depression

Depression is often said to be higher in the gifted population. Yet, in her analysis of many studies, Neihart (1999, 2002a) concludes that gifted children experience depression at similar or lower rates than others. This stands to reason: given that depression is related to feeling helpless or out of control of one's life, gifted children would be less prone to such emotions as they are more likely to have an internal locus of control—that is, to feel in command of their lives. They are also more likely to have high levels of organisational perfectionism (which is a gracious term for being 'control freaks'), immunising them against depression (Lynd-Stevenson & Hearne 1999).

Suicide

Another claim of those who believe in the increased vulnerability of the gifted is that they have a high suicide rate. However, there is in fact no evidence that this is the case (Gust-Brey & Cross 1999; Lajoie & Shore 1981), and it is obviously impossible to conduct postmortem IQ tests, so data cannot be collected retrospectively.

The claim originally arose from reports that people who complete suicide are generally of above-average intelligence, whereas those who attempt suicide by non-lethal means tend to be less intelligent (Hayes & Sloat 1989). But this is a far cry from claiming that *gifted* people are more prone to suicide, as above-average IQ falls below the gifted range.

The contention can also be dismissed by examining the precursors of suicide in the general population. As might be expected, emotional disturbances (sometimes leading to and exacerbated by social withdrawal), family dysfunction and illicit drug use are all common precursors to suicide, particularly when combined with impulsiveness (Dixon & Scheckel 1996), but there is no higher rate of these characteristics in the gifted population than amongst others.

Despite the lack of data, two lines of reasoning keep the contention active. The first is the presumption that the gifted are vulnerable to suicide because of their emotional sensitivities, perfectionism and asynchronous development. However, as already discussed, the evidence in support of these characteristics is not compelling.

The second line of reasoning is that, if gifted individuals are sensitive, they will be more vulnerable to suicide because their feelings of helplessness, hopelessness and worthlessness are more likely to be trivialised by outsiders (Hayes & Sloat 1989).

Behavioural difficulties

Many writers and researchers (e.g. Clark 2002; Cornell et al. 1994; Gallucci 1988) report a low incidence of behavioural problems among gifted students. Delisle et al. (1987: 38, in Clark 2002: 542) report:

> Gifted students generally do not develop behavior problems when they are: (a) placed with a teacher who enjoys teaching gifted children and learning with them; (b) afforded frequent opportunities to learn with intellectual peers; (c) actively engaged in learning that is appropriately complex, challenging and meaningful; and (d) provided [with] guidance in how to understand and cope with their giftedness in society.

Because they are able to anticipate outcomes at younger ages, gifted children tend to be more careful and less impulsive than other children (Roeper 1995b). Nevertheless, some do evidence some behavioural difficulties:

- as a way of coping with boredom (Freeman 1995a; Plucker & McIntire 1996);
- to prove to peers that they are not so smart after all (Clark 2002);
- because of their heightened activity levels (Shaywitz et al. 2001);
- as part of an underachievement syndrome (Clark 2002; Delisle 1992; Freeman 1995a);
- when their emotional development has not caught up with their intellectual precocity.

As a result, the children might display intense emotional outbursts which look immature, compared with both their age and their ability levels. As well as these outbursts, other emotional and behavioural issues were identified by Damiani (1997), who found that 38 per cent of 32 parents of young gifted children reported sufficient behavioural difficulties at home to warrant their seeking professional advice. The behaviours of concern included being unable to be distracted from something which was forbidden, arguing at length over parents' directives, being bossy and becoming frustrated with other children. Nevertheless, these difficulties arise mainly from the children's attempts to think independently, rather than being motivated by a desire to be deliberately disruptive (Silverman 1997). The behaviours are not outright challenges to parental authority, unless parents interpret them as such—see Chapter 6.

In terms of antisocial behavioural difficulties, an elevated high school dropout rate has often been linked to giftedness. This, however, is a myth:

the rate is the same (around 17 per cent) for both gifted and other students (Irvine 1987). Even so, given their abilities, gifted young people could be expected to achieve better than this, so this dropout rate could be considered to be unduly high. Yet it seems that gifted students' personal reasons for leaving school prematurely are similar to those of other dropouts: school failure, not liking school, falling pregnant, or other personal or family problems (Renzulli & Park 2000). However, the families of gifted dropouts and those of students who remain in school differ in that the parents of gifted dropouts are more likely to come from minority cultures and have low incomes and low educational levels (Renzulli & Park 2000). These parents might have low educational aspirations for their children, be less involved in the school and in negotiating other options besides dropping out, and offer less academic support.

Delinquency has often been raised as a behavioural issue for gifted adolescents. However, the opposite is more likely to be the case, as persistent antisocial behaviour is related to lower IQ and less sophisticated moral reasoning (Neihart 2002b).

Underachievement is associated with a higher rate of adolescent delinquency, but both underachievement and delinquency are due to nonconformity to social norms, or antisocial attitudes and values (McCord 1993; Tremblay et al. 1992). In turn, these attitudes have familial and social causes which are unrelated to whether the young people are gifted or not.

Social difficulties

Developmentally gifted children are out of stage—which is to say that their cognitive development proceeds ahead of that of their age mates, resulting in talents that differ from the average. This, in turn, can lead to feeling *socially* 'out of phase' with age mates in that they have few interests in common (Manaster & Powell 1988). Together, these two facts cause some writers to contend that gifted children feel *psychologically* 'out of sync'—that is, they feel different and, as a consequence, believe that they *cannot* fit in with others. It is claimed that this sense of being different makes them vulnerable to social maladjustment.

However, being different can in fact be a source of pride for many (Freeman 1993, 1997); most will have gifted parents and other relatives with whom they share common interests, and it is possible that their developmental differences mean simply that gifted children face *different* social challenges, while still being able to maintain a good overall level of adjustment (Manaster & Powell 1988).

Psychiatric disturbance

The notion of the 'mad genius' still permeates lay understandings of giftedness, despite evidence that ongoing mental illness and gifted productivity are incompatible (Yewchuk 1995a, 1995b). There simply is *not* 'a fine line between insanity and genius', as the myth claims.

There is some suggestion that highly creative adults may be more prone to mood and thought disorders, at a rate of around 10 per cent (Neihart 1999, 2002a; Yewchuk 1995b). However, this could be an overestimation as it is typically based on retrospective biographies of famous achievers, accounts of whose lives are contaminated by the superstitions and limited medical knowledge of the times; while, for present-day creative adults, the higher incidence could be due to the effects of their fame or impoverished life circumstances rather than to their creativity as such (Kerr & Cohn 2001).

For the remainder of the gifted population, the incidence of emotional disturbance is probably lower than or the same as for all others (Gallucci et al. 1999b). Given that between 9 and 10 per cent of all children experience some emotional difficulties (Gallucci 1988), and that some of these children will be gifted, we know that *some* gifted children will experience emotional difficulties (Konza 1997). However, mental illness and giftedness are separate: although a person *can* have both, one does not *cause* the other.

Conclusion

Based on the evidence to date, two conclusions are justified. The first is that there is little evidence so far that gifted children are more prone to any of the emotional difficulties just discussed—that is, the weight of evidence leads to the conclusion that giftedness does not cause emotional maladjustment (Feldhusen & Nimlos-Hippen 1992; Freeman 1991; Gallucci 1988; Gallucci et al. 1999a, 1999b; Garland & Zigler 1999; Grossberg & Cornell 1988; Gust 1997; Gust-Brey & Cross 1999; Lehman & Erdwins 1981; Neihart 1999, 2002a; Robinson & Noble 1991; Rost & Czeschlik 1994).

Indeed, it is even possible that gifted children and adults are *better* adjusted than the average, both ultimately and during their childhood (Clark 2002; Grossberg & Cornell 1988; Janos & Robinson 1985; Kunkel et al. 1995; Moon et al. 1997; Nail & Evans 1997; Olszewski-Kubilius et al. 1988; Parker 1996). This can come about because, although being different can raise some challenges for gifted children, they generally have the support of well-resourced parents who are also gifted and highly achieving (Stedtnitz 1995). As well as these external resources, they also have internal skills— that is, sophisticated cognitive skills—for solving any problems they face, so can make satisfactory adjustments to being gifted (Freeman 1997; Webb 1993; Whitmore 1980). In the words of Clark (2002: 175), 'the very ability that creates the problem can supply the solution'. Furthermore, their gifted skills make it likely that they will experience considerable success and accolade which, in turn, may contribute to their positive adjustment (Garland & Zigler 1999; Joswig & Tuchow 1996).

The second conclusion is that, although their makeup does not generate emotional maladjustment, the lack of suitable provisions certainly can. This means that when children are displaying emotional, social or behavioural difficulties, we should look to their context and what is being provided for them, and adjust that. The problem is the fact that their needs are not being met, rather than that their makeup is flawed.

Reasons for the persistence of myths about gifted children's emotional status

If we continue to claim an association between giftedness and emotional problems, we make parents reluctant to identify their children as gifted, we cause children who do have emotional difficulties unrelated to their giftedness to be overlooked, and we maintain misconceptions and misunderstandings of gifted children's characteristics and needs (Gust 1997). We also disempower parents, causing them to feel that they do not know how to make wise choices for their child or guide their child's emotional development.

Despite these negative outcomes, misconceptions about the emotional status of gifted children continue to circulate. This can be partly due to the complexity of research, the findings of which depend on the culture, age, gender, placement and ability profiles of the children being studied, while sample bias and errors of reasoning lead to findings about specific groups being over-generalised to all gifted children.

Culture

The first and most fundamental reason for discrepancies in conclusions is the culture of the children being studied and of the researchers themselves. In Western cultures, the distrust mentioned in Chapter 7 of any elite group (outside of sport) leads to negative reactions to giftedness which can cause gifted children to perceive themselves negatively. This is in contrast to countries such as Singapore and China, for example, where parents and teachers with whom I have discussed this express amazement that Western cultures could have anything but deep respect for highly able learners. In these Asian countries, I am told, being gifted is literally seen as a gift, so there is no assumption that it would cause emotional difficulties (although the pressure to achieve in those cultures could create stress for gifted and average learners alike).

Sample bias

The next reason for overstating the emotional difficulties of gifted children is that, as could be expected, this topic is dominated by clinical psychologists' accounts. However, parents and children consult psychologists only when there is a problem to be solved. That is, virtually 100 per cent of those consulting psychologists have problems, but for every child attending a psychologist's consulting rooms, there could be 99 who do not: we simply do not know the ratio. Psychologists' accounts are valuable for telling us the *types* of difficulties that gifted young people can experience, but they do not tell us about the *rate* of these—that is, how common the difficulties are.

Another possibility is that the myths about gifted children's vulner-abilities lead to stereotypes about giftedness, which in turn mean that individuals with emotional problems disproportionately come to adult atten-tion, while those who are well adjusted are less likely to be recognised as being gifted (Freeman 1983, 1991, 1993, 1997).

The reverse could also be true in that children are selected to attend gifted programs because they are so soundly adjusted that they can perform well at school and therefore come to be identified as gifted. In that event, those in gifted programs would appear to be better adjusted than average learners, but it could be argued that it was their emotional status—not their giftedness alone—that allowed them into the program in the first place.

Placement

The preponderance of studies of children in gifted programs also raises the issue that these programs could either be meeting the children's needs so the children will have fewer difficulties, or the programs could raise expec-tations for the children's achievement and thus generate more emotional difficulties for them. We do not know the extent to which findings about children in gifted programs apply to gifted children elsewhere.

Age of subjects

Although I concluded earlier that gifted young people and adults ultimately achieve a high level of emotional adjustment, it is possible that there are key periods during childhood when they experience difficulties. For example, there appears to be a downturn in young people's self-confidence during the early to middle high school years, with some improvement thereafter (although not necessarily reverting to former high levels) (Klein & Zehms 1996; Kline & Short 1991; Kunkel et al. 1995; Lewis & Knight 2000; van Boxtel & Mönks 1992). If younger and late high school students are studied, there is little evidence of social or emotional problems, whereas difficulties do emerge in the middle adolescent years.

Although there has been no research conducted on the social adjust-ment of young gifted children, I believe early childhood to be a sensitive time also. This comes about because these children's additional needs are only just being discovered and responded to at this age; parents are just becoming acquainted with the implications of these needs for their parent-ing role; and young children generally have access to only a narrow age range of peers.

Over-generalisation

Another reason for overstating gifted children's vulnerabilities is that descriptions of the emotional patterns of exceptionally gifted children are often wrongly applied to those with more mild levels of giftedness. The life experiences of someone with an IQ of 180 are very different from those of someone who has an IQ of 130, so we cannot assume that what characterises the exceptionally gifted population is true for the whole gifted group.

Syllogistic reasoning

In my view, the most fundamental reason for the persistence of the myths is the erroneous assumption that life challenges will necessarily lead to emotional difficulties. This is an error because challenges do not lead to difficulties in some linear fashion. To claim so is a case of syllogistic reasoning, which states that if *a* leads to *b* and *b* leads to *c*, then *a* must lead to *c*—thus gifted children feel different; feeling different leads to adjustment problems; therefore, gifted children must have extra adjustment problems (Neihart 1999, 2002).

However, even if gifted children do experience challenges, this does not necessarily mean that these will generate emotional difficulties for them. They are likely to possess more intellectual coping mechanisms than most others, while individuals of any ability level can be protected from negative reactions to adversity by a caring relationship with at least one adult beyond the immediate family, family cohesion and support, an internal locus of control and problem-solving skills (Bland et al. 1994; Compas 1987; Dole 2000; Neihart 2002c; Rutter 1985). While the gifted population may have no superiority in these external support factors, they generally have an advantage in terms of internal coping skills.

Second, no characteristic or trait is positive or negative in itself (Delisle & Galbraith 2002): how it is channelled governs how it affects individuals' lives. This is reflected in Box 3.1, which details some commonly cited emotional characteristics of gifted children and illustrates that, well harnessed and disciplined, the same traits that could lead to emotional difficulties can instead result in a positive and rich emotional life. As examples even conscientiousness can lead to stress if the worker does not rein in the drive to do too much, while students can benefit in the long term by drawing on their stubbornness to complete a course of study that has become tedious.

Type of ability

Research conclusions about the effects of giftedness can depend on the domain in which the children are talented. Verbally gifted children are more socially obvious in more settings, so could have extra adjustment difficulties compared with those whose skills are confined to a restricted domain, such

Box 3.1 Positive and dysfunctional expressions of some common emotional characteristics of gifted children

Trait	Positive expression	Dysfunctional expression
Sensitivity	Perceptiveness Empathy Imagination	Over-reaction to criticism or mistakes Early appearance of fears
Perfectionism	Striving for excellence High achievement Self-esteem from success	Procrastination Frustration Disappointment, whatever the standard of one's work Punitive expectations of self High demands of others
High task commitment	Exuberance Enthusiasm Curiosity Sustained concentration High motivation Focus Persistence	Boredom with repetitive tasks Underachievement with routine activities Irritation at being interrupted Insatiability Stubbornness Fatigue
Independent thinking	Creativity Wide range of interests Responsible, independent Autonomous	Lack of interest in details Scattered and disorganised Difficulty working with others Nonconformist
Internal locus of control	Learns from mistakes	May blame self for mistakes
Social perceptiveness	Sense of humour Insight Leadership	Self-deprecation Manipulation of others Alienation/isolation
Sense of justice and idealism	Empathy Interest in social issues Cynicism about authority	Disappointment/outrage when others do not abide by rules Stress from helplessness to effect social change

as mathematics (Ablard 1997; Brody & Benbow 1986; Dauber & Benbow 1990; Swiatek 1995).

Levels of ability

There is an hypothesis that, as IQ rises, the uniqueness—and, in turn, the emotional difficulties—of gifted individuals becomes more pronounced, as illustrated in Figure 3.1 (Brounstein et al. 1991; Delisle 1992; Gross 1997, 2004; Kline & Meckstroth 1985; Kline & Short 1991; Tannenbaum 1992; van Boxtel & Mönks 1992; Whitmore 1980). This is the curvilinear model of socio-emotional adjustment (Grossberg & Cornell 1988). However, although it seems intuitively appealing, and despite the difficulty of locating enough highly gifted subjects to test this hypothesis rigorously, the few studies on the issue have found no significant difference in adjustment between moderately and highly gifted students (Garland & Zigler 1999; Oram et al. 1995).

Comparison group

Some writers (e.g. Lehman & Erdwins 1981) observe that, when compared with children of the same mental age, gifted children's adjustment is similar, but that when compared with same-aged children, their adjustment is better—particularly in the social skills domain. So conclusions about the gifted population largely depend on with whom they are being compared.

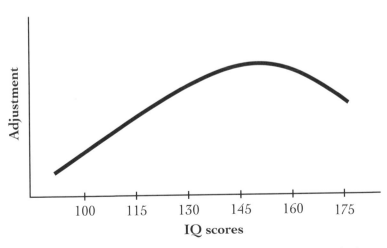

Figure 3.1 Hypothesised curvilinear relationship between IQ and emotional adjustment

Conclusion: Persistence of myths

There is a risk of over-generalising findings about gifted children's vulnerabilities, and particularly of applying to the wider gifted population observations about those who present with clinical conditions, those in gifted programs, or those with extreme levels of giftedness. At the same time, gifted children can have some atypical needs, frustration of which might provoke emotional difficulties. Any difficulties, then, arise not from the children's inbuilt characteristics but from the mismatch between their needs and what is being provided for them.

A model of emotional needs

It is my contention that gifted children share the same human needs as anyone else, but that what satisfies these might not be typical: adults and babies both feel hunger, but the curry that satisfies an adult's appetite is unlikely to be suitable for the newborn. Similarly, a fast-paced educational program that meets the needs of gifted learners will be unsuitable for those who need to learn more slowly.

To detail these needs, I have generated a model based on one originally developed by Abraham Maslow (1968), in which he proposed that individuals' emotional needs can be ranked in a hierarchy, whereby they must fulfill earlier needs before they can focus on meeting their higher-level needs. I have extended his model into the one depicted in Figure 3.2.

As you can see, the model is founded on a tree. At its root—the source of all growth—is the need for physical survival: for food, shelter, warmth and procreation. This first level of human need requires that adults supply the fundamental physical requirements to sustain life and do not inflict injury on children. It is a common adage that hungry children will think only of food, implying that poverty can directly affect the ability of children to engage in an educational program and so will limit their skill development and thus the realisation of giftedness.

At level 2 (depicted in Figure 3.2 as the trunk of the tree) is, first, the need to feel safe, both physically and emotionally. Whereas adolescents and adults can choose to take part in activities and to associate with people who bolster their self-esteem and support the growth of their natural skills, young children in particular are at the mercy of the contexts in which we place them. This means that during their early years in particular, children rely on adults to create an accepting environment which supports experimentation, so that they are emboldened to attempt new challenges and grow intellectually.

The second level 2 need is for well-being. I have experienced many unwell children whose parents reported that their children had low self-esteem despite the parents' best efforts. I have come to understand that this is simply because, when children must maintain a constant focus on getting

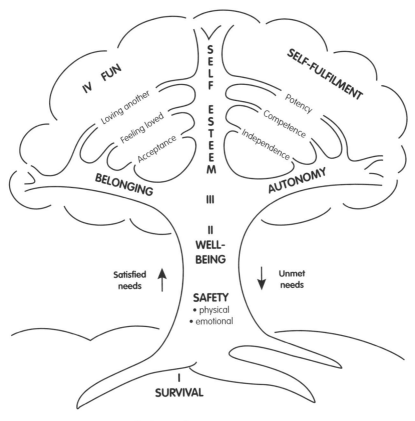

Figure 3.2 A model of individuals' needs

well and staying well, they do not have sufficient energy left over to focus on the next, higher, level of needs.

At the next level are the core emotional needs, depicted in Figure 3.2 as the tree's three limbs:

- self-esteem: the need to value oneself;
- belonging: the need to love and be loved;
- autonomy: the need to be self-determining.

In the model in Figure 3.2, self-esteem is the central of these three emotional needs, but it cannot exist in isolation: individuals cannot feel positively about themselves without relating warmly to others and feeling in command of themselves. So, in the model, the three needs have connections, depicted as branches, with self-esteem and belonging both requiring that children experience acceptance, love and the opportunity to love at least one other person; while self-esteem and autonomy both require that children can exercise increasing independence, develop competence and feel a sense of potency. This triumvirate are the core emotional needs which are the focus of Chapters 4 to 6.

Finally in the model is the first level 4 need for fun (depicted in Figure 3.2 as the tree's foliage). This is the intangible joy that we experience when our lower needs are met (Glasser 1986). Adults cannot compel children to have fun, but we can provide the conditions that meet their needs and so make it more likely that they will enjoy their educational experiences. As gifted children are typically aware early that they are different from their age mates, experience a lack of intellectual peers, and are often frustrated in their quest for intellectual challenge, there is an increased risk with these children that their lower-order needs (especially those at level 3) will not be met. Therefore, they may not necessarily find enjoyable those things in which their age mates delight.

The second level 4 need is for self-fulfilment. This refers to our drive to develop our abilities fully. This need implies that the goal of any program for gifted children must be to embolden them to use their skills—not because they have any greater moral obligation than average learners to 'meet their potential', but because it is assumed that we as individuals will be self-fulfilled only when we fully exercise our qualities and abilities. This self-actualisation also entails making contributions to the well-being of those around us.

The final aspect of the model is the arrows on each side of the tree's trunk. In line with the hierarchical nature of the model, the upward arrow indicates that individuals are free to pursue their higher-level needs only when their lower-order needs are satisfied. Alternatively, the downward arrow indicates that if higher-order needs are not satisfied, individuals can react as if their very security and survival are being threatened.

Conclusion

The evidence detailed in this chapter shows that gifted children are no more prone to emotional threats than others and that, even if they were, emotional challenges would not necessarily lead to maladjustment.

So when gifted children experience emotional difficulties, it is unlikely that these are caused by their giftedness as such. Instead, two processes are likely to be occurring. The first is that the same mechanisms which lead to emotional disturbance in the rest of the population similarly affect gifted children (Gallucci et al. 1999a; Garland & Zigler 1999)—namely, adverse family or environmental events acting on a genetic predisposition. The yacht with a defect in its mast will be safe in calm sailing conditions, but a storm will cause the flawed mast to fracture. In other words, there can be hazards in the environment, but these will not result in difficulties if individuals' constitution and supports are intact.

Second, their difficulties *could* be related to their giftedness; although not to their psychological makeup as such, but rather the negative reactions and educational neglect that they may endure. In other words, external reactions to their giftedness may generate the problems. This conclusion is supported by findings that when schools appropriately adjust their programs to meet these children's needs, in the absence of other triggers, the children's emotional difficulties improve. It is also endorsed by Schauer's (1976) findings that the majority of gifted individuals who were showing signs of poor adjustment in fact had undetected learning difficulties which were not being catered for educationally.

It seems plain to me that most of what we know about meeting the needs of all children applies equally well to gifted youngsters. Our job in raising or educating children—gifted or not—is to help them develop resilience in the face of life's inevitable setbacks by minimising the risk factors in their lives, teaching them coping skills, and providing outside support to supplement their internal resources (Dole 2000). This then leads us into the three chapters that form the remainder of Part II, each of which examines one of the three core emotional needs, with a particular focus on their implications for young gifted children.

Suggested further reading

Delisle, J. and Galbraith, J. 2002 *When gifted kids don't have all the answers: how to meet their scoial and emotional needs* Free Spirit Press, Minneapolis, MN.
Neihart, M., Reis, S.M., Robinson, N.M. and Moon, S.M. eds 2002 *Social and emotional development of gifted children: what do we know?* National Association for Gifted Children, Washington, DC.

SELF-ESTEEM
four

Self-esteem is not a trivial pursuit that can be built by pepping children up with empty praise, extra pats, and cheers of support. Such efforts are temporary at best, and deceptive at worst. Our children need coaches, not cheerleaders. (Curry and Johnson 1990: 153)

Introduction

The model introduced in Chapter 3 places self-esteem at the centre of the three core emotional needs, but it cannot exist in isolation: it is intimately connected to feelings of belonging and autonomy, as illustrated in the model in Figure 3.1 (See page 61.). In other words, to feel positively about themselves, children need to feel loved and to be competent at worthwhile skills.

The nature of self-esteem

Children learn about themselves through feedback from their parents and other important people in their lives. By a process called 'reflective appraisal', they interpret this feedback to build a picture of the type of people they are (a self-concept) and the type of people adults want them to be (their ideal self). They then judge how much they measure up to this ideal. Therefore, self-esteem has three parts: the self-concept, the ideal self and self-esteem itself (Burns 1982; Pope et al. 1988). This is depicted in Figure 4.1 as overlapping circles. In this model of self-esteem, the self-concept and ideal self will never overlap entirely, as we all need goals for which to strive; so whenever we achieve one important goal, our ideal self expands to set new horizons for our next achievement.

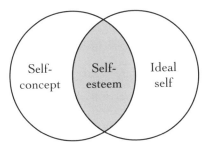

Figure 4.1 Self-esteem as the overlap between the self-concept and ideal self

The self-concept

Also termed self-perception, this is our image or description of ourselves. Individuals' self-concept results from prior successes and failures and, to a lesser extent, contributes to their subsequent performances (McCoach & Siegle 2003). Young children's self-concept has very few elements, encompassing the basics of how they look, what they wear, their state of health and their possessions. However, their view of themselves expands as they grow older to encompass differential perceptions of their relationships, abilities and talents at sport and academic work, temperament, religious ideas, and ability to manage their lives (Burns 1982). Their ancestors, family, racial and cultural membership will also be part of children's self-concept.

The ideal self

The ideal self is a set of beliefs about how we 'should' be. It ranks our skills and qualities according to how important or valued they are to other people, particularly our parents. Then we internalise these value systems into a set of aspirations, goals or ideals for ourselves. These ideals can be explicit—such as expecting only distinction grades in academic work—or implicit, with standards that individuals hardly know they are imposing on themselves and which therefore can be difficult to identify and challenge (Pope et al. 1988).

Self-esteem

Our self-esteem is an overall judgment about whether our qualities and performances meet or fall short of our ideal standards. This judgment is an internal one, whereby we compare our skills in one domain with those in others, and an external one whereby we compare our skills to those of our peers (Plucker & Stocking 2001). This means that gifted children with uneven skill levels or those with an able peer group may be more vulnerable to low self-esteem.

It is likely that the various facets of self-concept have variable influence on overall self-esteem across individuals and cultures. For example, academic self-concept might have more influence on overall self-esteem than physical self-concept for intellectually gifted children, but the reverse would be true for athletes; while in cultures that value collectivism rather than individual distinction, children's social self-concept might have more overall influence than, say, their academic abilities (Worrell 2002).

A mathematical way of conceptualising self-esteem could be (Mruk 1999):

$$\text{Self-esteem} = \frac{\text{perceived success}}{\text{aspirations}}$$

This formula tells us that individuals' self-esteem can improve either by becoming more aware of their successes (expanding their self-concept) or by making their aspirations (ideal self) more realistic and achievable (Mruk 1999). I will return to this theme shortly.

Self-esteem issues for gifted children

Most of the information that we have about gifted children's self-esteem comes from school-aged children and adolescents. These findings are summarised here, but we have to be cautious when applying them to a younger age group, as these children have received very little research focus.

Box 4.1 Characteristics of individuals with low versus healthy self-esteem

Low	Healthy
Anticipate failure and so resist challenges	Approach new and challenging tasks in the confident expectation of being successful
Lack assertiveness	Show initiative
Do not resist peer pressure	Trust their own ideas
Seek external approval and recognition	Seek to develop competence and to satisfy their own goals
Are harshly critical of their own shortcomings	Have a balanced perception of their qualities and shortcomings
Attribute failures to personal inadequacies	Interpret failures as a need to exert more effort

---

Early development of self-concept

From an earlier age than usual, gifted young children become aware of more facets of their personality and of their differences from their age mates (Hoge & McSheffrey; Sekowski 1995; van Boxtel & Mönks 1992). They realise early that other children cannot speak, play games or reason as proficiently as they do and, unless given the correct reason for these differences, will assume that other children will not play with them either because there is something wrong with themselves, or there is something wrong with everybody else. The first explanation contributes to low self-esteem; the second could make the children confused or arrogant or, in a multi-step reasoning process, could also lower self-esteem through a sequence of thoughts along the following lines: other children are being deliberately stupid; they are doing this to annoy me; they must want to annoy me because they do not like me; there is something wrong with me.

At the same time, it is worth emphasising that it is not healthy for children to grow up being the cleverest person they have ever met, as this can unrealistically inflate their self-esteem. They need at least some contact with intellectual peers so that they can identify with other children rather than inhabiting only an adult world. This has implications for their academic program and placement, which is examined further in Chapter 9.

Acceptance

All children need to feel accepted, especially within their family. Acceptance of children feeds both their self-esteem and their sense of belonging, so is depicted in Figure 3.1 as one branch of the tree, linking the level 3 emotional needs for self-esteem and belonging.

However, children's giftedness often receives a cool reception from outsiders and sometimes even from their own family members. In the literature on acceptance of cultural diversity, the point is made that being 'colour blind' about another person's race is little better than bigotry, communicating that a person's culture is not important. But it is important to the other person, and rightly so. So it is with giftedness: people often claim that giftedness does not matter and that we are all of equal worth. The second of these statements is self-evident, but the first minimises the significance of being gifted to those who are, and denies the reality of their lives. So for gifted children, acceptance includes acceptance of their giftedness.

Children's giftedness can mean that many of them are 'high-maintenance' children. Parents often describe to me the extra effort required to keep their gifted child stimulated and the extra emotional guidance their child requires. (Keep in mind, of course, that parents would not be consulting a psychologist unless there was a concern, so not all gifted children necessarily fit this pattern.) It can be difficult to accept a child who upsets the equilibrium in the household, who requires constant advocacy with the school and who challenges parents' status as household leaders. It is also demanding when an introverted parent has a child who needs constant stimulation and company: some of these parents can feel personally smothered by the demands, even while wanting to meet their child's needs. Last, parents with placid emotions can find a child who is prone to emotional displays disconcerting—even a little frightening—making it difficult for them to accept this seemingly alien creature.

Perfectionism

It is often claimed that gifted children are commonly impaired by a dysfunctional form of perfectionism whereby they strive to achieve unrealistically high standards and are seldom satisfied, no matter how well they do. However, this contention has little research backing. One study in apparent support of this hypothesis asked students participating in a seminar on perfectionism to complete a questionnaire about this aspect of their lives and found that most were perfectionists (Orange 1997)—but this is be expected, as few would attend such a seminar unless it were personally relevant to them.

Another study distinguished between perfectionism that is oriented to one's own expectations versus others' expectations (Siegle & Schuler 2000). It found differences along these two dimensions in gifted children attending grades six to eight, with the participants reporting a healthy degree of concern about making mistakes and parental expectations (reflecting a healthy outward orientation), but higher levels of inward-oriented concerns about being organised and meeting their own personal standards (Siegle & Schuler 2000).

When perfectionism is dysfunctional, individuals' feelings of self-worth are linked to being successful but their often punitive attitude towards their own efforts can sabotage their performances (Prichard 1985). In the model of self-esteem presented here, this means that their ideals are too demanding. I find that those who are most prone to this dysfunctional form of perfectionism are those who think that being gifted means they should be highly capable at everything; those who have uneven development and unfavourably compare their lower with their upper skills; and those whose parents are perfectionists and so treat their own mistakes caustically, thus inadvertently teaching their children that making mistakes is negative. These children sometimes avoid taking intellectual risks and concentrate predominantly on their area of special skill, with the result that the gap between their upper and lower skills widens and they progressively lose confidence in their weaker areas. They might put off starting something in case they are not able to do it perfectly. Alternatively, they can become workaholics as their achievements are their only measure of self-worth (Hess 1994). They may fear failure, partly because they have little experience of it (Hess 1994).

The bulk of findings, however, report that gifted students are perfectionists in adaptive rather than dysfunctional ways (LoCicero & Ashby 2000;

Parker 1996; Parker & Adkins 1995; Parker & Mills 1996). They strive for excellence because they know they are capable of achieving it so, in this sense, their perfectionism is the engine that drives their achievements. As such, it is not a problem for the children themselves, although it can be misunderstood and poorly tolerated by other people (Silverman 1994; Taylor 2004).

Imposter syndrome

Despite their advanced skills, many gifted children secretly feel that they are imposters—that one day someone will find them out to be fakes or frauds. This can come about when they expect themselves to be the most gifted person in any room and realise that they are not, when they believe that, as they are not gifted in one particular skill, this means that they are not gifted at all, or they are learning so rapidly that they do not detect the metacognitive skills they are using to manage their own thinking and so believe it to be outside their control. Others find their own achievements unsurprising and expect that soon everyone else will too.

Sense of 'getting dumber'

At some stage in every child's life there comes a task that cannot be learned instantly. Up to that point, many gifted children have thought that they learn well only because the activities are easy for them. Their learning happens so quickly that they do not notice the skills they are using to be successful. So, when the work gets harder, they do not realise that they know how to work through its challenges. They are so accustomed to being able to do things the first time that a lack of instant success makes them worry about themselves, to assume that they cannot learn. This can cause them to think that they are 'getting dumber' when in fact the task has just become more complex and cannot be learned instantly.

Dual exceptionalities

When gifted learners also have learning difficulties or disabilities, they can become confused about themselves, as they know how easily they learn some things and cannot understand why it is so difficult to learn others. They interpret their lesser skills as a sign that they are not gifted—and others can do the same, which magnifies the problem—thus devaluing all of their skills. As already mentioned, this uneven skill profile is one of the main contributors to a dysfunctional form of perfectionism.

Multi-faceted self-concept

Self-esteem has many aspects, with global or overall self-esteem being an amalgam of five relatively distinct facets: social, emotional, academic, family and physical (Hoge & McSheffrey 1991; Pope et al. 1988; van Boxtel & Mönks 1992). Each of these aspects is further divided into subfacets which could be termed 'self-confidence', which is very specific to a given skill and situation. A person with a healthy overall self-esteem can still lack confidence at public speaking, for example.

This multifaceted view of self-esteem is particularly relevant for understanding gifted children, and accounts for some of the differing research findings about their self-esteem. To begin analysing the findings, it is widely recognised that gifted children of all social classes, ethnicity and gender tend to have high *global* and *academic* self-esteems: most feel most positively about their area of talent (Ablard 1997; Brounstein et al. 1991; Chan 1988; Chapman & McAlpine 1988; Davis & Connell 1985; Hoge & Renzulli 1993; Karnes & Wherry 1981; McCoach & Siegle 2003; Pyryt & Mendaglio 1994; Robinson & Noble 1991; Sekowski 1995; Tidwell 1980; van Boxtel & Mönks 1992; Van Tassel-Baska et al. 1994; Wright & Leroux 1997). They set realistic expectations for themselves, are willing to risk failure and can notice their achievements. Even so, as many as 20 per cent seriously underestimate their abilities (Phillips 1984, 1987), with girls in particular underrating their maths skills (Marsh et al. 1988). Meanwhile, children can have differing levels of self-esteem across the various school subjects, with separate general, verbal and maths self-concepts emerging by adolescence (Marsh 1990; Marsh et al. 1988). Furthermore, their internal comparison across subjects can result in low self-esteem even in subjects where they achieve well, if they perform still better in others (Plucker & Stocking 2001).

These high academic self-concepts are sometimes offset by gifted children's lower opinion of their abilities in other domains such as physical skills and social relationships (Ablard 1997; Brounstein et al. 1991; Kelly & Colangelo 1984). In terms of *physical* appearance, gifted female adolescents in one study had a more positive body image than their male counterparts (Leroux 1988). In terms of physical prowess, unless the children happen also to be very able at sport, most intellectually gifted children of school age will be aware that they are less able physically than they are academically. Because of their advanced moral reasoning, some will reject the competitive element of many school sports and, in turn, their lack of participation deprives them of the practice that would increase their skill level. As a result, their physical self-esteem can be lower in comparison with their more physically able classmates and, in turn, this can contribute to negative perceptions of them by their peers.

Socially, many gifted children are aware that, although they themselves value their special skills, many others—including their parents, teachers and peers—do not (Colangelo 2003; Coleman & Cross 1988; Cross et al. 1991, 1992; Kerr et al. 1988; Swiatek 1995; Tidwell 1980; van Boxtel & Mönks 1992). Nevertheless, although unpopular gifted children have a lower overall self-esteem than their popular counterparts, both groups still have higher self-esteem than average learners (Norman et al. 2000). And acceleration—

which is so often shunned in the name of social adjustment issues — was found by Gross (2004) to *improve* gifted children's social self-esteem, as they now fitted in with their older, more capable classmates.

Although gifted children in general are likely to have a healthy *emotional* self-esteem, emotionally sensitive gifted boys in particular are perhaps more prone than others to be teased for their sensitivities. If they heed others' derision, they might feel negatively about the emotional aspects of their personality.

Anecdotal and other evidence about the families of gifted children describe many as warm, supportive and close (Gross 2004). Furthermore, as giftedness runs in families and contributes to adults' high achievements, it could be that gifted children feel proud of their highly achieving parents, as long as they are not under pressure to be equally successful. So, although gifted children can be subjected to the same fortuitous or negative life events as all other children, it could be that their *family* self-esteem is higher on the grounds that their family is responsive to their needs and their parents are highly capable.

The self-esteem of gifted children on each of these facets can also differ according to their achievement levels, age, gender and placement. Taking each in turn, having high potential is not enough to bolster children's self-esteem: they must be performing well too (Delisle 1992; van Boxtel & Mönks 1992; Vespi & Yewchuk 1992), although the findings about the self-esteem of underachieving gifted children are mixed.

As for age, it appears that a need for social conformity in mid-adolescence temporarily lowers young people's self-esteem, while younger and older children and adolescents are less subjected to peer pressure and so experience a higher level of social self-esteem (Klein & Zehms 1996; Kline & Short 1991; Kunkel et al. 1995; van Boxtel & Mönks 1992).

In terms of gender, there are no consistent differences between the self-esteem of gifted girls and boys that are not apparent in average girls and boys (Czeschlik & Rost 1994; Hoge & Renzulli 1993; Tong & Yewchuk 1996). Younger boys may have higher physical self-esteem than girls, while younger girls tend to have higher academic, behavioural and social self-esteem than boys (Chan 1988; Feldhusen & Nimlos-Hippen 1992; Lea-Wood & Clunies-Ross 1995; Lewis & Knight 2000). In one study, female adolescents saw themselves as more well-adjusted than did the boys (Leroux 1988).

For gifted children the self-esteem of the two genders balances out — both in terms of their overall or global self-esteem and across time. Gifted boys see themselves as independent, whereas gifted girls place a high premium on the social aspects of self, so may have a higher social self-esteem than boys (Leroux 1988; Luscombe & Riley 2001). Their social inclusion might not be impaired because, although being successful is probably more acceptable for boys, many gifted girls are likely to have strong role models in their talented mothers and so do not regard themselves as misfits

(Howard-Hamilton & Franks 1995). On the other hand, because they may be concerned about the social stigma attached to being gifted and female, girls' academic self-esteem lowers as they get older, while boys' academic self-esteem improves (Kline & Short 1990).

The last factor affecting gifted children's self-esteem is their educational placement. Some studies (e.g. Feldhusen et al. 1990; Kolloff & Moore 1989; Maddux et al. 1982) report that involvement in gifted programs has a neutral effect on gifted children's self-esteem, while others demonstrate that the children's self-esteem is improved. A closer look reveals that children's social and physical self-appraisals are enhanced—probably as a result of finding friends who have similar interests to themselves—while their academic self-esteem may be lowered (Chan 1988; Craven & Marsh 1997; Gross 1997; Olszewski et al. 1987).

Although some writers expected this drop in academic self-esteem as gifted children felt pressure to live up to increased expectations arising from being identified as gifted, many others had expected that validating gifted children's academic skills by placing them in a gifted program would instead raise their academic self-esteem. The decrease is explained by the fact that children in gifted programs now have more capable youngsters with whom to compare themselves and their ranking within a more able group can change: they are no longer the brightest child in their class (Chan 1988; Jenkins-Friedman & Murphy 1988). This results in a lowered—although perhaps more realistic—picture of their own academic skills (Coleman & Fults 1982; Craven & Marsh 1997; Hoge & Renzulli 1993; Marsh & Craven 1998; Marsh et al. 1995; Moon et al. 2002; Schneider et al. 1989; Wright & Leroux 1997). Craven and Marsh term this 'the big-fish-little-pond effect'.

On the other hand, those children with high skill levels across domains can maintain a high internal comparison so do not suffer from deflated external comparisons (Plucker & Stocking 2001). Second, adjustment difficulties tend to be short-lived (Moon et al. 2002). Third, children who are interested in *doing* their best, and so compete to improve their own performances, appear to fare better in gifted programs than children who compete to *be* the best (Craven & Marsh 1997; Gross 1997). If they expect to outperform others, they might avoid risk and challenge as their failure to win would threaten their self-esteem (Feldhusen et al. 2000).

Causes of low self-esteem

Low self-esteem can come about in one of three ways. First, individuals will have low self-esteem if they *cannot perform a valued skill* and are aware of this. If the skill they want to achieve is within their grasp, this source of low self-esteem is positive in that it can drive them on to become more competent.

The second route to low self-esteem is when individuals have many valued skills and qualities but do not realise it. They do not sufficiently appreciate their skills: their *self-concept is impoverished*. These children need more information about their attributes.

Third, some people have low self-esteem because their *standards are too high*. Sometimes they will need to be taught more realistic standards; sometimes it could be more relevant to give them the confidence to strive for their goals.

Routes to healthy self-esteem

These three routes to low self-esteem, combined with the model of emotional and social needs introduced in the previous chapter, suggest some methods for building a healthy level of self-esteem in children.

Promote competence

If children lack self-esteem because they know that they are being unsuccessful in important ways, they will not feel better while they continue to be unsuccessful: success—at something meaningful—breeds confidence. They will not be deceived by easy tasks (Bandura 1986), nor helped by encouragement to lower their standards, but instead adults will need to boost their self-confidence that they will be able to achieve their goals (Silverman 1989b, 1994). At the same time, the children will require coaching to build their skills at tasks that have personal meaning, are purposeful, offer choice and autonomy, and increase their perception of their personal skill (Hay 1993; Seligman 1975).

Give specific feedback about successes

The second cause of low self-esteem is an impoverished self-concept. So that they can develop a comprehensive picture of their skills and qualities, children will need information (or feedback) about themselves and their accomplishments. This feedback needs, first, to be authentic or honest. But it is difficult to be honest about what the children produce: it is very unlikely you will tell young children that what they have achieved is worthless. But you will be able to be honest if you focus on the *processes* that they have employed, rather than the end product itself. You can comment on the thinking or emotional dispositions that children exercised: for example, 'I'm impressed that you tried so hard to figure that out' (thus focusing on persistence) . . . 'I respect that you took a chance and tried something new' (commenting on creativity and risk taking) . . . 'I admire that you planned that so carefully' . . . and so on. (See Chapter 9 for a comprehensive list of valued dispositions.) Commenting in this way on the processes rather than the products means that all children—whatever their abilities—can receive constructive guidance about their efforts, even when the outcomes they produce differ considerably in quality. This will also minimise competitiveness between children.

Second, feedback must be *specific*. It should verify, highlight and expand on what children have achieved while also, when appropriate, giving them information about what their next goal might be.

Third, feedback does not need to patronise children. If a waiter said that you were a 'good girl for using your manners' when you thanked him for bringing your meal at a restaurant, you would find this condescending as you are perfectly capable of monitoring and assessing your own behaviour. If we similarly teach these self-management skills to children, there is no need to tell them that they are good people (as if there were some doubt about this previously), but rather we should make it clear that we appreciate their actions. The waiter would say 'You're welcome' after being thanked; we can do the same with children.

These criteria imply that adults should avoid giving children *judgmental* feedback in the form of praise or other rewards, as this tells them about what you regard as *ideal* behaviour. This evaluative feedback feeds children's ideal self, raising their standards, and runs the risk that they will come to believe that they can seldom attain what you expect of them: the circles in Figure 4.1 will separate further apart. At the same time, outside praise and other rewards can detract from children's own natural motivation (Amabile 1990; Csikszentmihályi 1991; Kohn 1996, 1999; Ryan & Deci 1996; Sternberg & Lubart 1992). (For a contrary opinion, see Cameron & Pierce 1994, 1996; Eisenberger & Armeli 1997). This gives rise to the following principle.

Guiding principle for delivering feedback
If you want children to develop a healthy self-esteem, do not praise them.

Informative feedback could, for simplicity, be called *acknowledgment*, whereas *judgmental feedback* that is delivered for performances that we approve is usually termed *praise*. Specifically, the two differ in the following ways (Porter 2003):

- Acknowledgment teaches children to *evaluate their own efforts*: 'What do you think of *that*?' . . . 'Was that fun?' . . . 'Are you pleased with yourself?' . . . 'You seem pleased that you did that so well'. In comparison, praise approves of work that meets *adult* standards.
- Unlike praise, acknowledgment *does not judge* children or their work, although you could give them your *opinion* of their achievement. For example, 'I like the colours you used', or 'I'm impressed that you tried something new' can replace the judgment that a painting is 'beautiful',

while 'I appreciate that you tidied up' replaces the judgment that a child is a good boy or girl for helping.

- Acknowledgment is a *personal* interaction that does not show children up in public or compare them with each other. Unlike praise, it does not try to manipulate other children into copying a child who has been praised. Acknowledgment simply describes—in private—what the adult appreciated: 'Thanks for helping to pack the toys away'.

When we give children information about the skills and qualities that they already possess and are exercising, we are telling them about who they are: we are feeding their self-concept. Equipped with this information, they will realise that they already possess many of the standards that are part of their ideal self, so their self-esteem will improve. It might help to picture the circles in Figure 4.1 moving closer together, so that they overlap more.

Even so, informative feedback (acknowledgment) will improve children's self-esteem only if they value the qualities that you are commenting on. So Katz (1995) advises focusing on enduring skills and traits, such as being able to try when a task gets difficult or being a considerate friend, rather than such skills as being able to ride a bike, which virtually every child can do. Similarly, if you acknowledge children's inherited characteristics, their self-esteem will not improve because they had no control over those characteristics and cannot take the credit for them. Instead, acknowledge *effort* rather than cleverness, *personality* rather than appearance, learning *style* rather than outcome (Katz 1995).

Provide balanced feedback about mistakes

There are two sources of negative feedback: children's own perception that they have failed at something (and this may or may not be accurate); and feedback from others, which also might or might not be valid.

Accurate self-appraisal of failure

At some time, everyone will fail at something or will be snubbed or rejected by other people. It is important to notice this sort of negative feedback, especially when it is valid, as it will propel us to make improvements. But it is also important not to let a single failure define ourselves as failures as people, or to take other people's opinions more seriously than we take our own (Katz 1995).

When children are rightly disappointed in their efforts, they will not benefit from attempts to placate them with messages like, 'There, there, it doesn't matter'. Instead, we need to reflect their feelings: 'I understand that you're disappointed' and follow that up with asking if they would like to try to improve on what they have achieved and, if so, whether they want to do so immediately or after they have recovered from the disappointment. In the longer term, coaching in planning, sequencing and other self-regulatory skills can help them become more successful at all tasks, while skill-based coaching will make success more likely at specific tasks.

Also, teach children how to cope with failure by reacting to your own successes and mistakes in a balanced way. If you acknowledge your successes, they will learn that it is okay to notice their own; if you are gentle with your own failures, they will similarly learn to tolerate theirs.

Unrealistic self-expectations

The second occasion when children receive negative feedback is when they believe that they have failed, but their efforts may be perfectly reasonable given their age. When children are being too hard on themselves it is tempting to try to reassure them. However, this can be an inadvertent message to 'get over it'. So your task is to accept that they feel as they do, even if you do not understand why. Your first response will be to listen and accept what they feel, then you could gently ask whether they are being realistic, without giving advice or telling them off for feeling as they do. Maybe they are expecting themselves to be as capable as their older sibling, or as an eight-year-old, perhaps? In that case, you can reassure them that they will be more able when they are that age, but in the meantime it is their turn to be younger.

To help children to establish realistic expectations (ideals) for themselves, and thus to cope with setbacks, it can be useful to teach them the following maxims:

- Strive for excellence, not perfection.
- Have the courage to be imperfect.
- Don't let failure go to your head.
- On worthwhile tasks, strive to *do* your best, but not to *be* the best.

Expectations from others

The third occasion when children will receive negative feedback about their achievements is when other people are critical of their efforts. Gifted children in one study complained that their parents expected them to do their best all the time, and that adults often highlighted deficiencies in their performance rather than what was good about it (Ford 1989). These children felt obliged to make their teachers look good by achieving well, and were annoyed at the expectation that they be perfect. They also felt irritated at receiving so much 'constructive feedback' while their less able classmates received extensive praise for lesser achievements.

To overcome external pressures to be perfect, it is important to teach children from an early age that no one has to get things right every time and that not all mistakes have to be corrected. Our predilection with correcting children's mistakes comes from an erroneous belief that this is how to help them to learn, but focusing on their deficiencies and overlooking their strengths discourages effort and contributes to continued failure (Balson 1992). Mistakes indicate a lack of skill, and skill is acquired only through practice, but discouraged children refuse to practise and so do not learn. So when children have not been as successful as you would have expected, it is still important to comment on what they *did* achieve: if they have written their name backwards, you can congratulate them for beginning to understand how to write their own name, rather than pointing out the error.

Also, do not require children to fix every mistake. Most errors do not really matter, and most children realise that making mistakes is a part of learning, in the same way that falling over was a part of learning how to walk. If you can already perform a task perfectly, without errors, this means that you already know how to do it—and that is not called learning: it is called *practising*.

Conclusion

To promote healthy self-esteem in children, we need to help them to be successful at worthwhile tasks; guide them to appreciate their achievements; and assist them to set realistic expectations for themselves. While communicating faith in their abilities, our own expectations of them need to be reasonable, so they are emboldened to strive for lofty ideals that fulfil their personal dreams.

Suggested further reading

For a detailed look at self-esteem:
Curry, N.E. and Johnson, C.N. 1990 *Beyond self-esteem: developing a genuine sense of human value* National Association for the Education of Young Children, Washington, DC.
A lay title which discusses perfectionism and its relationship to self-esteem for gifted and other individuals is:
Adderholdt-Elliot, M. 1992 *Perfectionism: what's bad about being too good* Hawker Brownlow Education, Melbourne.

SOCIAL NEEDS
five

My life is spent in a perpetual alternation between two rhythms, the rhythm of attracting people for fear I may be lonely and the rhythm of getting rid of them because I know that I am bored. (Joad 1948, in Gross 2004: 176)

Introduction

The second emotional need shared by all individuals and outlined in the model introduced in Chapter 3 is for people to feel that they belong in their families, care or educational environments, neighbourhoods, wider community and culture. In this model, both self-esteem and social needs require that children feel accepted and loved by others. For gifted children, this raises two issues: the first is that, while younger gifted children are often more popular than their averagely achieving peers, this advantage tends to disappear by adolescence (Rimm 2002). Second, parents' acceptance of their children's giftedness can be compromised when the children's additional needs make them 'high maintenance', as mentioned in Chapter 4.

The second aspect of belonging is that the children themselves need to feel connected to others. Being popular and accepted is one thing, but emotional well-being is actually more reliant on having someone else to love. It is this aspect that is often raised as a core concern for the gifted population. Given that individuals choose friends who share their skills, interests and values, but that gifted children have restricted access to such companions, there is a risk that they will be lonely.

Friendships

Children's friendships matter as much to them as adult friendships matter to us. Moreover, they serve many important functions. Developmental benefits are that friendships help children to become socially skilful, teach self-control, give children experience at problem solving, provide practice at using language, and allow children to exchange skills and information that they do not readily learn from the adults in their lives (Asher & Parker 1989; Asher & Renshaw 1981; Hartup 1979; Johnson & Johnson 1991; Kohler & Strain 1993; Perry & Bussey 1984; Rubin 1980).

On an emotional level, friendships supply reassurance, promote healthy self-esteem, enhance confidence in stressful situations, prevent loneliness, provide fun and foster individual happiness. Friends also offer practical and emotional support through giving information, advice and counsel. Intimacy is necessary to sustain one's drive to excel, and contributes significantly to individuals' perception of satisfaction with their lives (Gross 1996). Indeed, children report that the presence of other children is the most important factor to them in their early childhood setting—more important than toys, activities and staff (Langsted 1994, in Pugh & Selleck 1996). This verifies that friend-ships are valued by young children and that making friends is the most important developmental task of early childhood (Cooper & McEvoy 1996).

Social issues for gifted children

The problem-solving and metacognitive skills that enhance gifted children's cognitive performances also contribute to their social acumen (Freeman 1995b; Jones & Day 1996; Moss 1992). Their high levels of social knowl-edge mean that most gifted children are socially accepted by their peers: they are less disliked and are identified as being less aggressive than others (Austin & Draper 1981; Cohen et al. 1994). Nevertheless, despite their intel-lectual advantages, it can be a challenge for gifted children to adjust socially to being different, even when their difference is a source of pride and so feeds their self-esteem (Freeman 1993, 1997).

Friendship is a voluntary, ongoing bond between individuals who have a mutual preference for each other and who share emotional warmth. There are three issues in relating to peers: inclusion/exclusion, control and affection (Schutz 1958, in Webb et al. 1991). The most basic of these for children is whether they are included in the group. This sense of belonging can be threatened for gifted children, as their skills and interests might not be shared by their age mates.

At the next level, the group establishes who is a leader and who is a follower. Gifted children, on the one hand, often have the developmental maturity to act as leaders; on the other, they may not have the emotional maturity to handle that role with grace, and their leadership might not be accepted by others in the group.

The third issue for groups is whether the group members feel any lasting affection for each other. As Webb et al. (1991: 146) observe: 'Typically you feel affection only for those whom you can count on, and whose behaviour is predictable.' As I discuss later in this chapter, gifted children might find other young children's less mature behaviour confusing and even upsetting, making it more difficult for them to establish affectionate ties in a group of age mates.

In addition to these background issues, gifted children can experience some challenges to their social acceptance and inclusion, particularly when placed exclusively with age mates rather than intellectual peers.

Isolation from peers

The six-month-old at playgroup who is talking will soon realise that other infants do not respond verbally to her, yet few older children are available. While this disparity in skill might not make gifted children disdainful of others, neither does it give them a chance to learn that others can be satisfying companions. In turn, this could lead to a pattern of introversion that was not inbuilt but is an inexorable response to isolation.

Attachment and separation

In my observations, young gifted children often develop deep attachments to their primary caregivers and some other close family members—but not a breadth of attachment to peers. As just mentioned, this comes about not because they shun other people, but because the difference in the development between themselves and their peers means that they do not learn that peers could be a relevant source of intimacy for them. Meanwhile, their thirst for stimulation means that they come to rely on their parent to translate the world to them and explain them to the world.

The result is that they are more than usually vulnerable if separated from their parent, while being less consoled by the presence of age mates. Given that separation requires both leaving someone and going somewhere else, separation problems can arise when the children are reluctant to leave the parent on whom they have relied for so much of their stimulation and intimacy, and are unwilling to remain in a place where there is no substitute source of companionship. This is exacerbated if the intellectual demands of the setting are low.

This reliance on a parent (in the absence of other deep relationships) is also partly the reason for parents' sense that these children are 'high maintenance'. The responsibility to be all things at all times for your child can be exhausting and worrying. This topic is addressed again in Chapter 13.

Feeling different

Children choose friends whose skills are at the same level as their own and who share their interests (Clark 2002; Oden 1960, cited by Delisle 1992). Young gifted girls are less likely than other girls to play with dolls, and instead favour games involving structure and logic, which makes their play styles incompatible with those of their age mates (Gross 1996). Also, gifted children tend to show less interest in competitive games (Janos & Robinson 1985), perhaps because they feel empathy for the loser. This can make it hard for them to find friends.

Friendship problems may be most acute in early childhood, because same-aged peers do not share gifted children's interests and level of organisational and conceptual play, but older children regard them as infants and so do not want to play with them (Whitmore 1980). Also, older children may not be accessible, as they are likely to be in a separate group in a child (day) care centre, or already at school.

Belonging in one's family

An extreme sense of feeling different and not seeming to belong in one's own family has been manifested in a handful of gifted adults whom I have met who, for one reason or another, were the only ones in their families to achieve at high levels. Some of these adults reported that, as children, they worried about whether they were adopted, as they felt so out of step with the rest of their family and were often criticised by family members for their giftedness. I do not know if this sense of not belonging with one's family is more common in gifted than average learners or even if it is a widespread experience among the gifted but, when it occurs, it is likely to have profound emotional effects.

Loneliness

Their popularity does not necessarily mean that the gifted children themselves are satisfied with the intimacy of their relationships. Even though they can relate well to their age mates, they do not necessarily find age peers to be soulmates and instead tend to form their closest friendships with other gifted children, older children or adults (Cohen et al. 1994). On the other hand, it is important to keep in mind that isolation does not necessarily create loneliness.

Introversion

If children have few friends, parents and educators often become concerned about their social well-being. However, most people of all ages have just one or two friends (Porteous 1979), and the number of children's friendships is less important than their quality: children might have few friends but appreciate and enjoy the ones that they have. Also, children might spend little time playing with others, but when they do they play entirely appropriately and glean satisfaction from doing so. Thus the important measure is *how*—not *how much*—children play socially. Solitary play can be beneficial if the children are occupied when alone, and will be detrimental only if they are doing something that is better done in a group (Perry & Bussey 1984).

Silverman calculates that gifted children are introverted at twice the rate of average learners. With a referred population, of course, it is difficult to judge the accuracy of this statistic but, even if correct, introversion is not necessarily a characteristic of the children themselves but can be imposed on them by a lack of intellectual peers. Their introversion can cause their gift-edness to be overlooked, however, as teachers more readily recognise extroverted children as gifted (Silverman 2002).

Nevertheless, being introverted is not a social handicap, as Silverman (2002) emphasises. For example, in adult life individuals who are comfort-able with their own company are less likely to marry unwisely as they will choose solitude over a dysfunctional relationship, whereas those who are desperate not to be alone might choose an unsatisfactory relationship over none at all.

Lost friends

When gifted children's older playmates move up to the next group in the child (day) care centre or go to school ahead of them, they have to make new friends. However, as they near the age to move on, there are fewer and fewer older children available to provide the stimulation they need, and so their last terms in child care or preschool can be a particularly isolated time.

Exploitation

Gifted children's advanced moral reasoning and sense of empathy can result in their being assigned roles as peer tutors or buddies to less able or younger children. This, however, amounts to exploitation and might communicate that they are worthy *only* if they help others, while robbing them of time to develop their own skills.

Peer pressure

At a younger age than normal, gifted children move from measuring them-selves against their own standards to comparing themselves to others (Gross 1996). Not only does this mean that they develop their self-concept earlier, as already mentioned in Chapter 4, but it also causes them to feel peer pressure earlier than usual. Particularly beyond the early childhood years, many feel conflict between their need to achieve and their need for intimacy, realising that remarkable achievements can lead to peer disapproval or even complete ostracism (Gross 1996). So their play can become a compromise between their own interests and the need to maintain relationships.

High demands of others

Because gifted children often have the verbal abilities to direct play, and be-cause their play ideas are sophisticated, they might manipulate or intimidate other children into playing games their way (Clark 2002; Hay 1993). Meanwhile, their high expectations of others might deter their companions, which can cause them to feel still more isolated and lonely or to stop showing how bright they are so that other people will like them (Delisle 1992).

Misunderstandings of other children

The reverse can also occur. Gifted children can be intimidated when other children do not abide by their advanced social mores. They can mistakenly assume that another child's aggression, lack of empathy or lack of planning is a deliberate attempt to hurt them instead of the normal developmental ignorance that it is, and so they are more deeply hurt than usual. For example, the gifted child who plans ahead and can consider other people would not start down a slide until the previous child was safely off the equipment; a child with normal development might forget to plan this far ahead, go down while another child was still on the slide and kick him or her in the back. The gifted child who is injured will not understand that it was accidental because he or she thinks first and simply does not have such accidents.

Need for tact

It is often said that gifted children need to be tactful about displaying their abilities in front of others. However, many young gifted people—especially girls and the exceptionally gifted—are often *too* reticent about showing their true abilities (Swiatek 1998). This may be due to their awareness of the social stigma attached to being gifted (Cross et al. 1991, 1992), although it is equally possible that the children are merely being tactful with peers, as they tend to be happy for peers to know that they are interested in learning but are careful not to parade their academic accomplishments (Cross et al. 1991).

Either way, in order to maintain their achievement levels, these children need support to recognise their talents. When they understand their own abilities, they will also understand that other children are different from them, without regarding this as a deficit. Instead of thinking that other children are being 'deliberately stupid', they will be more likely to accept individual differences.

Leadership

Young gifted children's early sensitivity to the needs of others and mature moral reasoning skills enable them to lead their peers (Clark 2002; Hensel 1990, 1991; Rothman 1992). Their leadership skills are enhanced by an early development of verbal skills, which allow them to convey their ideas to their playmates; a precocious imagination, which allows them to envision possibilities; problem-solving skills; and organisation abilities (Hensel 1990, 1991). These same traits can conversely be enhanced by being placed in leadership roles (Rothman 1992).

These advanced social and intellectual skills might mean that other people are willing to confer leadership status on gifted individuals, whether or not they seek it. However, some school-aged gifted children resent always being expected to take leadership roles in the class (Ford 1989). And, unlike their older counterparts, young gifted children might not have the emotional resources to cope with social dilemmas.

Effects of identification of giftedness

Some writers report that gifted children find it difficult to live up to the gifted label once they have been so identified. While giftedness can confer higher status, it can also create a barrier between gifted individuals and their age mates (Buescher 1985). However, it is not clear whether it is the label which they find difficult to bear, or whether it is the circumstances that caused parents to request an assessment in the first place, such as the observation that their child was bored or not fitting in socially.

Family conflict

Inter-generational relationships (between parents and their highly achieving gifted children) are typically described as emotionally supportive, with girls often feeling closest to their mothers (Leroux 1988). With respect to sibling relationships, intellectual discrepancies between siblings can lead to exaggerated competitiveness and jealousy between them (Chamrad & Robinson 1986; Freeman 1995b). This can be exacerbated by parents' uncertainty about how to respond to each child—see Chapter 13.

Factors influencing gifted children's social adjustment

Many older gifted children report having been teased by their less able peers. Those who cope best are those children whose sense of self is intact and so can withstand verbal jibes, who can express their feelings and communicate these with others, and who can find people with whom they can communicate honestly (Galbraith 1985). Regarding their own gifts positively can also cause peers to view them similarly (Ring & Shaughnessy 1993).

Aside from these personality features, some aspects of their giftedness itself can affect gifted children's social adjustment.

Ability levels

The majority of moderately gifted children have positive peer relationships even when they lack intellectual peers (Janos & Robinson 1985). When comparing moderately and extremely gifted children, one study found that children of both ability levels said that they preferred playing with other children to being with adults or playing alone. Very few reported that it was hard for them to make friends, and all thought of themselves as being 'about as friendly or friendlier' than other children (Janos et al. 1985).

This picture is not so uniformly positive for highly gifted children, however (Brody & Benbow 1986; Silverman 1997). Compared with the more moderately gifted, extremely gifted children report that it is harder for them to make friends, an observation that is verified by their parents (Brody & Benbow 1986; Dauber & Benbow 1990; Janos et al. 1985). Therefore, it does appear that a significant minority of highly gifted children—perhaps 20–25 per cent (which is twice as many as average or moderately gifted children)—experience social difficulties (Janos & Robinson 1985; Janos et al. 1985). This is compounded by the fact that very young children are less mobile than their older counterparts and so cannot independently locate intellectual peers in their vicinity.

Rural children with exceptional advances are disadvantaged still further (see Chapter 10). Nevertheless, their social isolation does not represent an emotional disturbance or lack of social skill, as their difficulties disappear when true peers can be located (Gross 1992, 2004). That is, the problem is not inherent in the psychology of highly gifted children, but simply in the mismatch between their needs and their social environment.

Talent profile

The social experiences of gifted children can depend on the skill domain or domains in which they are advanced. For example, as already reported in Chapter 4, verbally gifted children may be less socially accepted than mathematically gifted children, perhaps because extreme verbal talent is more obvious in more social situations (Ablard 1997; Brody & Benbow 1986; Dauber & Benbow 1990; Swiatek 1995, 1998).

Age

There appear to be two periods of development that are particularly challenging socially for young gifted people: the early childhood years and adolescence, although these two critical times occur for slightly different reasons. In the early childhood years, gifted young children are isolated because they typically do not have access to older children who would be their intellectual equals. Adolescents, on the other hand, are more likely to have access to older intellectual peers but can experience more pressure to fit in with their age mates, with the result that they must choose between hiding their talents or facing isolation.

Gender

Gifted girls report receiving less social support from their classmates and friends than do gifted boys (Van Tassel-Baska et al. 1994). Girls appear to feel more keenly than boys the conflict between displaying their talents and winning social approval. The risk is that gifted girls will underachieve in order to gain social status and to conform to peer group expectations (Luftig & Nichols 1991).

Methods to promote social adjustment

Children who cannot locate a true peer are more likely to be lonely, so an intervention will be necessary. Nevertheless, it may be more benign to change the environment that gives rise to social isolation than it is to attempt to change individual children. Many gifted children already have the necessary social skills but do not have peers who share their interests and with whom they can exercise their relationship skills.

Place children with intellectual peers

Peer relationship skills can be practised only within peer relationships, so gifted children need access to some others who share their abilities and interests, while also relating with age mates (Cohen et al. 1994). Therefore, the single most important intervention for promoting gifted children's social satisfaction is to find them some intellectual peers with whom they can play at least occasionally (Galbraith 1985; Gross 1996; Janos & Robinson 1985). Without this, they are at risk of not understanding their own abilities, concealing their true skills and blaming themselves for not fitting in with their age mates.

When gifted children find acceptance within an intellectual peer group, their social confidence grows and they find themselves better able to relate to average learners as well (Silverman 1997). Being with intellectual peers changes their sense of who they are and what they can achieve, their ability to make contact with strangers, their sense of being accepted by people whose opinions they value, their sense of freedom to express themselves and their ability to find others who are excited about the same things as they are (Coleman 1995). The children no longer feel that they in a minority of one. As discussed in Chapter 4, their academic self-esteem may decline somewhat from comparing themselves with more able peers, but their social self-esteem will improve as a result of having more successful relationships with the other children.

Provide solitude

Paradoxically, one way to encourage social interaction is to allow children some solitude and privacy. Around one-quarter of children can be expected to prefer their own company to being surrounded by numerous other individuals. In contrast with extroverts, who are invigorated by social contact, those who are introverted find it draining to have many others around them for extended periods, and so are likely to seek even more solitary time than they otherwise might. For these introverted children, and those who occasionally seek some solitude, having a corner to which they can retreat can encourage their social participation at other times. Some solitude will give the children contemplation time—time to think, plan ahead, adjust to changes and manage pent-up emotions.

Facilitate social play

Although you cannot guarantee that children will develop friendships, you can create the conditions in which friendships may flourish. A basic way to encourage peer interaction is to ensure that the children know each other, as they are more willing to play with someone whom they know. In group care or educational settings this requires that, where possible, you maintain a stable group membership and on a daily basis incorporate the likes of name songs in your group sessions so that the children become familiar with each other. This step can be particularly crucial in occasional care settings, where membership of the group fluctuates from day to day.

Next you can ensure that the activities on offer are intellectually challenging and so invite engagement and social interaction and thus are more attractive than being alone. Toys that tend to invite isolated or parallel play include small building blocks, play dough, books, sand play, computer games and craft activities; while those that promote social cooperative play comprise the likes of dress-up clothes, dolls and doll houses, large blocks, housekeeping materials and vehicles (Ivory & McCollum 1999). On the other hand, providing dramatic play equipment (such as kitchen utensils with play dough) will allow children to engage cooperatively with otherwise solitary materials (Sainato & Carta 1992).

Finally, at a more directive level, you can coach children in their use of social skills if these seem to be lacking (see below).

Instigate cooperative games

You can actively foster cooperative play between children by instigating activities and games that require joint effort and cooperation. An example of a cooperative game is the frozen bean bag game. This requires children to move around with a small bean bag on their heads, freezing when it falls off and remaining still until another child helps by replacing the bean bag on their head (Sapon-Shevin 1986). Another example is non-elimination musical chairs, which involves removing a chair—not a player—whenever the music stops, so that all the children ultimately have to organise how to fit on the one remaining chair.

For gifted children, a crucial aim of such games is to engage those who are often isolated and to pair up those who might not ordinarily play with each other but who, as a result of playing together, might find that they have interests in common. In this way, cooperative games expand the pool of each child's potential friends, which is particularly important for isolated children—among whom are some who are gifted.

At the same time, you will need to curb those competitive activities that foster rivalry between children, in contrast with those that encourage children to achieve at their personal best. As mentioned in Chapter 4, the self-esteem of children who strive to outperform others is vulnerable to failure, and these children tend to be disliked by peers because of their aggressive behaviour (Udvari & Schneider 2000). Competitive games that emphasise winning involve the likes of taunting or teasing games (such as 'King of the castle'), grabbing or snatching at scarce toys (as in musical chairs), monopolising or excluding other children (for instance, the piggy in the middle game) or the use of physical force (such as tag ball) (Orlick 1982; Sapon-Shevin 1986).

Some cooperative or joint learning activities such as collages or murals can also be beneficial. In these activities, the children rely on each other to achieve a common goal (Robinson 1990a). However, within the school sector, there is a vigorous debate about the suitability of cooperative learning for gifted children, mainly centred on the fact that it usually involves mixed-ability groupings (Johnson et al. 1990; Slavin 1987b; Snowden 1995), although it does not necessarily have to (Fiedler et al. 1993; Joyce 1991). Its advocates (e.g. Slavin 1991) claim that gifted children can gain socially and learn more in a mixed-ability cooperative group by leading or teaching the less able children; its critics (e.g. Colangelo & Davis 2003; Robinson 1990, 2003) say that this 'Robin Hood' method of shifting instructional attention and robbing time from the able so that they can help the less able amounts to exploitation of gifted children, restricts their access to more advanced learning, and can frustrate them if their group-mates do not understand or are less motivated than they are (Matthews 1992).

The conclusion of this debate is that the effects of cooperative learning will vary according to the children's ages, ability levels, group size and the type of activity being undertaken (Li & Adamson 1992). Thus Rogers and Span (1993) advise that cooperative activities should be restricted to the social sphere, as with cooperative games. These can produce the social benefits of structured cooperative learning activities without incurring their disadvantages. Meanwhile, with young children, same-ability pairs might be more effective than larger or mixed-ability groupings, not only because dyads are more effective at enhancing active engagement and learning (Robinson 2003) but also because young children work best in smaller groups.

Explain degrees of friendship

Gifted children might need to hear that there are different levels of friendship. Some people will be acquaintances only—people who will be fine to pass the time of day with, but with whom they do not have much in common. At the next level are those who share one particular interest but beyond which there is little common ground. This type of specific friendship can be necessary when children have differing developmental levels across skill domains and so require different peers for different pursuits (Webb et al. 1991). Next are friends, who choose to spend time with each other and do not have to do anything in particular for the time to pass pleasantly. Finally, a rare few will be soulmates. These are the people who *know* us and confirm that it's okay to be who we are. We do not have to hide what we are good at, but we do not need to brag about it either, as our friends already know about us and believe in us. If at a particular stage of life, gifted children cannot find a soulmate, they will need guidance to appreciate the benefits of lesser degrees of intimacy.

Teach social skills

As already stated, gifted children are unlikely to lack social skills, but rather to lack social peers. But if some do appear to need some coaching to enter a group or maintain relationships, it can be helpful to guide their use of the following skills (Porter 2002a, 2002b).

- The first social skill is responding positively to other children's invitations to play.
- Next is surveillance: to enter a group, children need to take time to survey the group's activities and members' non-verbal behaviours. This allows hopeful entrants to make their behaviour relevant to the group's, which in turn makes it more likely that their bids to gain entry will be positively received (Asher 1983; Brown et al. 2000).
- Next, they should approach the other children and quietly observe their game, wait for a natural break to occur and then begin to do what the other children are doing (Putallaz & Wasserman 1990). This has been called the wait-and-hover technique. It is extremely useful, as long as it is followed by bids to enter; otherwise children remain on the periphery for extended periods (Brown et al. 2000).
- Having gained entry to other children's play, new entrants need to be supportive, signalling that they are keen to cooperate and can be trusted. Supportive actions comprise complimenting, smiling at, cooperating with, imitating, sharing, taking turns, assisting others and leading diplomatically to enlist other children in their play, but without being bossy.
- Meanwhile, they must avoid disruptive actions such as calling attention to themselves, asking questions, criticising the way the other children are playing, introducing new topics of conversation or new games, being too boisterous and thus out of keeping with the group, acting aggressively, or destroying others' play materials (Putallaz & Gottman 1981; Putallaz & Wasserman 1990).

- During play, children need to be aware of how their own behaviour affects others and be sensitive to the needs of their playmates.
- Finally, playmates will need to know how to resolve conflict peaceably. To achieve this, they will need to: be persuasive and assertive rather than bossy; negotiate play activities; obey social rules about sharing and taking turns as leader; suggest compromises when someone's actions have been disputed; and not accede to unreasonable demands from playmates but nevertheless decline tactfully by presenting a rationale for not accepting a playmate's idea or offering an alternative suggestion (Trawick-Smith 1988).

Early childhood is an ideal time to guide children's use of these social skills, as so much of their play is social and because guidance can occur in the natural setting without intruding on the play itself. At the same time, it must be emphasised that an environmental adjustment can be more important than attempting to improve individual children's skilfulness in isolation.

Conclusion

It is clear that satisfaction with our relationships depends not on how many relationships we have, but on how close we feel to our companions. So adults need to help gifted children to distinguish between friendship and the more superficial popularity so they can be true to themselves and do not have to sacrifice their own personal goals merely to gain popularity (Keirouz 1990).

Suggested further reading

For more detail on social skills for young children in general:
Kostelnick, M.J., Stein, L.C., Whiren, A.P. and Soderman, A.K. 2002 *Guiding children's social development: theory to practice* 4th edn, Thomson, New York.

AUTONOMY
six

Parents with authoritarian (high control, high demands) patterns are likely to produce children with high achievement but also high degrees of conformity and lack of originality. (Robinson & Noble 1991: 59)

Introduction

The third emotional need described in the model introduced in Chapter 3 and addressed in this chapter is individuals' requirement for autonomy, or to be self-governed: people need to feel in command of themselves and of what happens to them. In the model in Figure 3.2, both self-esteem and autonomy require that children be given the freedom to develop competence, independence and potency. Competence is so intimately tied into self-esteem that it was covered in Chapter 4; the remaining two issues will be the focus of this chapter.

After the age of two years, children use adults' reactions to their attempts at independence to judge whether they should feel proud or guilty about their efforts (Curry & Johnson 1990). Validation by adults of children's efforts at acting independently will simultaneously enhance their self-esteem and promote their sense of autonomy.

Potency is a belief in our ability to have an impact on our surroundings and on those around us. More centrally, though, it entails a realisation that we can make a difference to our own actions by staying in command of our thinking and emotions. Psychologists often refer to this concept as *self-efficacy*, a sense of *agency*, or possessing an *internal locus of control*. This means believing that our own actions affect outcomes, in contrast to thinking that external forces outside of our control (such as luck) determine what happens to us.

Autonomy issues for gifted children

The over-riding issue about gifted children's autonomy is their sense of control over their giftedness itself. Some see their giftedness as an entity: a 'thing' that they have been given and which will express itself without any effort on their part. Instead, they need to recognise that giftedness will flourish only with effort: it is something they can and must take charge of if they want to enjoy its benefits. Other challenges to autonomy not typically experienced by average learners are described below.

Independence

As mentioned in Chapters 1 and 5, gifted children can be a paradox of independence coexisting with strong dependency. When learning a new task, they might fiercely insist on doing it independently but, having mastered it intellectually, have little interest in repeating it and so demand that adults do it for them. If intellectual peers are not available to them, they can develop a depth of attachment to parents but not a breadth of attachment to their age mates. Both of these characteristics can result in heavy reliance on parents for stimulation and emotional support.

Locus of control

An internal locus of control involves believing that one's own actions affect outcomes. Mastery-oriented children attribute their failures to aspects of the task or to changeable factors such as effort. This avoids discouragement and directs their energies towards finding a solution (Compas 1987).

In contrast, people are said to have an external locus of control or to display 'learned helplessness' (Seligman 1975) when they believe that events outside of their control are responsible for what happens to them. Helpless children display ineffective learning styles in terms of reduced effort and high discouragement, resulting in deteriorating performances (Compas 1987). They either make no attributions regarding the cause of their failures, or blame aspects of themselves such as their own lack of ability.

There is some evidence that highly achieving gifted children develop an internal locus of control earlier than less advanced children (Brody & Benbow 1986; Clark 2002; Kammer 1986; Knight 1995; McClelland et al. 1991). Their strong belief in personal control underpins gifted children's enhanced self-management and motivates them to use their problem-solving strategies effectively (Chan 1996).

On the other hand, although it is important that individuals take personal responsibility for their actions, some gifted children — particularly girls — take too much responsibility, blaming themselves for failures rather than attributing their lack of success to the strategy they used (see Chapter 10).

Excessive responsibility

Because verbally gifted children have an advanced understanding of adult issues and conversations, they sometimes involve themselves in adult business, with the result that they are often aware of and take responsibility for social issues from an early age when they are still too young to cope emotionally. They feel responsible but have no power to do anything about social problems, so can become stressed, lose confidence in themselves or become depressed about their helplessness (Galbraith 1985). This will be resolved as they get older and their advanced cognitive abilities help them to resolve their concerns earlier (Sowa et al. 1994); however, as young children, it can threaten their sense of personal control.

A sense of being grown up

Because of their advanced development, gifted children often are not in awe of adults' intellect and do not perceive a difference in status between themselves and adults. Their strong goal orientation causes them to adhere persistently to their own goals and to resist adult attempts to direct them (Maxwell 1998). They will assert their own opinions and will debate adult directives at length. The children fully expect adults to take them seriously as human beings, and are affronted if adults give them advice that they already know, or attempt to impose controls on them. This sense of themselves as already mature was illustrated in a comment on ABC radio by Janet Holmes à Court about her late husband Robert, in which she said that he was happiest after he was 40—as he had been 40 all his life but no one had realised it.

This trait—which is not unique to gifted learners but is exacerbated in many by their language and conceptual abilities—is a problem only if adults want to 'pull rank' on children and expect them to do as they are told. The children's chagrin at attempts to control them can be overcome when we act as leaders and guides rather than as children's bosses; when we make expert judgments about their needs rather than imposing power on them; when we listen to children, even though on occasions we will not grant what they want; and when we give children real opportunities to contribute to decisions that affect them. This issue feeds into behavioural guidance, so is expanded on later in this chapter.

Insufficient adult guidance

Alternatively, inappropriately lax discipline can come about when adults:

- have too much reverence for gifted children's advanced skills and so fail to offer appropriate behavioural guidance (Freeman 1995a);
- believe that gifted children are so exceptional that they do not have to abide by normal social rules (Prichard 1985);

- are confused by the children's asynchronous skills and so do not know what to expect of the children or of themselves (Freeman 1995a);
- accord gifted children higher status, compared with both siblings and, sometimes, the parents themselves (Keirouz 1990);
- allow children who are perceptive or gifted verbally to use these skills to manipulate and manage their parents (and siblings);
- become children's peers as a result of being their main play partner and their medium for interpreting the world (Roeper 1995b).

When children receive insufficient guidance about their behaviour, their parents' reduced authority and their own inflated power can put too much pressure on them, leave them feeling unprotected (Kitano 1986), create resentment in the other siblings who sometimes feel as if they have three parents (Chamrad et al. 1995; Hackney 1981) and put pressure on the parents' relationship, particularly when the spouses disagree about how to respond to the children (Keirouz 1990).

Emotional self-control

Gifted children's uneven development can result in over-generalised high expectations on the part of either adults or the children themselves (Kline & Meckstroth 1985). The stress of living up to high expectations can lead children to stretch to cope at an advanced level; then, when the stress gets too much, they behave even more immaturely than is usual for their years. The resulting emotional outbursts can look immature, compared both with their age and their ability levels, and are sometimes misinterpreted as a sign that the children are not gifted after all. They can also provoke controlling disciplinary responses from adults, which can excite further negative behaviours from the children.

Awareness of their metacognitive skills

Success at tasks involves not only being able to perform the skill, but also being able to organise oneself to do it proficiently. Gifted children are more able than most at both the performance and organisational aspects of tasks. But, by definition, their learning is happening more quickly than usual, which can make it difficult for them to detect the skills they are using in their learning.

So, even more than with average learners, gifted learners need us to highlight those skills. We might comment, for example, that they must have rehearsed some information (said it over and over in their head) so that they remembered it; that they must have thought about where to start a task before beginning it; that they noticed that this task needed them to remember something they had learned previously . . . and so on. It is important to highlight that the children know how to concentrate, plan each step of a task, check that their approach is working, persist and change approaches if necessary, so that when they encounter tasks that cannot be learned instantly, they do not give up but instead know that they are in control of whether they succeed or fail.

Ways to promote autonomy

Stress can result when people believe that they cannot control how events turn out. However, the factors that promote autonomy and thus minimise stress also promote the realisation of giftedness. Fortuitously, many characteristics of gifted children act as buffers against the development of stress reactions, including their sophisticated verbal and problem-solving skills, an internal locus of control, high self-esteem and self-awareness (Dole 2000).

Support independence

It is important for both their self-esteem and unfolding sense of autonomy that children acquire skills such as being able to separate from their parents and to perform self-care tasks at an appropriate age. Sometimes, our good intentions to help children mean that we do something for them that they could do for themselves. Instead, let children attempt tasks for themselves— even if they make mistakes along the way—so they develop faith in their ability to learn and are willing to take risks.

Offer choice

Children will develop autonomy through repeated opportunities to exercise choices, use initiative and be self-determining. Asking for their suggestions and listening to their ideas tells them that you value them and believe in their abilities to take responsibility for themselves. Allowing children to contribute to decision making about issues that affect them will both enhance their self-esteem and give them a sense of potency.

There are three levels of choice that we can offer children (Porter 2003, 2005). When the activity is optional, you can ask *whether* they would like to participate. But if the task is compulsory—such as washing hands before a snack—so you cannot give a choice of whether to do it, you can still give options about *how* (e.g. using the hand dryer or paper towels or going with a friend). If there is no choice about how to perform the activity, you can give a choice about *how to feel* about it—for example: 'I know that you don't want to wash your hands but, as it is something we all have to do, you can get upset about it or you can get on with it happily. It's up to you.'

Restrict children's responsibilities

Because of their advanced understanding, it is easy unwittingly to expose gifted children to concerns about adult issues. However, although they might appear to be intellectually able to discuss such things, emotionally it can stress them. When we tell young children something, they are likely to judge that (a) we want them to do something about it; (b) it is their fault; or (c) it is important, when it might actually be quite trivial. Therefore, it is wise to discuss with them only those issues about which they *can* do something. Given gifted children's tendency to take on early responsibilities, it is wise to censor discussions with them, using their emotional response as a guide to how much information they can cope with.

It can be useful to explain that adults are taking care of adult business, and that it is children's job to be children and to grow up at their own speed. They will be adults for a lot longer than they will be children, so they will have plenty of time to act to set the world to rights later. It is not their turn yet to be older. But you can help them to do age-appropriate things (such as writing a letter to a politician) so they feel satisfied that they have done what they can in the meantime.

One strategy that I use is to take these children to a tall building. One where I once worked had three storeys with 28 steps between each. We could do the maths and figure that this equalled 84 steps, which is perfect as it equates to one step per year of average life expectancy. I would then have the children count the steps to the first landing: fourteen. Then we would return to the ground floor and I would ask children to stand on the step corresponding to their age: if they were six years old, they would stand on the sixth step. Next, I would ask them to jump from there to the tenth step without holding the handrail. The children would always refuse, complaining that they would lose their balance.

'Precisely,' I would say. 'That is what is happening in your life. You are six and are trying to be ten and you're losing your balance . . . Can you still see the tenth step from where you are on the sixth step?' (Of course, they could.) 'And can you see that if you took one step at a time, you would get to the tenth step without losing your balance?' The point was made: they would make it to the age they wanted to be, but one step at a time and not yet: it was not their turn to be ten yet . . . but their turn *would* come.

The paradox about growing up is that the more responsibility children assume for issues that are not yet their business, the less responsibility they can take for themselves. So many children with apparently immature behaviour are actually, in my experience, *too* grown up. They cannot behave more maturely, however, until they can lose some of the inappropriate responsibilities that are burdening them: they will have to grow down before they can grow up. It's like already having a full-time workload and being asked to take on one more task: something has to be completed or delegated before you can attend to a new responsibility.

Support resilience

Self-efficacy or potency—our belief in our ability to have an impact on ourselves, our surroundings and other people—is the psychological basis of resilience. Support from others, as well as gifted children's problem-solving skills, internal locus of control, strong sense of purpose and healthy self-esteem, contributes to their resilience in the face of the everyday stressors likely to be encountered by anyone (Bland et al. 1994; Dole 2000).

Resilience does not come about by avoiding stressors, but by encountering them at a time and in a way that enhances children's self-confidence that they can master events and take appropriate responsibility (Rutter 1985). People who believe in their own abilities to overcome adversity are more likely to act and, in turn, are more likely to be resilient in the face of setbacks. Whether experiencing adversity because of outside circumstances such as family stress or challenges associated with their giftedness, gifted children will need emotional support and to be able to appraise challenges realistically so they can use both their intellectual and social problem-solving skills to bounce back from adversity. This is known as *coping*, and can entail any of three responses.

- *Problem-focused* action, as its title implies, involves solving the problem that is provoking stress.
- *Emotion-focused* strategies involve adjusting our thinking to change our emotional reactions.
- *Adjustment* processes involve changing our behaviour so that we can adjust better to circumstances that we cannot change (Compas 1987; Sowa & May 1997).

Gifted children use problem-focused coping strategies well in advance of their age mates (Reis & Moon 2002). But, in general, children will use problem-focused strategies most when they perceive that they have some control over a situation, whereas they will use emotional or behavioural adjustment to deal with issues that they cannot change (Spirito et al. 1991). Even so, it does not so much matter *how* children cope but *that* they take action about a stressful event (Rutter 1985). Doing so teaches them that they are in command of their lives.

Teach the link between thoughts and feelings

To teach children to manage their emotions, it can be useful to explain to them that their feelings, and subsequently their behaviour, are controlled by what they *think*. Other people and outside events do not *make* us feel anything: how we think about events leads to our feelings and behaviour. Our feelings help to make life interesting and signal when we need to change some aspect of our lives, but extreme emotions can get in the way of a happy life.

Bill Glasser (1998) says that behaviour has four parts: thinking, feeling, action and a physiological response (a change in bodily state). It might help to think of these as the four wheels of a front-wheel-drive car. The front two—the driving wheels—are our *thinking* and our *actions*. They pull along behind them our *feelings* and our *physical well-being*. When we wish to go some-where, we cannot wait until the rear wheels of a car 'get in the mood' to move, but instead we have to use the front, driving wheels to pull the rear ones along. Likewise, if we want to feel better, we have to change what we think and do—and our feelings and even physical health will improve in turn.

So when children habitually express feelings in ways that interfere with others or with their own social or emotional well-being, you can teach them that this comes about because they are thinking in ways that lead to extreme emotions. Some of the common dysfunctional thinking habits are listed in Table 6.1. Once children are aware of the patterns they often use, you can coach them to think in new, more productive ways which, in turn, will lead to more balanced emotional responses.

Table 6.1 Common dysfunctional thinking patterns of children

Thinking style	Common theme	Emotion
Robot thinking	I can't help myself	Feelings of failure
I'm awful	Everything is my fault	Avoidance of risks
You're awful	Everything is your fault	Belligerence
Fairytale thinking	It's not fair	Hurt, anger
Woosie (wimpy) thinking	I can't stand it	Anxiety Shyness Over-reaction to threat
Doomsday thinking	Things are always awful; they will never get any better	Depression

Source: adapted from Roush 1984 (in Kaplan & Carter 1995: 396).

In my conversations with children, I have found that wimpy and doomsday thinking patterns are common to those whose emotions get out of control. Both of these thoughts are often accompanied by one of the other four types—so you will need to explain more than one pattern to troubled children. Wimpy thinking is clearly inaccurate as individuals can 'stand' all sorts of things—even very negative events—and still survive, often happily. And doomsday thinking is inaccurate because nothing ever happens *always*, so things *can* improve—particularly when children learn to recognise the part they play in their own problems and understand that they can change the way they are acting.

You can challenge children to examine the accuracy of their thinking by asking the following questions, using the acronym AFROG to help you remember each (Roush 1984, in Kaplan & Carter 1995: 407).

- Does this thinking keep me *alive*?
- Does this thinking make me *feel* better?
- Is this thinking based on *reality*?
- Does this thinking help me get along with *others*?
- Does this thinking help me to reach my own *goals*?

Once children have recognised that their extreme thinking is leading to excessive emotional reactions, your next task is to teach them to generate an alternative, more helpful set of beliefs and to practise their new thinking with as much conviction as they had previously used to assert their unhelpful beliefs.

Teach children to make accurate attributions

An attribution is an explanation of the cause of an event. To help children develop an internal locus of control, you will need to guide them to attribute outcomes to their own efforts, rather than to uncontrollable factors such as inability or luck. This is called *attribution training*. The aim is to teach children that they are responsible for an outcome—without, however, taking personal blame, as that can feed into dysfunctional perfectionism. So you will need to guide them to: define failure as *temporary* rather than permanent; see failure as *specific* to the event rather than as a sign of a general or all-pervasive failing on their part; and explain the failure in terms of their *behaviour*, not personality (Seligman 1995).

So, when you hear children blame their personality for failings (such as when they say 'I'm hopeless at this') and when they assume that the problem is permanent ('I'll *never* be able to do it'), you can gently correct their statements with something like: 'You're right that it hasn't worked out . . . What could you do to fix it?' Without confronting them with their mistakes, you should not allow them to make excuses or teach them to do so—for example, by blaming a 'naughty' step for tripping them over, but instead comment that they forgot to watch out for the step.

Guide children's behaviour

The single most effective way to enhance children's autonomy is to use a guidance approach to behaviour management. For the past century, two traditions have dominated our thinking about children's behaviour: the behaviourist tradition, which upholds that behaviour is controlled by its consequences; and the humanist or guidance view, which maintains that behaviour is triggered by individuals' needs (as described in the model presented in Chapter 3).

The belief that behaviour is determined by outside conditions is actually an error in logic: if paracetamol cures your headache, this does not prove that your headache was *caused* by a lack of paracetamol. Similarly, if a change in a reward or punishment regime alters a child's behaviour, this does not prove that the behaviour was caused by the consequences that were in place at the time.

The guidance view that behaviour is governed by internal needs is supported by observations that adults sometimes volunteer for community agencies, give up a higher paying job for one with less pay but improved job satisfaction, or leave paid employment to bring up their children. Meanwhile, children (and older people too!) sometimes act in a way that they know will get them into trouble but take the risk because their need is great. None of these actions is controlled by external rewards, as they all entail some sacrifice (loss of a reward) or application of a punishment.

This non-behaviourist view of the world renders rewards and punishments virtually irrelevant because, although individuals will usually be aware of the regime of consequences that is in place and will factor this into their decision about how to act, if their need is great enough, they will act to satisfy it—even if this attracts sanctions (Glasser 1998).

Not only are rewards and punishments irrelevant in instances of strong emotional need, but they can also be counter-productive because they violate children's fundamental need for autonomy. In turn, this violation can provoke negative reactions—that is, excite the very disruptive behaviours that we are trying to discourage (Porter 1999). Over 30 years ago, Tom Gordon (1970) labelled these reactions as 'the three Rs' of resistance, rebellion and retaliation. He later added submission and escape as other reactions to being controlled (Gordon 1974). These responses were commonly observed in my research into behaviour management in child (day) care centres, where they constituted approximately three-quarters of the behavioural disruptions in centres using a controlling style of discipline—that is, those that employed rewards and punishments (Porter 1999).

For five reasons, a guidance approach aims to teach children to act considerately rather than to comply with adults' directives. The first reason is that training children to be obedient endangers them, as they might not resist abuse—and here I'm thinking mainly of sexual abuse—because they have been taught to do what adults say (Briggs & McVeity 2000). Second, teaching compliance is dangerous for surrounding children, as those who have been trained to follow others might collude with schoolyard bullying when directed to do so by a powerful peer. Third, whole societies would be safer if people did not follow the commands of a sociopathic leader who told them to harm members of a surrounding community on racial or religious grounds. Fourth, if we want children to experiment intellectually, we must also be ready for them to experiment behaviourally, even though this will sometimes result in mistakes. Finally, gifted girls in particular are likely to be disadvantaged by being trained to be compliant and dependent, as that can result in their being under-ambitious (Kline & Short 1991).

Instead of teaching compliance, then, I advocate that we teach children how to be considerate of others—to think about the potential effects of their actions on others. Having empathy for others is the essence of a compassionate society and comprises (Porter 2003):

- developing in children a *sense of right and wrong* so that, even without supervision, they will act considerately—not because they might be punished for doing otherwise, but because it is the right thing to do;
- teaching children to *manage their emotions* so that their outbursts do not disturb those around them but, more importantly, so that they themselves learn to cope with setbacks in life;
- teaching children to *cooperate* so that they can satisfy their own needs without violating the needs of other people;
- giving children a sense of *potency*—that is, a sense that they can make a difference to their own actions and emotions and can act on their values.

Rewards and punishments cannot teach considerateness, as they focus children's minds on what will happen *to them* if they act in particular ways, when instead a guidance approach wants them to appreciate how the behaviour affects *others*.

Instead of administering rewards such as praise, privileges, stickers or awards, a guidance approach teaches self-appraisal through acknowledgment (which was described in Chapter 4). And, rather than punishing children for lapses in behaviour, it teaches children both the skills they need to solve problems and the ability to exercise emotional self-control so that they can employ their skills, even when distressed. It *teaches*; it does not punish—because punishing children for behavioural mistakes would be to punish them for *being* children, as children will inevitably act thoughtlessly sometimes.

Its specific methods cannot be detailed here for reasons of space, but in brief I recommend the following practices (Porter 2003):

- Prevent outbursts by meeting the children's intellectual, emotional and social needs and by not pulling rank on children through authoritarian discipline.
- Explain in non-judgmental terms the effect that a disruptive behaviour is having on others. This teaches children how to appreciate another person's perspective.
- Be assertive about an inconsiderate behaviour using three steps: reflecting children's needs; stating your own; and then negotiating how the two can be reconciled. For example: 'I know that it is difficult to wait for me to help you with that, but I am busy with the other children just now, so what would you like to do until I can get there?' By acknowledging that their need is important—that is, by listening to the children—you help them to be willing to listen to and negotiate with others in return. It shows them how it *feels* to be understood.

- Negotiate a deal or contract with individual children that describes how you need them to behave and reciprocates by specifying what you will do to help them achieve that.
- When children veer out of command of their emotions, keep in mind two guiding principles: first, that you cannot reason with people while they are being unreasonable; and second, that the outburst is not due to a lack of information about how they should or should not be behaving, but results from a lapse of self-control. (When we eat 'junk' food, we do so not because we lack factual knowledge about its low nutritional value, but because we lack self-control.) In that case, do not preach about the behaviour itself, but help children to calm down. You already know how to do this: use the same soothing approaches that you use for hysterical babies—a cuddle, a sympathetic ear, an offer to help. This applies for protesting tantrums, whining and sulking, angry outbursts with others, or for those times when children will not cooperate with a reasonable directive out of distaste for what they are being asked to do. In other words, even when the behaviour seems nasty or malicious, it is simply a sign that the children's emotions are governing their behaviour, rather than their intellect being in command—and that they need support to regain self-control.
- If bringing them in close either physically or emotionally does not work or is impractical in the circumstances, guide the children to withdraw to a solitary place and do a soothing activity. Individuals will differ in what soothes them, but they might choose to listen to music, read, tinker with their collectables, watch a video . . . or whatever. Even we adults sometimes need to calm down our perturbed nervous systems, but we prefer not to do so sitting on a chair in the laundry facing the wall: we choose a soothing pastime. This is the essence of the difference between time out and time away: one is a punishment and the other a solution to an overwhelmed nervous system.

Conclusion

The essence of resilience is for children to develop confidence in their ability to take charge of themselves and to recover from disappointments. To achieve this, adults can give them personal support to be independent, exercise choice, take appropriate responsibility, cope with stressors and stay in command of their own thinking. As well, our disciplinary methods must support rather than censure children. This applies to all young people, but gifted children's advanced intellectual skills mean that they are particularly prone to reacting to unjust disciplinary approaches and to rebelling against authoritarian methods which rob them of their autonomy (Niebrzydowski 1997). The need of all individuals to be autonomous requires adults to act as leaders rather than bosses, and to teach considerate behaviour rather than punish its opposite. Only then will society be protected from the behavioural excesses of its members and will individuals exercise responsibility for themselves.

Suggested further reading

A lay discussion of resilience is provided by:
Seligman, M.E.P. 1995 *The optimistic child* Random House, Sydney.

A guidance approach to children's behaviour is outlined in:
Gartrell, D. 2003 *A guidance approach for the encouraging classroom* 3rd edn, Delmar, New York.
Kohn, A. 1996 *Beyond discipline: from compliance to community* Association for Supervision and Curriculum Development, Alexandria, VA.
Kohn, A. 1999 *Punished by rewards: the trouble with gold stars, incentive plans, A's, praise and other bribes* 2nd edn, Houghton Mifflin, Boston, MA.
Porter, L. 2003 *Young children's behaviour: practical approaches for caregivers and teachers* 2nd edn, Elsevier, Sydney/Paul Chapman, London/Brookes, Baltimore, MD.
Porter, L. 2005 *Children are people too: a guide for parents to children's behaviour* 4th edn, East Street Publications, Adelaide.

EDUCATIONAL
PROVISIONS

Part III

A RATIONALE FOR
GIFTED EDUCATION

It is wishful thinking to suppose that hard-working teachers without sufficient content knowledge, without special knowledge of gifted children, without time to plan programs, and with limited assistance from supervisory personnel, will be able to alter the educational situation for gifted children to any meaningful degree. (Rogers 1989: 149)

Attitudes to giftedness

It seems that everyone has an attitude towards giftedness. When teachers' lay opinions have not been counteracted by training in gifted education, misinformation can taint their willingness to make educational provisions for gifted learners. So this chapter describes some of the most commonly expressed attitudes and details how these affect gifted children. The eight views are as follows.

- Many lay and education professionals have an outright prejudice against gifted children.
- Some believe that, as giftedness is a construct that has been created arbitrarily, it is not meaningful. This can be simplified down to the notion that 'no one is gifted'.
- Others believe that everyone is gifted at something.
- Some contend that some children (and adults) are gifted, but believe that this is not an educational issue as these children will be able to progress without specific help. This can be simplified into the view that giftedness does not matter.
- There is also a view that giftedness matters but not as much as other educational needs, so it must remain a lower priority for resource allocation.

- Others contend that society should invest in gifted education, as talented children will grow up to become our political leaders and key people in industry. This is the national resources rationale for gifted education (Borland 1989).
- Some proclaim that those who are gifted need additional support in order to reach their potential.
- The special education view is that those gifted children who have additional needs now have a right for those needs to be met *now*, regardless of how the children later develop.

The remainder of this chapter examines each of these perspectives, building a rationale for gifted provisions for those children who are not presently having their needs met within regular programs.

Prejudice

Many researchers have found that teachers tend not to have positive views of gifted children or of educational provisions for them, with attitudes ranging from indifference to outright antagonism (Cramond & Martin 1987; Forster 2002; Lee 2000; McBride 1992; Sankar-DeLeeuw 2002; Sharma 2001). Forster speculates that this prejudice might materialise because teachers do not like children who are cleverer than themselves. Or it could be that, during their own school careers, those who later become teachers were typically the students achieving at the upper end of the middle-ability group and, given that young people resent peers who are more able than them (Carrington 1993), they may continue to do so as adults. Carrington and Bailey (2000) extend this by adding that preservice teachers least prefer gifted students who are studious or who make frequent contributions to the class. An explanation for this finding is that perhaps the preservice teachers see these learners as not adequately balancing their academic and other life.

Alternatively, teachers' prejudice might not be due to their own personal psychology, but to the perceived threat to their authority posed by knowledgeable parents. Fifty years ago, professionals dominated those whom they were advising, as in the medical sphere where 'the doctor was always right' (see Porter & McKenzie 2000). Over time, however, this professional dominance model has been eroded—but not completely, and not in all quarters. Some teachers still see themselves as the experts who alone will determine what children need. Instead, a collaborative relationship with parents respects their intimate knowledge about their own child, listens to their aspirations for their child's education, and enables the teacher to learn from parents about their child and his or her needs. This collaborative stance is not threatened by well-educated, articulate parents with in-depth knowledge of giftedness . . . but a dominant, expert relationship *is*. The solution for teachers, then, is simply to define their relationship with parents as collaborative, with complementary roles and a reciprocal exchange of expertise. In that case, there would be no need to perceive parental expertise as a threat to their superior authority, as the two parties are equal after all.

A different explanation is offered by Forster (2002), who contends that preconceptions about giftedness are sustained by a lack of teacher training in gifted education, although training alone may not be enough to overcome prejudice: increased contact with gifted students and gifted provisions seems essential as well (Carrington & Bailey 2000).

Others assert that some of the prejudice against gifted learners has a wider cause—namely, a cultural distrust of intellectuals. This may be peculiar to Western cultures, as the many Chinese and Singaporean students and conference delegates with whom I have discussed this prejudice find it incomprehensible within their values system. But across the cultures of the United States (Gallagher 1991), the United Kingdom (Eyre 1997), Australia (Bailey 1998; Wilson 1996) and New Zealand (Fraser 2004), the message is the same: we value the products of high achievers but denigrate 'bookishness'. Perhaps the pioneer history of most of these countries is the cause—it was brawn, not brains, that was necessary to carve out a new civilisation in a foreign land (Wilson 1996). Added to that, Australia's penal history generated a suspicion of authority and the intellectuals who made and carried out official policies (Wilson 1996). This history means that many Westerners use words such as 'intellectual' or 'precocious' as terms of derision (Christie 1995) and, while keen to allocate extra money for elite sports training programs, are less willing to give it for elite intellectual training (Gross 2004).

This anti-intellectual view of giftedness is the most troublesome of those to be detailed here, as prejudice is less open to scrutiny than mere misinformation (as represented by many of the remaining attitudes). Furthermore, it would likely cause teachers not to attend discretionary professional development sessions, and to gain little from compulsory training. Yet knowledge about giftedness is essential for delivering an appropriate education (Plunkett 2000). Finally, prejudice is troubling because teachers do not get to pick and choose who they will teach, so must be able to cater for all the individuals within their care. This does not suggest that they should know everything, of course: the essence of professionalism is knowing what you do *not* know, and setting about locating resources (such as reading material, specialists or parents) to fill the gaps.

No one is gifted

This second misconception denies the usefulness of the *concept* of high ability. It states that giftedness is merely something we have invented to explain various learning behaviours. The argument goes that we have constructed the category of 'giftedness' statistically by choosing where to place the demarcation between gifted and average abilities. This decision was entirely arbitrary and probably had as much to do with how many resources were

available for addressing advanced learners as it had to do with any characteristics that distinguish them from average learners.

This is acknowledged (Sternberg & Davidson 1986)—but that fact
alone does not make the concept of giftedness useless. For example, we have
invented notions of short-term and long-term memory stores to explain
memory function and, although it is unlikely that there are dedicated
sections of the brain for each type of memory, we continue to use these
constructs because they help guide research and practice. So it is with high
ability. We have created a definition of high ability but this does not mean
that we invented high ability itself. Giftedness is a psychological reality in
that there *are* individual differences in ability (Gallagher 1996; Pyryt 1996).

The denial of individual differences is actually political rather than
psychological. Whereas psychology accepts that differences exist between
individuals, politics rejects the elitism inherent in regarding gifted learners as
superior to others (notwithstanding the cultural ambivalence towards giftedness that has already been mentioned) (Sapon-Shevin 1994, 1996b). This
tension between the psychological and political aspects of a label can be
overcome, however, when we acknowledge that people can have differing
abilities while still having equal worth as individuals.

A variation on the theme that no one is gifted is the assertion that there
are too few gifted students to warrant special attention, as claimed by some
teachers in the study by Forster (2002). This is ridiculous: by definition,
there are few gifted students; if more students were included in the gifted
category, some could argue that there were so many of them that the
category had become meaningless. Furthermore, given that by definition
there are as many students with disabilities as there are gifted learners, this
line of reasoning would have to apply equally to children with disabilities,
resulting in an argument for the cessation of special education for those with
learning difficulties.

The problem with the view that no one is gifted is exemplified by the
saying taken from the child protection literature that 'I wouldn't have seen it
if I hadn't believed it'. In other words, denial of advanced abilities and their
significance for their possessor means that teachers fail to identify and to
provide for those whose exceptional abilities provoke additional needs. We
would not deny the significance of individuals' gender or race to their sense
of self, yet some deny children's abilities as being relevant to who they are or
what provisions they might require.

Everyone is gifted

A third view is that all children are gifted at something, and so they all
require or deserve special provisions. This view is easily dismissed, as it
simply cannot be true that all are 'above average' in their abilities: to claim
so is arithmetically absurd. If everyone were above average, being above
average would now *be* the average, so everyone would be average.

This view is often aligned with the concept of multiple intelligences, whereby it is claimed that, although individuals might not be gifted in one domain, they will be in another. However, Gardner (1997) himself refutes this. While it is true that each child will have individual strengths, these abilities will seldom fall so far above the average that the children will need special programming in those domains (Braggett 1992; Gagné 1997; Gross 2004; Runco 1997). Not only would it be difficult for teachers to cope with so many children for whom to make special provisions, but it would also use resources that could otherwise be directed at children whose abilities *were* extreme (above or below the average) (Maker & Nielson 1995).

The view that everyone is gifted is akin, in my mind, to asserting that everyone is 6 feet (180 cm) tall — and that those of us who appear not to be are just being stubborn about it, or there is something wrong with how we are being measured. The parallel argument in gifted education is that, if individuals are not recognised as gifted, this must be because our assessment is inaccurate. But while the accusation that IQ tests overlook certain forms of ability is true in some cases, in others testing does not recognise individuals as being gifted because they actually are not.

Giftedness does not matter

Given that you are reading this text, you are probably not one who subscribes to this fourth view of giftedness. However, others see gifted learners as already having a huge advantage so assume that there is therefore no need for a special focus on them within the education system. But although it is true that gifted children are advantaged in that they can learn more easily than most, they are still children and still need to be taught how to learn (Braggett 1994). As Webb et al. (1991: 10) observe: 'Although gifted students possess exceptional capabilities, most cannot excel without assistance.'

Giftedness matters but is a low priority

The low-priority view of gifted education acknowledges that gifted children have particular needs, but that these needs are not as grave as those of children with learning difficulties. This argument states that society's scarce resources have to be allocated to the most needy, and that allocating funds to gifted children would detract from funding for those with learning difficulties. This is not a denial of the needs of the gifted, but merely a debate about the willingness of society to fund meeting those needs.

Sapon-Shevin (1994) contends that the resources used for gifted education represent favouritism. However, reports from the United States tell us that gifted education there receives 2 cents out of every $100 spent on education — that is, 0.02 per cent of the educa- tion budget (Sternberg 1996), compared with 33 per cent of the education budget going to special education (Stanley & Baines 2002); or just $1 per gifted child per year (Ford et al.

1993). In Australia, $6.60 was allocated for each gifted child for each of the three years between 1993 and 1995, which compares with the almost $600 each allocated to Olympic divers (Wilson 1996). Many writers thus conclude that critics are correct that the resources used for gifted education are inequitable, but contend that they represent neglect, not favouritism (Borland 1989; Ford et al. 1993).

This accusation of favouritism or elitism is frequently contrasted unfavourably with notions of democracy, which demands that everyone be given equal opportunities (Gross 2004). However, egalitarianism states that all children have an *equal right to develop* from their present skill levels: this should not be confused with a *right to equal development* (Gross 2004; Stanley & Baines 2002). Although children have an equal right to access *appropriate* educational experiences, justice does not demand that these experiences be the *same* for all children (Benbow 1992; Strike 1983). Furthermore, when gifted children are singled out on the basis of *need*—that is, are offered a modified curriculum because their present program is not meeting their needs—this is not elitism or favouritism: it is what schools are supposed to do when children have atypical needs (Borland 1989).

Giftedness matters because gifted learners are a national resource

According to this utilitarian view, the main reason to foster the skills of gifted children is to ensure that they ultimately contribute to society in some exceptional way. Two often-cited slogans stating that 'Our children are our future' and 'The gifted are our future leaders' reflect this focus on children's future value to the community, rather than their present needs or value.

The claim that gifted children will become leaders in their chosen disciplines has very little supporting research evidence, and even common sense would refute the contention. This is because, as we saw in Chapter 2, it takes more than ability alone to become prominent: success requires a fortuitous blend of ability, hard work, good chance and advantageous social circumstances. This commonsense appreciation is confirmed by both Terman's longitudinal study of gifted children (which followed a cohort of gifted individuals from the 1920s until the present) and the Hunter College Elementary School study, both of which showed that, rather than becoming world leaders, the gifted participants in these studies tended to become well-rounded and well-adjusted professional adults (Bailey 1998; Feldman 1984; Freeman 1995a, 1998; Gallagher 1996; Hastorf 1997; Sears 1977; Subotnik et al. 1989; Winner 1996).

A second issue with the national resources rationale is that it regards young children only as having the *potential* for giftedness, and so generates no imperative to focus on them in their early years, as there is no way of knowing at that age who will continue to excel significantly. This leads to a neglect of giftedness during the early childhood years.

Gifted education is necessary for children to reach their potential

Yet another claim about gifted education is that gifted children need special educational provisions if they are to achieve their potential. The first problem with this argument is that there is no evidence that students in gifted programs excel over those gifted children who receive a standard education. Furthermore, if gifted individuals cannot excel without special provisions, virtually all members of the past generations have had their potential curtailed — because very few indeed received gifted educational provisions.

Second, the whole notion of potential is as absurd as it is worrying. It is absurd because it is meaningless, as there is no way to measure potential, and therefore no way to assess whether anyone has achieved it. And it is worrying because it puts unnecessary strain on parents who feel that every waking hour must be devoted to their child's needs, as otherwise the child supposedly will not reach his or her potential. A parent I met recently told me that when she reduced her child's dance classes from three to one lesson per week, the other parents accused her of jeopardising her child's potential. The child was aged three-and- a-quarter!

This pressure is then transferred to educators, whereby parents demand that teachers perform some special magic for bright children, on the grounds that otherwise the children will not reach their potential. Given the impossibility of measuring whether they are attaining their potential, teachers cannot answer this pressure to anyone's satisfaction.

Giftedness matters because some gifted learners have additional needs

In contrast to the previous two positions, the special education view is that children have rights and needs now and deserve to have these met, regardless of how they later develop. In short, the special education approach treasures children for being themselves, rather than for what they can do now or might do in the future (Corrigan 1994).

The special education approach recognises that some gifted children will already be receiving what they require educationally, while others will need special provisions to meet their atypical needs (Borland 1989). This view endorses the following statements:

- Children with atypical learning patterns often have some needs in addition to children whose development is typical for their age.
- There is no debate that we must identify — and identify early — children whose learning capacities fall significantly below the average so we can deliver a curriculum that is more likely to meet their atypical needs. The same can be said, then, for children whose skills are significantly above the average — that is, for those whom we call 'gifted'.

- Having identified children whose needs are not being met, we must set about providing a program which more routinely provides what they require. Naturally, this is true for all children, whatever the need—not just for those whom we recognise as having advanced development.

This special education view contends that gifted children have as much right to have their needs met as other children—but are no *more* deserving than anyone else (Peterson 1993). Thus advocacy for gifted education becomes advocacy for individualised education for all children, not for better treatment for the gifted. Eyre (1997: 91) is clear about this: 'Time for the most able should not be achieved at the expense of other pupils.'

A rationale for gifted education for the young

Despite ample evidence of the efficacy of early provisions for educationally disadvantaged children, these findings are seldom applied to gifted children. Special provisions for gifted children are rarely available prior to the middle primary (elementary) school years (Gillman & Hansen 1987). Yet a core tenet of early years education is that high-quality early programs have crucial benefits both for children's development and for their attitudes towards both learning and themselves as learners (Field 1991; Gallagher 1988; Phillips & Howes 1987; Sylva 1994). It is well accepted that the brain is most malleable in the first five years of life, so early childhood is a critical period for facilitating children's development.

There are few studies of the effectiveness of early enrichment for gifted learners (Karnes & Johnson 1991). However, one study (Fowler et al. 1995) offered early language-enrichment training to parents of infants aged between three and 24 months. The researchers found that, whereas 4.8 per cent of children whose parents were university educated could be expected to be gifted, a massive 68 per cent of these children who also received early enrichment were later identified to be gifted. Even more astonishing is the finding that, whereas only 0.001 per cent of children could be expected to be gifted when their parents did not complete high school, 31 per cent of those children (many from minority cultures) who received early enrichment training were later defined as gifted. Another meta-analytic study concluded that school-based enrichment programs make the most difference to children's achievement in their first few years of school (Vaughn et al. 1991). Together with our knowledge of the benefits of early intervention with children who have disabilities, such studies indicate that early enrichment can promote the development of young children's learning capacities.

Some gifted education advocates also claim that underachievement can be identified in the earliest years of school, in which case it seems obvious that prevention of underachievement should begin prior to this —namely, in the preschool years, when children's attitudes to learning are most malleable (Karnes & Johnson 1991; Karnes et al. 1985; Wolfle 1990). Evidence for this claim may be fairly scant, and the underlying assumptions about the permanency and definition of underachievement need some careful analysis (which is offered in Chapter 11), but it seems self-evident that failing to meet children's needs during their induction into the education system could discourage them from the outset, while their lack of access to intellectual peers renders their social and emotional needs at this age a particular priority. At the same time, early childhood is the time when parents are most likely to encounter for the first time the notion that their child has exceptional needs, so they may need some additional information to maintain their confidence in their own ability to satisfy these needs (Creel & Karnes 1988) (see Chapter 13).

Nevertheless, there is some disquiet about identifying the very young as gifted. Because young children have such a short life history on which to base diagnoses and prognoses, there is a justified reluctance to label them in any way, and the gifted label is no exception. Some commentators express deep concern for the effects on neophyte personalities of being labelled as gifted—fearing, for example, that early identification will make these children conceited or pompous, or will isolate them from their peers (Gross 2004; Mares 1991). However, as Mares (1991: 12) observes: 'This is sheer nonsense. The child is gifted, whether she is identified or not.'

Others think that the gifted label will lead to some children being 'hot-housed' to the point where they lose interest in their special talent, are withdrawn from social and playful contact with other children, or come to define themselves as valuable only because of their exceptional abilities (Mares 1991). However, a focus on giftedness during children's earliest years does *not* mean hot-housing children such that they are force-fed information in advance of their interests. Pumping children full of information is *not* the same as encouraging them to develop their own special gifts and abilities (Smutny et al. 1989). Hot-housing promotes adults' ambitions; gifted education seeks to nurture the skills and interests of the children themselves.

The range of gifted education provisions

When children have disabilities, their access to special education services is determined on the basis of *need*: if the children need a service, they are generally regarded as having a right to one. (For reasons of limited resources, this is not always supplied, but the aim is to do so.) However, with gifted children, access to special provisions is often based on a determination that they *deserve* these: they must behave in exemplary ways, have tidy handwriting or display uniformly able performances before they are considered for a gifted program (Borland 1989). However, the very fact that such children are meeting expectations within their present setting suggests that this setting is mostly meeting their needs. In that case, these are the children who least need modified provisions; those who need adjustments are the ones who are not coping within the present arrangements. We do not give medical treatment to those who are healthy, but instead to those who are unwell (Borland 1989).

The criterion, then, should be the same for gifted learners as for those who have a disability: *need* should provoke the implementation of special provisions. The issue then becomes what form those provisions should take. Three main options are possible: fully segregated gifted education; partial segregation—or 'pull-out' programs; or inclusive education for all.

Segregated gifted programs

Segregated programs give rise to the most strenuous objections to gifted education. However, it must be said that, even in the school sector, segregated programs are uncommon—especially beyond the United States—while such programs for gifted children are rare indeed in early childhood (Hall 1993; Kitano 1982; Wolfle 1990). This neglect can be traced back to the attitudes to giftedness already outlined here—and key among these is the equity argument.

The first criticism of segregated gifted programs on equity grounds is the protest that educationally disadvantaged children are under-represented in these programs. Advocates recognise this reality, but counter with the argument that this neglect would not be righted by denying identified gifted children an appropriate and meaningful education on the grounds that not everyone who is eligible receives it (Borland 1996b; Borland & Wright 1994; Braggett 1992; Gallagher 1996; Pendarvis & Howley 1996). Furthermore, if gifted provisions were withdrawn, wealthy parents could secure enriching experiences privately, while poor gifted children would receive even less than they do now (Borland 1996b). Therefore, advocates of gifted programs claim that, instead of disbanding segregated programs, we should get better at recognising and including children whose giftedness may be disguised. However, Sapon-Shevin (1996a: 196) scornfully dismisses this suggestion with the retort of Calvin Coolidge: 'There is no right way to do the wrong thing.'

Another criticism is that segregated gifted education perpetuates a special educational approach in which students with additional needs are regarded as deviants and are withdrawn from the mainstream, thus impeding reform of the school conditions that bring about these children's lack of success in regular classes (Pugach 1988; Sapon-Shevin 1996b). A related claim is that regular teachers are deskilled and insulted by the implication that they cannot adequately cater for atypical learners. Some counter this by saying that teachers cannot be expected to have expertise in all of the specialised techniques needed to teach all atypical children (Gallagher 1996; Stephens 1988); without minimising the challenges of providing for all children in the one setting, Sapon-Shevin (1996a) accuses this segregation-ist view of a lack of vision.

It could be argued that, like special education in the past, gifted educa-tion needs to concentrate its students into segregated settings to give teachers intensive experience in programming for them so they can gain sufficient expertise before disseminating it back out into inclusive settings. However, two problems arise with this idea—both of them probably insur-mountable. The first is how to select the children for these segregated programs and whether it is justifiable to use what would be considerable resources in this identification and selection process. The second is that the segregated model would not overcome the fact that those gifted children who were overlooked would still need to be provided for within the regular stream, so expertise would have to be accrued there after all.

Partial or 'pull-out' programs

Pull-out programs have children attending their regular class for most of the time and being pulled out of that class for enriching activities. Like segre-gated programs, these pull-out sessions are widely criticised as being subjected to insufficient scrutiny or evaluation, with the result that many are mediocre and ill-serve the children whom they are designed to help. Many involve trivial or irrelevant activities which lack a clear rationale and are not coordinated with the regular curriculum (Belcastro 1987; Ford et al. 1993; Irvine 1991; Vaughn et al. 1991).

This lack of coordination with children's regular curriculum also raises the philosophical objection that the class and school 'community' are disrupted when children are singled out for particular treatment and, in a more practical vein, that when individual students are withdrawn for enrich-ment activities, the teachers and children who remain in the regular classroom must alter their program so that the absent children do not miss anything significant (Sapon-Shevin 1990, 1994, 1996a, 1996b). These are legitimate concerns which, while not yet adequately researched, are never-theless not easily dismissed—at the school level at least (Belcastro 1987; Borland, 1996a, 1996b). However, the looser structure of early years educa-tion renders this objection less potent in that setting, as young children are often taught in small 'pull-out' groups so establishment of a small group with a gifted focus would neither excite attention nor disrupt the usual routine.

Another criticism of pull-out programs is that these might imply to the children's regular teachers that they are now being catered for, and so there is nothing more that they need within the regular classroom (Delisle 1994c; Sapon-Shevin 1994, 1996b). But an even more telling criticism comes from parents, who assert that 'their children are gifted all of the time, not just during pull-out time' (Vestal 1993: 10), and so require more continuous enrichment than pull-out programs can provide (Taplin & White 1998). This analysis is supported by Gallagher (2000), who asks what a gifted educator can possibly offer in just one or two hours per week that could come close to overcoming children's frustration at not having their needs met for the rest of the week. He likens this low dose of enrichment to a child receiving a non-therapeutic dose of asthma medication on the grounds that there is not enough for everyone, and concludes that pull-out gifted programs come 'perilously close to educational fraud' by claiming to offer a real intervention when that cannot be delivered in the timeframe allocated (Gallagher 2000: 10).

Inclusive gifted education

The debate about segregation versus inclusion for gifted learners is actually somewhat academic in early childhood education, as few gifted programs exist at all in the early years. This means that there simply *is* nowhere else to place gifted young children and, even where local education authorities permit early entry to school, there is nevertheless a lower age limit to early admission so the very young still have to be accommodated in early childhood centres.

Furthermore, even where segregated or pull-out programs are in existence, only a minority of advanced learners will ever be selected to attend. The conclusion is that, as most gifted children are already in mainstream settings, this is where we must direct our efforts: to improving provisions in these settings so that they more adequately meet the needs of all children.

Arguably, early years education is better equipped than most levels of schooling to incorporate the needs of gifted children, for a range of reasons. First, proportionally there is a narrower range of ability levels in a group of very young children compared with older children. When four-year-olds are learning 50 per cent faster than usual, they are still functioning only two years ahead of their actual age, but when ten-year-olds are developing 50 per cent faster, this represents a five-year gap between their skills and those of average classmates. This wider disparity in the developmental levels within a group of older children could conceivably pose a greater challenge for teachers attempting to accommodate their various needs.

Second, early childhood education is inherently child-focused and has a staunch history of inclusion of children with atypical development, while the naturalistic approach to programming that pervades early years education is a sound basis for individualised programming for gifted learners.

Third, the early childhood sector has a strong reliance on authentic and naturalistic assessment, which involves assessing not by contrived measures but by providing curricula that allow children's abilities and interests to emerge (Vialle 1997). This form of identification does not aim at singling out a few children to receive an enriching program but instead all children are exposed to open-ended activities in a wide range of content domains. All will engage with the curriculum at their own level, to which subsequent programming can respond in order to develop the skills that emerge (Braggett 1992). In this way all can extend their skills, although only some will come to function at significantly advanced levels and so could be said to be gifted.

This reality that gifted education for the very young has been, and will continue to be, conducted within their regular setting does not imply that educators can meet gifted young children's needs without support. In order to fulfil this responsibility, we must equip them to do so through some additional training and advisory support (Christie 1995; Feldhusen 1985, 1997; Hansen & Feldhusen 1994; Plunkett 2000; Reis & Purcell 1993; Reis & Westberg 1994; Van Tassel-Baska 1995).

Early childhood teachers will also need to come to grips with the fact that the children who enter preschools today are not the same as they were a generation ago. Average IQs are going up three points per decade, so today's children are more skilled (except in fine motor skills) and have more exposure to outside influences (including centre-based child care) that have the potential to advance their development. Entrants to preschools nowadays have often 'been there and done that': they have already experienced many of the activities on offer, either in centre-based care or at home as a result of the availability of affordable, commercially produced educational toys and activities. So it is probably safe to conclude that children whose development is advanced may already have mastered most typical preschool tasks, especially when they come to preschool having profited from extensive prior learning opportunities.

In light of these social changes, the challenge then becomes how to advance children's skills beyond entry level without imposing on such young children the structured, academic teaching that characterises the schooling of their older counterparts.

Conclusion

Rather than being a preparation for 'serious' learning, early childhood education and the first years of school provide a rich education in themselves (Gillman & Hansen 1987). Early childhood centres are not just a downward extension of the schooling system: they are uniquely equipped to cater for children with a broad range of developmental abilities and thus to offer gifted children appropriate programming in a naturalistic setting.

Research tells us that when educators expand their provisions for their more able children, overall provisions improve (Eyre 1997). This is a powerful incentive to gain competence in providing for these children—as all will benefit.

Suggested further reading

For a succinct overview of the key issues pertaining to gifted education, I recommend:

Freeman, J. 1998 *Educating the very able: current international research* Office for Standards in Education, London.

For collections of articles giving an overview of contemporary issues in gifted education:
Colangelo, N. and Davis, G.A. (eds) 2003 *Handbook of gifted education* 3rd edn, Allyn & Bacon, Boston, MA.
Vialle, W. and Geake, J. (eds) 2002 *The gifted enigma: a collection of articles* Hawker Brownlow, Melbourne.
For academic readers:
Heller, K.A., Mönks, F.J., Sternberg, R.J. and Subotnik, R.F. (eds) 2000 *International handbook of giftedness and talent* 2nd edn, Pergamon, Oxford.

ASSESSING DEVELOPMENTAL
ADVANCES IN
YOUNG CHILDREN
eight

The most important prerequisite of [assessment processes] is that they should fit neatly with the existing structures and systems so that the identification of ability and talent can be an integral part of the [centre's] activities . . . Otherwise, the link between identification and provision is tenuous: although certain pupils may have been identified, this process has not led to a change in classroom provision for these children. (Eyre 1997: 11)

Introduction

Imagine that you have been experiencing back pain increasingly over the past few months. It is now beginning to limit your functioning so you consult a doctor. She listens to your description of your symptoms and then begins to fill in a form to order tests: x-rays and some blood analyses. Your response is: 'Oh, I don't want you to give me any tests. I just want you to tell me what to do to stop the pain.'

But how could the doctor decide how best to treat the condition without knowing what it is? So it is when we refuse to assess giftedness. We do not want to complete a comprehensive assessment — and we particularly do not want to perform any tests. The result is that when parents and educators are being asked to cater appropriately for a child, they are having to shoot for a target whose whereabouts is unknown: they have no information about what *is* appropriate. So this chapter argues for a comprehensive assessment of gifted children and outlines the assessment measures that are most suited to this task.

Some key terms

Educational *assessment* is a systematic process of gathering information about children's learning levels, styles and skills to inform educators about how best to meet the children's needs (McLoughlin & Lewis 2001). *Testing* is but one element of educational assessment and involves eliciting children's responses to a range of tasks that are administered under structured conditions (McLoughlin & Lewis 2001).

These two definitions tell us that there is far more to educational assessment than purely testing alone—that is, assessment requires gathering information in a range of ways from a variety of sources, in several situations over time. This process will need to be both *systematic* and *collaborative*, and follow a logical sequence from data collection to the design of an educational program (McLoughlin & Lewis 2001).

Principles of assessment

In Chapter 7, I concluded that all children have a right to an education that meets their needs. In early years education, a cornerstone for achieving this is to provide a program that is developmentally appropriate. However, it is self-evident that it is difficult for educators to provide such a program if they do not know individual children's developmental levels. The only way to know this is through comprehensive assessment. This, then, is the core principle of assessment which, along with other basic principles, will now be discussed with reference to the identification of advanced development in young children.

Comprehensiveness

Assessment will need to be capable of generating a comprehensive picture of children's particular strengths and relatively weaker skill domains in order to design a suitable program. To achieve this, assessment should be an ongoing process, rather than a one-off event (Fatouros 1986), and should employ multiple methods from multiple sources over all developmental domains and settings (Neisworth & Bagnato 1988). A proposed model for achieving this is shown in Figure 8.1, with each step discussed in the next section.

Pragmatism

Comprehensiveness must be balanced with pragmatism—that is, the need for assessment methods to be efficient in terms of the financial and personnel resources that they require. This is both a social requirement—to restrict unnecessary spending—and also a personal requirement to ensure that children are not burdened by unduly prolonged assessment procedures.

Advocacy

Assessment should uphold the interests of children and aim to improve services for them (NAEYC 1988). This includes avoiding any negative effects on children that might arise from labelling them or through misuse of the assessment findings.

The goal of advocating for children is often seen to be at odds with the classification (labelling) function of assessment—in our case, classifying children as gifted learners. However, the concept of giftedness is by definition comparative: it means that individuals are advanced *compared with the norm*. Therefore, classification is inevitable. But this is not to say that all labelling or classification is negative, as it can perform the social justice functions of highlighting the plight of educationally disadvantaged groups in the community, identifying that individual children need special provisions and directing educational funds to the most needy.

Utility

Assessments must measure skills that are relevant either to children's educational programs or to their lives (Feldhusen & Baska 1989; Hansen & Linden 1990)—that is, the information gained must be educationally useful; otherwise there is no point in assessing. This is a common criticism of tests, based on the recognition that, as test items are selected simply because they distinguish among children of varying developmental levels, some have little functional relevance in children's lives. This makes it difficult to design teaching activities based on test content: all the tests can do is indicate a general area in which modified instruction could be useful (Bondurant-Utz & Luciano 1994; Neisworth & Bagnato 1992). Conversely, when test content *is* used to guide programs, educators might teach skills that have little educational value. Perhaps, however, we are asking too much by expecting one instrument to be a tool both for assessment and for determining teaching content.

Defensibility

Assessment methods should be based on the best available research and knowledge. This means that any test that is part of the assessment process should be used only for the purpose for which it was designed and must be valid and reliable—that is, technically sound in its construction and suitable for the ages and ability levels of the children being tested (Hooper & Edmondson 1998; NAEYC 1988).

There is widespread agreement that the commercially available tests used to assess intellectual giftedness are reliable. Reliability means that individual children attain similar results on repeated administrations of the test, and that different testers will score the same child similarly. Evidence in support of test reliability has two strands. First, as long as children's environment is stable (so that their natural rate of learning is not altered), their IQ scores will be similar from one testing to the next. The actual score will change by perhaps 5–9 points over one to six years (Cahan & Gejman 1993; Spangler & Sabatino 1995), but in the main, children's rankings within a group will alter very little (Tannenbaum 1992).

Second, children who are identified as being gifted in the early childhood years are highly likely to maintain their advanced skills, at least into the early primary (elementary) years (Cahan & Gejman 1993; Spangler & Sabatino 1995).

Nevertheless, tests produce less reliable results with young children than they do for their older counterparts. So, for individuals—and young children in particular—we cannot be confident of their future developmental trajectories. This is not a fatal flaw, however, because the aim of assessment is to understand children's needs *now*, in which case, prediction of their future development is not essential.

Paradoxically, reliability is both strengthened and threatened by the structure of the tests—that is, the rigour that makes them reliable also makes them inflexible and unresponsive to the requirements of young children, who can find the testing process demanding. In turn, this can impair their performances. This is particularly true for gifted children, who complete more items in each subtest than do average learners, which means that they must be able to concentrate for longer than expected for their age. Despite this, however, fewer gifted than average learners are untestable at young ages (Morelock & Morrison 1996).

Having conceded that IQ tests are reliable, critics nevertheless claim that the tests are not valid—that is, they do not measure anything worthwhile. Critics assert that the inflexible administration procedures that enable consistent scoring and the inclusion of only those items that *can* be scored uniformly mean that the tests sample a narrow range of content and processing skills (Sternberg 1986). Detractors conclude that, because the sample of items in these tests is so limited, the resulting score is itself of limited use. This tension between reliability and validity is exemplified by Pruzek (in Jenkins-Friedman 1982: 26), who claims: 'It is better to provide imprecise answers to the right questions, than precise answers to the wrong ones.'

This complaint is true, to some extent. However, other more valid or relevant skills could be included in the tests but could not be scored accurately. This would be like measuring length using a piece of elastic. Measuring length is, on occasion, a very valid thing to do, but if your instrument is unreliable there is no point in using it at all. The result would be even less meaningful than a reliable but restricted measurement. As long as we recognise the tests' limitations and do not put them to uses for which they were not designed, their use is, in my view, defensible when the information they yield cannot be obtained in other ways.

Accuracy

It is important that assessment is as accurate as humanly possible, so that expectations for children are not inflated by 'false positive' assessments — that is, a classification that the children are gifted when they are not — and so that children who truly are gifted are not overlooked, an error which is termed a false negative. With gifted children, false negatives are the more likely errors, because:

- children's environments might not offer adequate opportunities to display their skills, with the result that their everyday behaviours show little evidence of their true abilities;
- factors that are unrelated to ability can impair children's performances, particularly during testing;
- tests that may be part of the assessment process typically have low ceilings — which means that there are too few very challenging items — and so the most able children will not have the opportunity to demonstrate the full span of their skills (Burns et al. 1990; Kaufman 1992).

All these can result in children's giftedness being overlooked. In contrast, false positives are unlikely because children cannot demonstrate more skill than they are capable of achieving, so it is less likely that they will be diagnosed as gifted if they are not.

The need to avoid false negatives is why screening measures should not be used when children are already suspected of being gifted. In effect, the children have already been screened and so they now need a thorough assessment — often including testing — that is capable of generating a comprehensive picture of their developmental advances.

Equity

A principle that is related to issues of accuracy is that of equity. This upholds that assessment methods must be culturally fair, which means that they should not disadvantage any groups within the community (Hooper & Edmondson 1998).

Three equity problems arise with the identification of giftedness. The first is that our definition of giftedness is based on what the dominant culture values and understands to be gifted, meaning that skills that are valuable in other communities can be overlooked. Second, children — such as those living in chronic poverty — who have restricted opportunities to acquire and practise the skills that are valued by the dominant culture may have the *potential* to be gifted but may not be given the experience and support for their skills to flourish. These gifted children who do not display talents are seldom recognised for their innate abilities.

Third, testing is a particular hazard for children for whom English is not their primary language or whose cultural experiences do not prepare them for the formality of a testing session.

Advocates of testing recognise these limitations, but claim that bias would not be eliminated by abolishing testing and would still leave us with many decisions to make, with less defensible bases on which to make them: subjective impressions of children by privileged members of the dominant culture would disadvantage certain children even more than testing presently does (Pendarvis & Howley 1996; Worthen & Spandel 1991). Thus, the argument continues, until something better can be devised, the tests are still the most technically sound instruments presently available. They should not be displaced by less robust assessment measures out of an aversion to their results being given too much credence within the wider assessment process (Kaufman & Harrison 1986).

Tests do not allow us to see everything, so we must supplement their objectivity with sensitivity for atypical manifestations of giftedness (Passow & Frasier 1996; Smutny et al. 1989). Supplementing test findings with other sources of assessment information, across developmental domains and across settings (home, preschool, child care and the community), will be assisted when teachers are aware of atypical manifestations of giftedness, in a range of domains, and in children from diverse backgrounds (Bailey & Harbin 1980; Pendarvis & Howley 1996).

At the same time, we must recognise that the lower test results attained by children who are educationally disadvantaged are not in themselves proof that the tests are biased. Indeed, the test results accurately reflect the fact that these children *are* less likely to excel at school and beyond (Borland 1986; Pyryt 1996; Richert 1987; Tannenbaum 1983; Taylor 2000). This is a social flaw, not a fault of the tests, and calls for social action rather than abandoning testing altogether.

Skilled administration

The final criterion that must be satisfied by assessment processes is that those who are charged with the responsibility of recognising giftedness must be trained for this task. This applies both to educators and to psychologists who, when employed to administer IQ tests, need experience both with the gifted population and with assessing very young children. Not only must the assessment itself be carried out competently, but results—particularly from tests—must be communicated to educators and parents in meaningful language, devoid of jargon so that the findings can be applied accurately (Hansen & Linden 1990).

The assessment process

Figure 8.1 illustrates a proposed series of steps for assessing young children's abilities and needs. It could be called an 'identification by provision' approach: by providing an enriched curriculum, educators give children the opportunity to display their talents (Braggett 1997; Passow & Frasier 1996; Wallace 1986a; Zorman 1997). The model thus begins not with individual children but with the program, in phase one calling on parents and educators to provide stimulating activities then, in phase two, to observe how the children respond to these.

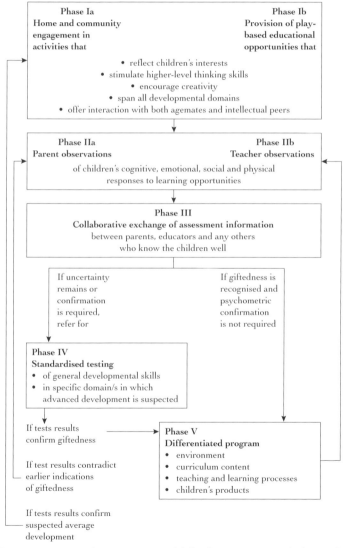

Figure 8.1 An assessment-by-provision model for the recognition of advanced development in young children

The third phase of the model involves collaboration between parents and educators so that they share information about the child's skills. The fourth phase of assessment will then employ formal testing for children whose developmental status is still a puzzle or for those who, for eligibility or placement reasons, need a standardised assessment. This layered approach will ensure that the focus is on *assessment*, not on *testing*. In accordance with Eyre's advice (1997), as cited in the opening quote to this chapter, the model also ensures that assessment information can be used directly within the curriculum, as most of the assessment is carried out by the people who are also responsible for programming.

Assessment measures

As just described, assessment comprises many facets. As Figure 8.1 shows, when assessing children whom we suspect of having significantly advanced development, the range of measures includes parental and teacher observations, checklists and IQ tests.

Parental observations

Imagine that a parent approached an early childhood educator to enrol a new child and advised that the child had cerebral palsy. I guarantee that the parent's report would not be met with: 'There, there, dear. Everyone thinks their child has cerebral palsy.' But when parents report that their child is gifted, this patronising message is a common response.

Instead, we must recognise that parents have detailed knowledge of their child's milestones, motivation and personality, and this allows them to be skilled reporters of their child's abilities. Various studies have found parents to identify their child as gifted with an accuracy rate of between 61 per cent (Louis & Lewis 1992) and 76 per cent (Ciha et al. 1974; Jacobs 1971). Generally, when parents in these studies inaccurately described their child as gifted, the children were advanced—just not to the extent of being gifted. But in a study by Silverman and colleagues (1986), *all* the children who were nominated by their parents but not identified as gifted on the IQ test had histories of recurrent ear infections. The researchers concluded that these children could be considered gifted-learning disabled, as indicated by their sequential learning difficulties and markedly lower verbal than performance scores on the tests. In that case, the researchers concluded, the parents' nominations could be regarded as 100 per cent accurate.

Despite this recorded accuracy of parents' reports of their child's developmental milestones, parents' impressions are often dismissed as biased. Some people think either that parents typically exaggerate their child's accomplishments or that they are pushy and might exploit their child. Contrary to these popular myths, it is more usual for parents to underestimate their children's abilities than to overestimate them (Chitwood 1986), especially when well educated themselves (Roedell et al. 1980).

Parental underestimation can come about when:

- parents do not notice that their children's development is advanced, possibly because they themselves, their own siblings, nieces and nephews, friends and friends' children are all bright so their children do not appear to be unusual;
- parents are not acquainted with any other young children with whom to compare their own child's skills; or
- the child's advanced skills are in domains where milestones are less well-defined, such as spatial abilities (Robinson 1993).

Other parents have an inflated view of giftedness which is based on an image of the child prodigy so, while recognising that their own child is 'bright', they do not realise that she or he might indeed be gifted (Mares & Byles 1994). Thus, even though parents can often judge the *direction* of their child's atypical development, they do not necessarily have the skills to judge the *extent* of any advances (Smutny et al. 1997).

More than this, some parents do not *want* their child to be gifted. Some mistakenly think that gifted children are not well adjusted, so deny the talent that is right in front of their eyes. Parents also worry about the effects of the 'gifted' label on identified children and their siblings, so resist assessment (Colangelo & Brower 1987). Finally, some parents and some members of particular minority cultures can be reluctant to single their child out from the group by applying the gifted label (Feldhusen & Baska 1989).

For these and other reasons, many parents are reluctant to raise the issue of their child's precocity, and many teachers will not raise it with them. The result is an underidentification of giftedness, especially during the preschool years (Chamrad & Robinson 1986; Mares & Byles 1994).

Teacher observations

Teacher nomination is the most widely used means of identifying gifted children (McBride 1992). However, early studies indicated that teachers were generally poor at recognising giftedness, especially in children from minority cultural groups (Hadaway & Marek-Schroer 1992). In a meta-analysis of studies about the accuracy of teacher identification of gifted children, Gear (1976) reports accuracy rates of between 4.4 per cent and 48 per cent, while Jacobs (1971) found that teachers' ability to identify gifted children was lowest during the early childhood years, when their accurate identification was just below 10 per cent.

Some of the reasons for this low accuracy rate are teachers' prejudices against giftedness (as mentioned in Chapter 7), a reluctance to label young children in any way, and stereotypical views about giftedness that focus only on the intellectual domain. There is also a justifiable desire to leave identification of giftedness to those who know more about it (McBride 1992). Whatever the cause, educators' deficient knowledge is sustained by a lack of training in gifted education which leaves many educators with inaccurate understandings of giftedness and results, among other things, in inflated views about how exceptional a child has to be in order to qualify as being gifted (McBride 1992).

As well as these general impediments, teachers tend to under-identify both slow-to-warm-up gifted children who hang back and only gradually become involved in activities, and children who are creative or non conforming, while overestimating the intelligence of children who plunge into activities readily and are cooperative and conforming to adult expectations (Jacobs 1971; Gross 1999; Roedell et al. 1980; Westby 1997). Educators also might find it easier to recognise moderately gifted than highly gifted children (Roedell et al. 1980), possibly because they rarely come across the latter.

These barriers to identification can be overcome, however. Teachers' accurate identification can double without raising the rate of false positives when:

- they are trained to recognise advanced development (Gear 1978; Roedell et al. 1980), including atypical manifestations of giftedness in a range of domains, with children from minority cultures (Hunsaker et al. 1997), and for those whose giftedness is not evident in their behaviour (Richert 1987; Yarborough & Johnson 1983);
- they can refer to a list of signs of advanced development (Borland 1978);
- the children are given sufficiently challenging activities so that their talents can surface; and
- educators have time to observe these talents (Denton & Postlethwaite 1984).

Many young children virtually identify themselves through their advanced performances (Braggett 1997; Casey & Quisenberry 1976). Even so, structured observation can enhance assessment of this group of children and can help to identify those whose abilities are more mixed—those who, perhaps, have advanced knowledge but are unable to demonstrate it because of how they approach tasks.

Observation involves describing in specific terms what children do, either in spontaneous situations or in activities that you have contrived in order to observe specific skills. In particular, to identify advanced development you could instigate and observe activities that require the children to use and report on their metacognitive processes (see, for instance, Lowrie 1998). Observation could focus on four categories: exceptional knowledge acquisition; comprehension and application abilities; generation skills; and motivation (Coleman 1994; Shaklee & Viechnicki 1995).

- Exceptional *knowledge acquisition* abilities comprise quick and easy learning, exceptional memory for and retention of knowledge, and advanced understanding.
- Exceptional *use, comprehension* and *application* of knowledge comprise advanced use of symbol systems (language or numbers) and advanced reasoning abilities.
- Exceptional *generation* of knowledge involves creative, atypical thinking, self-expression, a keen sense of humour and curiosity.
- Exceptional *motivation to pursue knowledge* involves perfectionism (in a striving-for-excellence sense, as defined in Chapter 4), initiative, reflective style, a long attention span on challenging tasks, leadership skills and intensity.

You could record the children's responses to the curriculum in notes or within portfolios in the forms of typical, notable or child-selected examples of their work, records of notable moments, photos of their constructions and observational notes about their language and behaviour which might signal their interests and thinking. Such portfolios are not merely a collection of children's products, but are a systematic compilation that documents their progress in all developmental domains, particularly in complex mental skills (Hadaway & Marek-Schroer 1992; Johnsen et al. 1993; Kingore 1995; Paulson et al. 1991; Seely 1996; Shaklee & Viechnicki 1995; Wright & Borland 1993). As an ongoing assessment technique, portfolios can be a basis for authentic assessment of individual children, and can also help you to develop and enrich the curriculum through reflecting on its impact on the children (Seely 1996).

Portfolios can offer evidence of advanced development, especially in non-traditional domains (Coleman 1994; Wright & Borland 1993). However, in order to recognise that the products in children's collections indicate significantly advanced development, you will still have to compare the children's achievements with age norms. Thus, for diagnostic purposes, portfolio evaluation will need to be supplemented by other assessment measures (Hadaway & Marek-Schroer 1992; Wright & Borland 1993).

Checklists

It has already been noted that both parents and teachers are more accurate in recognising giftedness when they can refer to a checklist of its common signs, such as the one given in Box 1.1 (see Chapter 1). At the same time, although checklists appear to be straightforward, they have a number of flaws. At the theoretical level, most have not established their reliability or validity (Hadaway & Marek-Schroer 1992), but rely instead on common-sense descriptors of giftedness. An exception to this criticism is the list proposed by Silverman and colleagues (1986), which has since been slightly expanded and updated (Silverman & Maxwell 1996).

At the practical level and in terms of using checklists as identification tools, the first issue is that it is difficult to know how much of each characteristic a child has to display in order to be defined as gifted: it can be difficult to judge what 'learning *quickly*' means, or what qualifies as 'most of the time' or 'often' (Roedell et al. 1980). Second, checklists do not indicate how *many* of these characteristics children have to demonstrate in order for the judgment to be made that their development is advanced. Some checklists are so broad that almost anyone could appear to be gifted, while other lists are so restrictive that no child would meet all or most criteria (Hadaway & Marek-Schroer 1992). Third, checklists can incorrectly imply that all gifted children are the same, when in fact they can display any combination of the attributes described. Finally, checklists rely on children's performances to identify giftedness, when we know that many gifted children underachieve or do not conform behaviourally, so would not be identified by observation of their behaviour.

So, in instances where there is still some uncertainty about a child's developmental status, ultimate confirmation of advanced development will still have to rely on a normed test, in which a child's abilities are compared with the typical skills of children of that age. To diagnose intellectual giftedness, this requires an IQ test.

IQ tests

Because giftedness means advanced development compared with the average, classification of a child as gifted will at times require a comparison with normal (or average) development. This is done using a developmental or 'intelligence' test. Results of the latter are reported as an 'intelligence quotient', thus yielding the abbreviated name of 'IQ test'. In recognition that there are more ways to be intelligent than are tapped by these tests, I shall refer to them by this abbreviated title throughout the coming discussion.

In most common use for testing two- to six-year-olds in Australia are the Wechsler Preschool and Primary Scale of Intelligence — Third Edition (WPPSI-III) and the Stanford-Binet — Fifth edition. Past the age of six years, the Wechsler Intelligence Scale for Children — Fourth Edition (WISC-IV) replaces the WPPSI-III. In less common use in Australia (although not necessarily elsewhere) are tests such as the Kaufman Assessment Battery for Children (K-ABC) and the McCarthy Scales of Children's Abilities. Only rarely would a child be referred for formal testing before the age of two years, in which event the Bayley Mental Scales of Infant Development might prove useful. Usually only a psychologist can administer these tests, so they constitute the final stage of the assessment process (as illustrated in Figure 8.1), instituted only after parents or educators have observed the child's skills and are still uncertain of the child's abilities or confirmation of giftedness is required — say, for eligibility reasons.

Capacities of IQ tests

IQ tests are reliable measures of intellectual giftedness, but it is an over-statement to say that they measure 'intelligence' (Borland 1986): it is widely recognised that they sample mainly analytical and convergent thinking rather than synthesis and divergent thinking (Borland 1986; Fuchs-Beauchamp et al. 1993; Renzulli 1986; Sternberg 2003)—although the authors of the WPPSI-III and WISC-IV claim to have given greater emphasis in these new editions to reasoning versus recall skills (Wechsler 2002, 2003). It is clear that doing well on IQ tests is *one* form of giftedness, just not the *only* form. Although they cannot measure every intellectual skill, when specific information is required about individual children's intellectual functioning, these tests can be a useful tool within the wider assessment process.

It is also well recognised that IQ tests often overlook advanced development in children from minority cultures or disadvantaging backgrounds (Borland 1996b; Braggett 1998; Davis & Rimm 2004; Gallagher & Gallagher 1994; Maker 1996; McKenzie 1986; Richert 1987, 1997; Scott et al. 1996; Tannenbaum 1983). However, the principle of comprehensive assessment dictates that testing should never be the only assessment measure. This applies for any children, but particularly for members of disadvantaged groups.

Having examined their limitations, in my clinical practice I find that IQ testing can benefit children, their parents and their teachers in ways that identification by other means cannot. (See also Box 8.1.)

- Unlike other assessment measures, IQ tests not only indicate *that* children's development is advanced but can also quantify the *extent* of this advancement. This information can assist parents and educators to understand and plan for individual children's needs.
- IQ test results that highlight children's strengths can replace previously negative explanations—such as behavioural problems—that have formerly attempted to account for children's difficulties.
- Testing can clarify a child's uneven developmental pattern and can identify gifted children who also have learning disabilities or difficulties—such as attention problems—that impair their ability to perform at advanced levels, despite having the capacity to do so (Kaufman & Harrison 1986; Pyryt 1996). In this way, testing can overcome parents' and educators' confusion about the child's developmental status and, when necessary, signal that both gifted and remedial provisions need to be planned for the child.
- Children's test-taking behaviour and score patterns can alert examiners to the potential for certain emotional difficulties such as the risk of low self-esteem in children with an uneven profile of abilities.
- Parents are empowered to advocate for their children: it is more difficult for educators to dismiss a psychologist's report than to set aside parents' impressions of a child.

- I find that, once equipped with formal testing results, parents can cease wondering about their child's development, which can be a relief for them and can allow them to be less watchful: they no longer have to scrutinise their child's performances in a search for an explanation of his or her behaviours. The results can also instigate a search for information about giftedness, which advances parents' understanding of their child's needs.
- When the results are explained to them, the children themselves receive an accurate explanation for their feelings of being different from others. (See Chapter 13 for more on this topic.)

Having listed these benefits, we must always keep in mind that the IQ test should not be the only assessment measure: test content is inherently restricted, and there is a limit to what an examiner can find out about a child in a 90-minute session. Interpretation of results must *always* therefore occur in light of other assessment findings, tempered with more authentic assessment information from parents and teachers and, if the two are at odds, more data should be gathered. IQ scores should not be trusted over the other measures (Borland 1986): they should be used to verify that a child is gifted, but scores alone should never be used to define a child as 'not gifted' (Borland 1986; Mares 1991; Rimm 1984; Yarborough & Johnson 1983). Moreover, it is a simplification to assume that all children with similar IQs are alike: programs have to be individualised, even for children with similar IQ scores.

Any IQ test that is administered in the preschool years will need to be repeated at least once at later ages. This is because development is dynamic so children's strengths and needs can change with maturation. You would not prescribe glasses for a child on the basis of an old vision test; similarly, you should not design an educational program on the basis of an outdated intellectual assessment (Gallagher & Moss 1963).

Finally, it is important to highlight that the difference between an exceptionally gifted child (with an IQ of over 160) and a moderately gifted child (with an IQ of 130) is not the same as the difference between a child with average skills (an IQ of 100) and one with disabilities (with an IQ of 70). The reason that this rather attractive notion is not true is that the IQ scale has unequal intervals between its numbers (Sapon-Shevin 1994). Instead of each number being evenly spaced—as is the case, for instance, when measuring temperature in degrees—an IQ scale is more like the street numbers on letterboxes, whose distance apart will depend on the size of each block of land.

Reasons for discrepancies between assessments

Sometimes assessment findings can differ simply because one source is inaccurate. A common reaction, though, is to dismiss parents' reports or an IQ score if these point to giftedness when, say, teacher observations do not.

Box 8.1 Advantages and disadvantages of IQ tests for gifted learners

Advantages	Disadvantages
Tests can diagnose the extent of developmental advances. This allows children's programs to be adjusted accordingly.	Because of long-term and immediate influences on test performances, tests can under-estimate children's skills.
IQ tests provide a profile of children's relative strengths and needs. This can allow gifted children with disabilities to be identified.	Test items are poor guides for program planning, as the items are not necessarily functional.
Tests can help parents and educators to understand and advocate for children's needs better.	Test results can be misused to 'hot-house' children.
The tests are a relatively quick, inexpensive way to reliably sample a range of intellectual skills.	The requirement to ensure reliability: • restricts the range of skills that can be tested (which limits validity); • leads to inflexible testing procedures (which can impair children's performances during testing).
The tests are less biased than purely subjective assessments.	The tests sample only majority cultural knowledge and skills.
The tests can fulfil a social justice function of highlighting social *groups* that are routinely disadvantaged educationally.	The tests underestimate the abilities of *individual* children from educationally disadvantaging backgrounds.

However, it is possible that even discrepant assessments are both accurate, for the following reasons.

- Some gifted children disguise their giftedness from their teachers, perhaps because they think that their skills must be wrong, given that no age mates are performing at their level, to be tactful, or to avoid the spotlight. This means that teachers do not see their advanced performances (Hodge 2004).

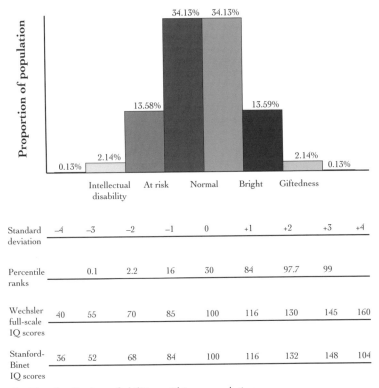

	−4	−3	−2	−1	0	+1	+2	+3	+4
Standard deviation									
Percentile ranks		0.1	2.2	16	30	84	97.7	99	
Wechsler full-scale IQ scores	40	55	70	85	100	116	130	145	160
Stanford-Binet IQ scores	36	52	68	84	100	116	132	148	104

Figure 8.2 The distribution of abilities within a population

- The activities on offer in the educational setting are age appropriate and so do not incite gifted children to display their advanced skills.
- The children's average fine motor skills impede their ability or motivation to produce sophisticated products in writing or drawings. The mechanical aspects of putting ideas on paper can discourage or impede the flow of creative expression. Seeing average performances in these domains, educators can incorrectly conclude that the children's thinking or creative skills are average also.
- The children are creatively or emotionally gifted, which parents might observe but which skills emerge less on IQ tests or in school performances, so can be overlooked in educational settings.
- The children are intellectually but not academically gifted. There are more ways to be advanced than in reading, writing and mathematics, and some intellectually gifted children manipulate information in sophisticated ways but are not especially advanced in these core academic subjects.
- The children are visually or spatially gifted. This can have a range of effects: the children may be less motivated to apply themselves to

non-visual tasks; they can get lost in the visual scenes that they generate in their minds and so do not pay close attention to verbal directives and instruction; they do not achieve well in the auditory mode as that is not where their special abilities lie; or their pictorial information processing requires them to switch modes in order to process auditory instruction, leading to a split-second time lag as they achieve this, which makes them appear to be a little 'slow'.

These examples tell us that both sources of apparently contradictory assessment information can be correct: the parents' judgments or an IQ score diagnosing giftedness can be accurate at the same time that the children do not perform at advanced levels in educational settings. In this event, a full picture of children's abilities is attainable only through collaborative reflection on assessment information, as depicted in phase III of the assessment process illustrated in Figure 8.1.

Box 8.2 Some interpretive statistics

Reports on IQ testing will contain some numbers that are important to understand so that the information is meaningful and can be used to help plan individual programs for children.

The first statistic to be aware of is the *average* (or mean) score. For IQ tests, the average is 100 points.

Second, if a child's score is other than 100, you will need to know whether that score is different enough from the average to warrant special programs. For this purpose, we need another statistic called a *standard deviation*. This figure tells you whether a particular child's score falls near to or a long way from (that is, deviates from) the average. If the score falls near the average, a child is likely to be well provided for by a regular program; if the score deviates a long way from the mean, the child is likely to need some special educational provisions.

When a child's score is converted into a standard deviation, an average (or normal) score obviously has a standard deviation value of zero, because the score does not depart at all from the average. However, because not all individuals achieve each developmental milestone at exactly the same age, scores with values near to zero are also regarded as normal. In terms of standard deviation values, this normal range falls between −1 and +1 standard deviations. Children achieving scores within this range are developing typically. This comprises just over 68 per cent of children and is represented by Wechsler IQ scores of 85–114 and Stanford-Binet scores of 84–115 (see Figure 8.2).

As to scores above this range, children whose results fall between +1 and +2 standard deviations are said to have abilities in the 'high average'

---

or 'bright-normal' range. Just over 13 per cent of children achieve at this level, which equates to Wechsler IQs of 116–129 and Stanford-Binet IQs of 117–131. Meanwhile, standard deviation scores of +2 and above (IQs of 130+) have traditionally been taken to indicate significantly advanced development, or 'giftedness'. Just over 2.5 per cent of children fall within this band and so are considered to be gifted. (See Chapter 2 for a discussion of conservative versus liberal definitions of giftedness, however.)

A final statistic that you might encounter is the percentile rank (PR). This number tells us that this child 'did as well as, or better than, x per cent of the cohort'. For instance, if a child's percentile ranking was 83, this means that she achieved as well as or better than 83 per cent of children of her age. However, this score quickly becomes extreme: for instance, within the normal range of –1 to +1 standard deviations, percentile ranks span from 16 to 84 (see Figure 8.2). This points to two disadvantages of percentile rankings: first, they incorrectly give the impression that tests are capable of making very fine discriminations between skill levels. Second, they imply that these differences are clinically significant, when in many cases they are not: all the children between PRs of 16 to 84 are within normal limits, and yet their numbers seem very disparate. By definition, all gifted children will be at or above the 97th percentile ranking, so using that statistic imparts no more information than the gifted label does alone.

The problem with all the statistics mentioned so far is that, even when children have been allocated a standard score or IQ number, it can still be difficult to know their developmental level unless this has been quoted in a report. One way to gauge this level is to use the ratio formula for converting an IQ score into a mental age. This was the original method of calculating IQ scores and for technical reasons is not strictly accurate, but it can be a useful guide. The formula is:

$$IQ = \frac{\text{mental age (MA)}}{\text{chronological age (CA)}} \times 100$$

A typically developing four-year-old, then, will have an IQ of 100:

$$IQ = \frac{\text{MA} = 4 \text{ years}}{\text{CA} = 4 \text{ years}} \times 100$$
$$= 100$$

To convert IQ scores into mental (developmental) ages, the formula can be rearranged to read:

mental age $= \text{CA} \times \text{IQ} \times 100$
or
mental age $= \text{CA} \times \text{IQ}\%$

So, if a four-year-old child is reported to have an IQ of 150, but no mental age has been given, you can calculate the mental age as:

mental age = CA × IQ%
= 4 years × 150%
= 6 years

And, in years to come—say, when the child is aged six and you have only earlier test findings to go on—you can perform the calculation that:

mental age = CA × IQ%
= 6 years × 150%
= 9 years

If using this formula to assist in educational planning, you must always bear in mind that many factors can contaminate test results and that—particularly in children's early years—their results can fluctuate. So this calculation gives only a broad indication of the child's likely present functioning. There is also a logical upper age limit (probably fourteen to sixteen years) to which the formula can meaningfully be applied.

Testing for exceptional levels of giftedness

The most reliable tests of intellectual functioning—the Stanford-Binet Fifth edition and the Wechsler tests—all have low ceilings: they do not measure above four standard deviations (which equates to a Wechsler IQ of 160 and a Stanford-Binet IQ of 164). This is because the tests were designed to discriminate *between* broad levels of skills, rather than *among* individuals within a narrow band of ability. As a result, children who are still achieving perfect scores when subtests have concluded are typically reported as having IQs 'above 160'. This orthodox practice is based on the view that scores above this level are volatile and that, once children are achieving at this high end, their educational needs are already understood to be extreme so it is not necessary to be more specific about their actual IQ score.

However, many of those who work with exceptionally gifted children find it useful to discriminate within this population and, to that end, elect to use an earlier form of the Stanford-Binet—called Form LM. Children's scores on this earlier edition are typically higher than on the subsequent fourth edition (Kluever & Green 1990), perhaps for two reasons. First, the fourth edition includes abstract visual reasoning whereas Form LM emphasises verbal skills, in which case verbally gifted children are likely to do better on the earlier test (Kluever & Green 1990); second, given that IQs have been rising by around three points per decade for the past 50 years, a lower score on a new edition is to be expected. However, some argue that this increase is not occurring at the highest end of the IQ spectrum and that the Stanford-Binet Form LM is a better measure for this group than its successor and so continue to use it. Perhaps with the recent release of the fifth edition of the Stanford-Binet, the ceiling problems of the fourth edition will be overcome, allowing testers to use an updated test with more modern norms. This is important, as there remains a concern that use of outdated norms could inflate estimates of children's abilities, which could disadvantage them by creating unduly high expectations of their achievements.

Conclusion

Rowe (1990: 544) asserts that some professionals rely on tests 'like a drunk might depend on a lamp-post — for support rather than illumination'. It is now well recognised that IQ tests have many limitations and that they should be used judiciously as only one part of a comprehensive assessment. Our best assessment instrument is human (Borland & Wright 1994), which entails knowing individual children well (Shaklee 1992) and over time. As Borland (1989: 119) states: 'When all is said and done, as far as the identification of the gifted is concerned, all is not really said and done. This is because a good identification (process) is ongoing.'

It is important to remember that assessment is not the responsibility of the educator in isolation, but should be a collaborative endeavour between professionals and parents, in which case the job of educators is simply to know which questions to ask parents about their child's development (McBride 1992).

Naturally, assessment is not an end in itself, but a means to achieving an end — namely, translating the information gained into a relevant program for individual children (Wolery 1996). Eyre (1997) reports that once teachers are aware of children's high abilities, they tend to provide more educational challenge and, as a result of observing children's responses to an enriched curriculum, become more adept at identifying high abilities in future. This, then, leads into the subject of program planning, which is the topic of the next chapter.

Suggested further reading

Although few texts specifically concentrate on the assessment of giftedness, my suggestions for a general overview are:
Beaty, J.J. 2002 *Observing development of the young child* 5th edn, Merrill Prentice Hall, Upper Saddle River, NJ.
McLoughlin, J.A. and Lewis, R.B. 2001 *Assessing students with special needs* 4th edn, Merrill, Upper Saddle River, NJ.
Taylor, R.L. 2000 *Assessment of exceptional students: educational and psychological procedures* 4th edn, Allyn & Bacon, Boston, MA.

If you would like a detailed treatment of intelligence testing, the text on which psychologists often rely is:
Sattler, J.M. 2001 *Assessment of children* 4th edn, Sattler, San Diego, CA.

MEETING GIFTED
YOUNG CHILDREN'S
LEARNING NEEDS
nine

*It remains a source of astonishment . . . that the same sane and caring adults
who would not dream of forcing a child growing at a faster rate than average
into shoes too small for her feet will nonetheless insist on forcing a child whose
mental growth is faster than average into a learning programme too small for
her mind and imagination. (Cathcart 1996: 124)*

Introduction

Your decisions for gifted learners will be predicated on the political stance
you adopt in your wider program. To formulate this, you will have to reflect
on whether you regard your task as one of helping children conform to their
culture; of teaching independent thinking skills so the children are empowered to reform or advance society; or of challenging social, political and
economic inequalities and thus transforming the culture (MacNaughton
2003). Although this last aim might seem too ambitious, it is possible with
critical reflection to design your program so that it does not perpetuate the
inequities of the wider society.

A conformist approach to curricula reflects what has been called a *top-
down* model, whereby adults determine which skills and information are of
value to children and then set about teaching these. This approach is largely
adult driven, with educators framing programs according to their beliefs
about education, children and their learning, and in light of policies, parental
preferences and local contexts. This teacher-directed process of generating a
program is not necessarily unresponsive to children's needs, but is nevertheless largely originated by the educator.

The reforming and transforming views of education—sometimes described as *bottom-up* approaches—see children as already enriched and vibrant human beings whose need to generate identities and understandings of the world is the starting point for, rather than an afterthought in, curriculum planning (Dahlberg et al. 1999). Rather than attempting to instil a predetermined curriculum, a bottom-up approach respects and responds reflectively to the skills and interests of children and their parents. It does not simply indulge these or rely on improvisation or chance, however: it utilises educators' expertise and active teaching while also engaging children's (and parents') competence (Fraser & Gestwicki 2002). It is 'child originated and teacher framed' (Forman & Fyfe 1998, in Fraser & Gestwicki 2002: 168).

This, then, generates a reciprocal process of program planning, in which educators pay attention to children's thinking and analyse the topics that are engaging them, while also taking into consideration which topics will be of long-term value to the children (Fraser & Gestwicki 2002). This information will generate the basis of the program, to which the children and parents will respond, upon which further adjustments will be made, and so on.

Aims of early childhood programs

The broad aim of a reforming education is for children to grow in knowledge and skills so they can generate understandings of themselves and their world and solve personal and societal problems (Dahlberg et al. 1999; MacNaughton 2003). This general goal can be broken down into the following specific aims (Bailey & Wolery 1992; Katz & Chard 1989; NAEYC & NAECS/SDE 1991; Smidt 1998; Wright & Coulianos 1991).

Facilitate competence

Competence involves acquiring and applying a range of skills across all developmental domains. For gifted children, a program will focus particularly on high levels of competence in their strong domains; complex, abstract, creative and critical thinking skills; communication skills; and research skills (Davis & Rimm 2004).

Encourage positive dispositions towards learning

So that children will remain willing to put in the effort required to achieve, they need positive attitudes to learning and to themselves as learners. These attitudes have been termed *dispositions*, which Ritchhart (2001) classifies as the three thinking dispositions of creative, reflective and critical skills, with a fourth disposition being emotional.

- The *creative* dispositions include imaginativeness, being open to new ideas and experiences, having tolerance of ambiguity, curiosity, adventurousness, exploration, being playful, seeking alternatives.

- *Reflective* skills include the use of metacognitive strategies of self-awareness, self-control (including impulse control) and self-monitoring to regulate one's own thinking.
- *Critical* thinking skills include planning, and being strategic, inquiring, investigative, intellectually rigorous and logical (seeking truth, reason and evidence).
- *Emotional* dispositions include the *motivational* (internal *drives*) cluster such as interest, confidence and enthusiasm for learning; and the *volitional* (or goal-directed *behaviours*) that include engagement, persistence, patience, independence, cooperativeness and delay of gratification (Gagné 2003; Goleman 1994; Lambert & Clyde 2000; Perkins et al. 1993; Ritchhart 2001).

Emotional support for children

Early years education also aims to support children's emotional development by:

- establishing a safe and caring physical and emotional environment that supports and protects the children's right to learn and grow personally;
- helping children establish satisfying and successful social relationships;
- developing a healthy self-esteem in each child.

A supportive community

A final aim is to support children's social networks by collaborating with their parents or other primary caregivers and connecting with their cultures. A supportive climate also entails empowering educators both personally and professionally.

Educational challenges for gifted young children

Gifted children's advanced intellectual skills plus their social and emotional needs create some special challenges for curriculum planning. On the one hand, these young children need the intellectual stimulation that is typically given to older children; on the other, they generally do not require an academic curriculum with all the structure that is typical of school-based learning. Thus the curriculum for young gifted children cannot simply be an adapted early school program.

Reliance on adults

Young gifted children crave high levels of stimulation. The more advanced their development, the less likely they are to receive this stimulation from peers and the more likely they are to learn to rely on adults to teach them directly. At home, this can be demanding but manageable; in a centre, it has to be balanced with the needs of the other children. And in both settings it needs to be balanced with children's natural requirements for self-directed exploration.

Threatened self-efficacy

Self-efficacy is individuals' judgment about their ability to organise and execute a chosen action (Bandura 1986) and, in this context, refers to children's awareness that they know how to learn. This awareness may be impaired in gifted children because their learning can be so swift that they do not recognise the strategies they are using. Thus they will need help to notice their own achievements (see Chapter 4) and to develop their thinking (matacognitive) skills (discussed later in this chapter).

Boredom

Boredom results when tasks are too easy or lack meaning for the children. Of any children in schools, those who are learning the least on any given day are the gifted ones. Their quick information-processing capacity, high levels of energy and curiosity can make it difficult to keep them challenged. A teacher's knowledge of child development—which is valuable in all other circumstances—can also be a handicap for gifted children if it sets a ceiling on an educator's expectations of them in the belief that, because of their age, they are not ready for more advanced experiences.

Perseverance

For at least three reasons, gifted children might not learn to persevere in their learning. First, the ease of the tasks they are given means that perseverance is seldom necessary, so they lack practice at it. Second, because they are often interested in global issues rather than fine detail, they might not naturally learn how to focus on the specific elements of a task (Chamrad & Robinson 1986; Mares 1997). Third, some regard effortlessness as a sign that they are clever, so can become discouraged and begin to doubt their abilities if the task requires persistence (Martin 2002; Phillips 1984, 1987). As a result, gifted children sometimes need to be supported in order to practise seeing tasks through to completion.

Attention span

Their ability to solve problems quickly can mean that gifted young children appear to have a short attention span, as they leave an activity after only brief engagement with it when in fact they are merely refusing to repeat an activity that they mastered the first time. Given that most gifted children concentrate well, if they are restless this may be a sign that they need more challenge. This, however, is not the same as needing harder or even more work—just more *appropriate* work. They are likely to resist if you insist that they do more than anyone else (Braggett 1994).

Teacher disengagement

Many gifted children are left to their own devices because their teachers know that they are capable and well behaved, and they do not 'look stuck' and in need of help (Eyre 1997; Wolfle 1989). Yet, being young, they can no more learn by themselves than can any other child.

Curriculum differentiation

Differentiation refers to adjustment of all relevant elements of the curriculum in response to children's differing learning needs and preferences. This has two implications: first, it is important to identify those needs accurately; and second, children with exemplary behaviour might not need adjustments as they are clearly functioning well under the present arrangements—instead, the children more likely to need a differentiated curriculum are those with disruptive behaviour or other signs of frustration (Borland 1989).

When planning to differentiate the curriculum, it is necessary to consider what you want to offer the more able children that is not already provided for and relevant to everyone, as it is ethically indefensible to provide only to gifted learners activities that would benefit all children (Borland 1989; Eyre 1997). Further, selected curricular modifications need to be both justifiable and educationally valuable, rather than being something faddish that titillates rather than educates (Callahan 1996); entertainment is fine, but it should not be mistaken for academic rigour (Sawyer 1988).

In essence, this means that adjustments must be systematically structured to match the children's learning needs (Borland 1989). A differentiated curriculum must take into account gifted learners' precocity, complexity and intensity (Van Tassel-Baska 1995, 2003) so must allow for differences in both the pace (quantity) and depth (quality) of their learning (Piirto 1999).

Differentiation spans all four aspects of the curriculum:

- the *environment* in which learning and teaching will occur;
- the *content* that children are to learn, which encompasses the planned or spontaneous opportunities that will be provided;
- the teaching and learning *processes* to be employed—that is, what educators will do to help children grow in understanding of themselves and their physical and social world;

- the *products* through which children demonstrate their learning.

Although there are many models for differentiation of the curriculum at the school level (see, e.g., Colangelo & Davis 2003; Rogers 2002), the inclusive nature of early childhood education, the small group sizes that typically characterise child care centres and preschools, and the young age of the children themselves make less relevant many of the provisions for gifted older children, so only those that can be applied in early years education will be discussed here.

Differentiation of the environment

The environment refers to the physical structure of a setting, its organisation and its social climate. The structure of the environment communicates how the space is to be used; gives a message about whether educators care for the comfort of the children and adults who occupy it; and demonstrates respect for diversity through the range of available materials, ease of access by diverse children and the control the children can exercise over their setting.

Young children need a safe emotional climate in which they are supported to meet high but realistic expectations and, when they expect more of themselves, these pressures need to be balanced by the provision of extra supports. The children must feel safe about making mistakes as, when educators set great store by doing things right, the children are likely to underachieve (Eyre 1997; Harrison 2003; Harrison & Tegel 1999). Children need to accept that failure is a natural part of the learning process; if they are not making mistakes, this means that they were already competent at that skill so are only practising it.

Time allowances

Sometimes gifted children will need an accelerated pace of curriculum delivery because they can learn more quickly than usual. At other times, they need prolonged periods of time for contemplation, to refine their ideas, develop their play themes and deal with content creatively and with an appreciation of its subtleties and profundities (Dowling 2002; Harrison & Tegel 1999; Klein 1992; Tannenbaum 1983; Ward 1996). They can benefit from being taught fewer concepts but in greater depth—which Patton and Kokoski (1996) describe as the 'less is more' rule.

Supplementary resources

The environment will need to provide creative and flexible resources to enable you to respond to children's interests. Reference material, parents and other community members with special expertise and interests, community walks and field trips can all support the children's inquiries.

Placement

Placement decisions centre on the age and ability levels of surrounding children. As children choose friends at their developmental level, and as gifted individuals might not have other same-aged gifted peers available, they might need early access to an older peer group. If these are not available within your setting, no matter how intellectually stimulating you make your program, you might not be able to fulfil the children's social needs, in which case an advanced placement could be necessary—such as early entry to school.

Within-class grouping

Placing gifted children together with others of similar abilities for at least some of their day, and subsequently making instruction more complex, improves the children's achievement, attitude to learning, social skills and self-esteem (Allan 1991; Gamoran 1992; Hallinan 1990; Kolloff & Moore 1989; Kulik & Kulik 1982, 1992; Lando & Schneider 1997; Rogers 2001; Rogers & Span 1993; Rist 1970; Shore & Delcourt 1996; Slavin 1987a, 1990a; Van Tassel-Baska 1992). This is probably because the starting point for the task can be higher (Eyre 1997). At the same time, withdrawal of gifted children from the larger group does not reduce the less able children's self-esteem (Carter 1986; Chan 1988). Nor does it lower their achievements, as the less able children regard gifted children as dissimilar to themselves and so do not model from them (Schunk 1987).

Although 'pull-out programs' in school are rightly criticised for scapegoating gifted children's difference, for being culturally insensitive, for disrupting the regular classroom, for a lack of continuity with the regular curriculum, and for the provision of trivial content, in preschools withdrawing a group of similarly able children for a specific activity on a semi-regular basis need not disrupt nor intrude on the activities of the other children. Although it is true that part-time enrichment is no solution for full-time giftedness, the pull-out session can instigate the children's more independent, project-based learning—that is, the enrichment can continue beyond the time spent in the small group. To minimise interruptions for the participating children and so enhance their concentration, Eyre (1997) suggests instituting a 'teaching bubble' for such sessions, whereby you create a physical cue to signal the other children not to interrupt the group and instead to ask another adult when they need help.

Relatively permanent ability grouping is termed *tracking* or *streaming* and, although occasionally practised within the school sector, is seldom used in early years education so will not be described here. Another grouping strategy—multi-age grouping—is, however, a possibility in the early years. In this arrangement, children of a wide range of ages are educated and cared for together. This has the social benefit of allowing younger children to access older friends and so to find peers whose developmental level matches their own, but obviously this grouping arrangement does not benefit the older members of the group.

This type of grouping also gives teachers the flexibility to create both homogeneous and heterogeneous groupings as required by the children and the activity (Lloyd 1997). Nevertheless, multi-age grouping alone has a neutral effect: simply placing children of different ages together will not be enough to ensure that they benefit from the experience (Mosteller et al. 1996; Veenman 1995, 1996). The benefits appear to come from the adults' philosophical commitment to meeting individual children's needs without age norms dictating teaching (Lloyd 1997).

Differentiation of curricular content

Gifted children will not require that the whole curriculum be differentiated: some experiences are equally valuable for all children; others will be suitable for a group of bright learners; while still others will be unique to a particular child (Braggett et al. 1997; Shore & Delcourt 1996).

The most fundamental principle of curricular content is that tasks should be meaningful to the children (Dowling 2002). Second, the curriculum should be interdisciplinary, which means that topics are examined from a range of perspectives. Third, it will be integrated. This means that content across all domains is incorporated naturally into all activities and that the whole child is the focus: the curriculum is sensitive to children's intellectual, physical, emotional, social and cultural needs, rather than their intellectual skills alone; and children's worlds of home, preschool or school and community are integrated (Barbour 1992; Holden 1996; Nidiffer & Moon 1994; Van Tassel-Baska 1995).

Content differentiation measures are typically classified as *acceleration* of the pace of instruction to reflect gifted children's faster rate of learning, using advanced placement such as early entry to school or grade skipping; and *enrichment*, which refers to the provision of broader, deeper or more varied educational experiences. However, the goal of all provisions for gifted learners is enrichment, so the distinction between it and acceleration is probably obsolete (Gagné 2003).

Promote children's interests

Gifted children often develop a series of passionate interests. These are significant because they help the children to resolve inner conflicts, so it is important to help them explore their topics rather than redirecting them to more traditional tasks (Cohen 1998). Focusing on these interests avoids their erosion and children's consequent underachievement (Whitmore, in Cohen 1998).

While children's interests change over time, their underlying themes are remarkably similar throughout childhood (Cohen 1989, 1998). Cohen has identified six major themes, with the following titles:

- *control*—which refers to children's drive to be in command of themselves and their world, to master tasks, and to understand how things are organised;
- *nature–nurture*—where the children's interests centre on the natural world and on nurturing others or belonging;
- *putting it all together*—where the children are interested in the meaning, function and origins of things, and in transforming objects;
- *people and relationships*—where they seek to understand other people and roles and to make friends;
- *aesthetic–expressive*—where they are interested in and sensitive to beauty and the arts and express themselves artistically and emotionally;
- *symbols and symbol systems*—where the children are interested in learning words, numbers, grammatical symbols and body language.

Cohen (1989) reports that, because gifted young children are aware of their environment earlier and attempt tasks earlier, they experience from a younger age the traps or dangers inherent in performing tasks for which they are cognitively ready but for which their bodies might be too immature. As a result, she says, their play tends to be centred on a control theme. This begins with a thirst for knowledge, which must be satisfied as knowledge confers power. Next comes the need to 'put it all together' and to understand cause and effect. Alongside these themes might be the child's need to express ideas, perhaps aesthetically (e.g. through music) or symbolically.

Children's interests can be encouraged by helping them to gather resources, asking them questions, and extending an interest into a new area when the time is right (Cohen 1998). Having determined which theme or themes are driving a child, you can generate tasks in a range of curricular areas which address that theme and demonstrate the relationships between areas of content (Cohen 1998; Shaklee 1998). For instance, children who seek to control, master and understand could be helped to research an interest such as dinosaurs and then to explore this interest through science, maths, story-writing or art, then teach the other children what they have learned.

Offer tailored activities

The following features of activities can be varied in line with the ability levels of the children and the complexity of the learning task (Tomlinson 1996).

- *Simple versus complex tasks.* When children are dealing with content or processes that they are only just ready to learn, they will need the content to be simple; when they are working comfortably within their developmental level, they will be more motivated by tasks that are complex.

- *Concrete versus abstract examples.* At entry level, children will need concrete learning experiences; if children are advanced in the task at hand, they will be more able to apply their more sophisticated knowledge to abstract problems.
- *Small steps versus larger leaps.* When a task is intellectually demanding, children will need it to be broken into smaller steps; when they already possess the requisite subskills, they can take larger leaps in their learning.
- *Knowledge acquisition versus concept mastery.* Gifted learners will often have more prior knowledge than their age mates. Therefore, they will need less repetition, revision and consolidation time than less able children (Braggett 1998; Kanevsky 1994; Plucker & McIntire 1996). Thus there can be less need to teach them isolated facts, leaving time for them to focus on broader concepts.

In expressing the reasons that she did not like preschool, a four-and-a-half-year-old told her mother that she didn't think her teachers' brains 'learned very quickly'. When asked why, the child reported that the teachers put the same activities out on Tuesday that they had put out on Monday and that they read a book today which they had read last week. The child's conclusion was: 'I don't think they remember!' The repetition, usually necessary for young children to learn, was irksome to this gifted child and accounted for her intention to attend preschool only on Mondays.

- *Uni-dimensional versus multifaceted.* When children are novices within a field of interest, they might need to explore it along a single dimension; when they already grasp the basics, they can explore it in a more multidisciplinary manner, making more connections between ideas and examining issues from various perspectives.
- *Structured versus open-ended.* When children are comfortable with an area, they can cope with open-ended activities. These have no right or wrong answers, so call on divergent thinking, engage children in making choices about the direction of their learning and permit a variety of responses, thus allowing children to employ their most favoured learning style. In so doing, they differentiate content, process and product (Hertzog 1998).

However, when children are not sure of their grounding in a domain, they might prefer more structured activities. Very unstructured tasks such as 'Go and find out all you can about . . .' activities are not likely to appeal to many children, will under-utilise their skills as they attempt to stay safe, and could lead to discouragement or disruptions (Burton-Szabo 1996; Eyre 1997; Stewart 1981).

- *Breadth versus depth*. All children will need to acquire a broad range of skills across domains; when they have attained these, they can be encouraged to achieve deeper understanding (Patton & Kokoski 1996; Van Tassel-Baska 2003).

Provide tiered activities

Tiered activities take two forms (Montgomery 1996):

- differentiation of *inputs*, whereby you provide different activities which share a common theme with various levels of difficulty. The children could self-select which activities suit them or you could target certain children and support them to attempt the more demanding tasks;
- differentiation of *outcomes*, whereby you set a common task which children enter at their own level and then respond to according to their level of sophistication.

Offering tiered activities requires that you establish appropriate starting points for the children, based on your identification of their prior knowledge (Eyre 1997).

Curriculum compacting

Curriculum compacting means delivering curricular content at a faster pace to reflect individual gifted children's more efficient learning. It occurs in three phases: first, identifying the goals and outcomes of a given activity; second, determining whether individuals can already achieve those goals; and third, providing these children with extension activities instead (Reis & Renzulli 1992; Willard-Holt 1994). These activities might comprise special projects on topics in which the children are passionately interested.

Curriculum compacting is unlikely to be used formally in early childhood settings, but can occur in the junior primary (elementary) years when, for example, a Grade 1 child in a composite class of Grades 1 and 2 completes the work of both grades in just one year and then moves into Grade 3 the following year. For single subjects, compacting tends to be most relevant to those with a hierarchical structure, such as mathematics.

Early entry to school

It can benefit some children with developmental advances to begin school early. Although described as an acceleration measure, that term implies an attempt to speed up the children's development itself, when instead early entry is really an attempt at an *appropriate developmental placement* (Elkind 1988; Feldhusen 1989; Feldhusen et al. 1996; Rogers & Kimpston 1992; Southern et al. 1993).

The academic aims of acceleration are to avoid boredom, along with any resultant behavioural and motivational difficulties; to promote the children's development of good study skills such as higher-order thinking skills; and to capitalise early on young children's interests and abilities. Early entry to school can prevent later grade skipping, with its resulting dislocation from the peer group. I believe it also has at least equal significance as a modification of the social environment, giving children access to older peers who are more similar to them in interests and skill levels, with the aim of allowing them to be more successful socially.

Research consistently reports that acceleration meets all of these academic, social and emotional aims (Benbow 1991; Eales & de Paoli 1991; Heinbokel 1997; Janos 1987; Kulik & Kulik 1984; Paulus 1984; Proctor et al. 1986, 1988; Rimm & Lovance 1992a, 1992b; Robinson & Robinson 1992; Rogers & Kimpston 1992; Sayler & Brookshire 1993; Schiever & Maker 1997; Shore & Delcourt 1996; Southern & Jones 1992; Southern et al. 1989, 1993; Swiatek & Benbow 1991; Townsend 2004; Vialle et al. 2001). Acceleration produces double the academic gains achieved by enrichment (Kulik & Kulik 1992). One study found that, compared with their class-mates, early entrants' relative academic standing increased as they progressed through school (Proctor et al. 1986).

Socially, accelerants mostly adjust well (sometimes after some initial minor difficulties); and the children report preferring to be with the older children who are more nearly their intellectual peers (Vialle et al. 2001). Whereas schoolchildren reject as playmates those who are in lower grades, they will play with those same younger children when they are in their own class (Gross 1993b).

Most studies have found that accelerants display equivalent emotional adjustment compared with equally gifted children who have not been accelerated (Sayler & Brookshire 1993; Swiatek & Benbow 1991), and thus no benefit seems to have accrued. However, children who elect to be accelerated might have experienced harm had they *not* been allowed to accelerate: they might have become bored and unmotivated, with a consequent decrease in achievement (Heinbokel 1997; Montgomery 1996; Swiatek & Benbow 1991). Furthermore, the support of teachers is an important influence on accelerated children's subsequent emotional adjustment (Southern & Jones 1992).

Finally, it appears that the resulting early exit from school is not a problem for accelerants, who continue to do well into the university years and beyond, particularly with early career counselling (Olszewski-Kubilius 2002; Swiatek & Benbow 1991). And, even if problems do arise at a later age, the child is then that much older and thus better equipped to cope. Furthermore, my ideal of accelerating children through primary school and then having a 'gap year' between primary and secondary schooling can overcome many difficulties arising from their being younger and less sexually mature than their adolescent classmates.

On the other hand, a few authors (such as Freeman 1991) have found some harmful academic, social and emotional side-effects of acceleration. With respect to early school entry, one specific finding was that 20 per cent of early entrants performed poorly in school as assessed by teacher ratings (McCluskey et al. 1996), although this might not have been caused by their early entrance: they might still have performed poorly even if they had started school on time. It is also unclear whether subsequent difficulties are due to acceleration as such, to normal ups-and-downs of life, to negative attitudes by teachers which result in accelerated children receiving little support in their new placements (Heinbokel 1997; Southern & Jones 1992), or to the fact that acceleration is used so rarely that an accelerated child feels abnormal (Southern et al. 1993).

Despite overwhelming evidence of the mainly positive effects, many parents are reluctant for their child to begin school early because they believe that its structure is incompatible with young children's social and emotional needs. Some hold a child back because of his or her apparent social or emotional immaturity. Similarly, many teachers are reluctant — even antagonistic — about early entry and other forms of acceleration, mistakenly perceiving a dichotomy between academic and social adjustment, not recognising that the two are inextricably linked (Townsend 2004; Vialle et al. 2001). Rather than signalling that a child is not ready for school, 'immature' behaviour can be a result of being in a socially and educationally inappropriate setting and can improve once the child is more appropriately placed (Vialle et al. 2001).

This discussion gives rise to some recommendations for how best to assess which children are most likely to profit from early entry to school or a higher grade, as outlined in Box 9.1. The reason that these options should be considered for appropriately screened gifted young children is that, in the early childhood years compared with further up the schooling system, there are few other accelerative or enriching measures available to them and comparatively few intellectual peers whom they can access by other means.

Grade skipping

A second key method of acceleration involves allowing gifted school-aged children to skip a grade. This can be essential when there are few surrounding gifted children, although when the school has many able students, they might be well catered for already without individuals needing to skip grades.

Partial or subject acceleration involves moving a child up to a higher grade for certain subjects while attending at grade level for the remainder. This has the advantage of stimulating children in their areas of strength while allowing them to progress at a typical rate in other subject areas, but has the disadvantage that children may complete the primary school

Box 9.1 Criteria for early entry to school or grade skipping

Children and their next placement have to be carefully screened before early entry is contemplated. The following are important considerations.

Essential requirements

- The principal has to be willing to admit the child early.
- The classroom that the child is entering needs to be flexibly structured and the receiving teacher must be sympathetic to the idea of early entry or grade skipping and be willing to help the child adjust to the new setting.
- The teacher must be willing to fill any gaps in a child's skills that have resulted from early entry to a grade or school. (Keep in mind, of course, that many gifted children will have acquired the necessary skills independently or from an older sibling or parent.)
- The child will need sufficient fine motor skills for academic activities such as handwriting.
- Reading readiness is a crucial factor for early entrance to school.
- The child's skill levels across most domains should be above the average of the children in the receiving class. In terms of IQ, this will generally translate into an IQ of 130 or above. I would add that, on its own, an IQ of 130 is insufficient reason for a grade skip, as just over 13 per cent of students have skills just below this level, so mildly gifted children should be teachable within their age cohort, unless the peer group is unusually challenging. Second, a high verbal IQ is more significant than a high performance IQ, as most teaching is delivered verbally.
- The child must be motivated to start school early or to skip a grade, although adults must be careful not to give him or her the impression that it will solve all difficulties.
- The child will need to be comfortable about mixing with older children and being one of the youngest in the class—if not the school.
- The parents' wishes and support are crucial, as their comfort with acceleration will affect how well their child copes.

Desirable criteria

The following are less important and should not rule out early entry to school or grade skipping if all of the above factors indicate its potential value to the child.

- The child needs to be socially and emotionally mature enough to cope with school. Having said this, there is clearly a wide range in children's social and emotional maturity, and younger children tend to 'grow into' the social-emotional levels of those around them. Moreover, social and emotional difficulties can reflect a lack of intellectual peers or dissatisfaction with an unchallenging curriculum, which grade skipping or early entry to school can ameliorate.

- It helps if children are healthy and not small for age so they can participate in the other children's physical games and sports and do not look physically out of place among older classmates.
- For early school entry, the children will also need the physical stamina to cope with a longer day. On the other hand, if they become tired, they could attend school for only four days a week.
- It can help if the children have attended an early childhood centre for at least six months prior to school entry so that they have learned to separate from their parents, to concentrate, delay gratification and use negotiation rather than aggression to resolve conflicts with other children.
- It is best to time early entry or a grade advancement at a natural transition point, if possible.

The uneven development of gifted children means that few will be equally mature across all domains. Therefore, consultation between early childhood staff, parents and the selected school or classroom will be necessary to decide what is best for each individual child.

Any decision to enrol a child at school or in a higher grade early should be treated as a trial for at least one school term, with its effects monitored closely. Children for whom acceleration is not successful need to be able to return to their original grade; others for whom one grade skip is not enough may need a second.

Sources: Bailey 1997; Braggett 1992, 1993; Davis & Rimm 2004; Diezmann et al. 2001; Feldhusen et al. 1986; Heinbokel 1997; Mares & Byles 1994; Morelock & Morrison 1996; Rimm & Lovance 1992b; Robinson 1990a; Robinson & Robinson 1992; Rogers 2002; Schiever & Maker 1997; Vialle et al. 2001.

curriculum in their advanced subject years early, but cannot move on to high school and so are obliged to repeat the last year of the subject numerous times.

As with all accelerative measures, grade and subject skipping can be organisationally attractive, as they appear to avoid the need to provide special curricula for accelerated children (Bailey 1993; Eales & de Paoli 1991; Willard-Holt 1994): the children do all the adjusting to their new placement. However, early entry to school and grade or subject skipping are merely temporary solutions: the pace and complexity of gifted children's learning mean that, even in an advanced placement, they will still require an enriched child-centred curriculum (Feldhusen et al. 1996; Vialle et al. 2001). This is particularly true for exceptionally gifted children, for whom even radical acceleration or enrichment alone will be inadequate (Gross 1992, 1993b, 2004). These children will need both of these measures, plus opportunities to work alongside similarly gifted children and to meet with mentors in their field of interest (Gross 2004).

Differentiation of teaching and learning processes

Many elements of teaching and learning processes are relevant for all children. All need to learn through active engagement, discovery and play, with opportunities to make choices about what they learn and with adults deeply involved in their learning. All will need teaching methods to be responsive to their various stages of development, as detailed in Table 9.1.

Although process is conceptually different from content, in practice we cannot teach children how to learn without teaching some content that is worth learning. Problem solving is meaningless when there is no actual problem to solve: the process is only a means to an end, so that end must be important (Borland 1989; Sawyer 1988).

Mediated learning

Mediated learning—as distinct from direct learning through the senses— occurs when adults interpret the environment for children, reflecting the

Table 9.1 Young children's modes of learning and corresponding modes of teaching

Developmental level	Modes of learning	Modes of teaching
0–18 months	Imitation	Direct instruction • Showing • Telling • Describing
18–30 months	Exploration Discovery Questioning	Provision of a safe environment
30–48 months	Prediction testing (trial-and- error learning) Discovery	Mediation Explaining cause and effect
4+ years	Construction	Opportunities for learning Facilitation Mediation

Source: adapted from Belgrad (1998).

156

children's interests, needs and capabilities to make the task demands compatible with these (Klein 1992). This takes considerable teacher skill to set the stage, to recognise the children's responses and to follow through with support in order to advance their thinking skills (Barclay & Benelli 1994).

In mediated learning, adults initially direct children's thinking processes towards a higher level than they can achieve alone, and then the children progressively acquire the ability to take over this executive control function themselves (Moss 1992). That is, children first experience problem solving as an interpersonal process—in a dyad with an adult—and then develop the ability to solve problems independently (Moss 1992). To achieve this transfer, children need opportunities to participate actively in the joint problem-solving process (Moss 1992; Wallace 1983).

Prior to school age, young children are dependent on adults to regulate (that is, mediate) their approaches to tasks (Moss 1990). So, although early childhood curricula are based on children's exploration and discovery, you will need to guide children's learning. In so doing, you should invite their ideas and suggestions, provide cues, ask questions, identify problems, and offer and ask for feedback. You can do this through your comments and open-ended questions (Wallace 1983). These will incorporate the following five key strategies (Klein 1992).

- *Focus.* You can select salient aspects of the activity and help children to focus on these through accentuation or exaggeration (Klein 1992; Moss 1992). (With young babies, you might 'dance' a toy to within easy reach; with older infants, you could point out important features: 'Hey, look at this! What do you think it's for?')
- *Meaning.* You can convey your intellectual interest in and emotional excitement about an activity. Children will then internalise (learn) to find such activities interesting, and develop the commitment that is necessary for sustained effort and success.
- *Expansion.* You can expand children's cognitive awareness beyond their immediate activity by making spontaneous comparisons, pointing out strategies for memory storage and recall, and so on.
- *Feedback.* You can express excitement and satisfaction with children's achievements by, for example, making explicit positive statements about their efforts (e.g. 'Look how well it's going!'). This teaches children how to monitor and judge outcomes for themselves, and will enhance effort and reflection (Moss 1992).
- *Organisation.* You can help children to plan, regulate and monitor their activities by matching the task to their developmental levels and interests. This can be done in the infant years by working on tasks jointly until the youngsters gradually acquire the ability to use their organisation skills independently. Once children reach a devel- opmental level of around four years (regardless of their actual age),

they will begin to internalise your directives in the form of self-talk, which is the beginning of metacognitive control (Moss 1992).

Mediated sociodramatic play

Young children do not play or work: they simply *do* (Hein 1973, in Snowden 1995). Their play experiences teach them knowledge and learning processes that they could not readily acquire through outside instruction. However, you will need to set the stage so that high-quality play—and hence high-quality learning—can occur (Ward 1996).

When children are engaged in sociodramatic play, the temptation is either to interrupt their play to make it more 'educational' or to leave them to their own devices for fear of stifling or disrupting their play ideas (Ward 1996). In most instances, it is important to allow the children to direct their own play and to remain engaged until they have resolved its issues (Harrison & Tegel 1999). However, at other times you will need to help children to enrich their play (Harrison & Tegel 1999). Ward suggests the following strategies.

- You can play in parallel with children who, through observing what you are doing, begin to copy your play. This adds to or extends their own play ideas.
- At the invitation of the children, you can become a co-player, joining in their existing play and responding to their comments or actions, thus complementing and extending their ideas.
- At the next more intrusive level, you might take more control of the direction of the play, either by making suggestions from the side or by participating actively.
- You can initiate play for children who appear not to be able to engage in advanced play without adult prompts. Then you can ease out of the play as soon as the children assume control of its direction themselves (Ward 1996).

At all of these levels you can pose questions, make suggestions and add to the children's processing and cooperative skills through careful observation of their play and assessment of the type of guidance they need. By providing help in the children's zone of proximal development (that is, at the level just beyond what they can achieve independently), you can promote further learning in all developmental domains.

Teach thinking skills

To facilitate thinking skills, children need to grapple with concepts that are not 'truths' but are contestable or debatable (Bayley 2002). With their wonder aroused, one-on-one or small group discussion—which comprises expressing and listening to ideas—will allow children to search for meaning by thinking things through for themselves (Bayley 2002).

Critical thinking entails evaluating one's thinking 'to make it more precise, accurate and relevant, consistent and fair' (Paul 1990, in Montgomery 1996: 91). To trigger such thinking in young children, Bayley (2002: 256) lists some cognitively challenging questions such as: What do you think about . . .? What do you think it means? Why do you think that? Who agrees with this? Is that fair? What do you think will happen? and so on.

Thinking skills are hierarchical: lower-order skills comprise the likes of sequencing, ordering, sorting, classifying, comparing, contrasting, relating cause and effect, making predictions and generating hypotheses (Montgomery 2001). Many gifted learners will be capable of acquiring and practising higher-order skills, which entail more abstract and complex thinking such as:

- defining and clarifying problems;
- application of knowledge by solving problems;
- analysis of ideas;
- synthesis of information;
- creating, inventing and constructing original ideas or products;
- evaluation of outcomes (Braggett 1998; Montgomery 2001; Wallace 1986a).

As well as promoting critical thinking skills, you will also need to foster enabling dispositions such as curiosity, persistence, tolerance of ambiguity, and confidence (especially about taking intellectual risks).

Teach metacognitive skills

The main task of the early childhood years is the acquisition of metacognitive thinking—that is, knowledge about and control of one's learning—which begins earlier than usual for gifted learners (Horowitz 1992; Schwanenflugel et al. 1997). However, because their thinking occurs so quickly, some might not be aware of the skills they are using. Therefore, they need specific instruction in metacognitive strategies that explains why a strategy works, and where and when it should and should not be used (Schwanenflugel et al. 1997). While they are completing tasks, children need feedback about their learning processes that highlights, verifies and expands on the processes they are using to plan, monitor and evaluate their approach to tasks (Freeman 1995a; Schraw & Graham 1997). This ability to reflect on their own thinking allows children to become increasingly autonomous in their learning (Montgomery 2001).

Enhance motivation

Just as it is a mistake to view intelligence as an intrinsic trait of the individual, so too it is a mistake to view motivation as an inherent part of children's personality. Motivation refers to children's willingness to invest time, effort and skills in tasks that we define as educationally significant (Ben Ari & Rich 1992). If some children are choosing to invest their energies elsewhere, this will have at least as much to do with the way educational activities are structured as it has to do with their personality (Ben Ari & Rich 1992).

In order to be motivated, all children need appropriate levels of challenge; to have choice about their own learning; to believe that what they are achieving is worthwhile; to attribute success to their own efforts rather than external factors such as luck; and to receive authentic feedback about their efforts. Gifted children's intellectual skills accentuate these needs. In addition, they will need extra support for the intellectual risks they are capable of taking earlier than usual.

Some specific ways to enhance intrinsic motivation have already been mentioned in previous chapters, such as giving informative feedback (see Chapter 4), reducing rivalry between children by minimising comparisons between them (see Chapter 5) and teaching children to make accurate attributions about the links between effort and outcome (see Chapter 6). Other measures are implied by the following mathematical formula for motivation (Jones & Jones 2001; Rea 2000).

Motivation = expectation of success $\times$ anticipated benefits of success $\times$ work climate

This implies that children will be motivated when they believe that they are likely to be successful at a task, are passionately interested in it or believe that achieving it will benefit them in some way in the future, and they feel a blend of excitement and calm ('serious fun') within a supportive relationship with parents and educators so they are emboldened to try (Rea 2000). To foster these elements, educators will need to use the following measures.

- Supply enriched activities that provide an attainable and meaningful challenge (one that is *worth* achieving), and teach the skills needed to be successful at them *at a time* when those skills are indeed required, rather than when the children are succeeding anyway (Siegle & McCoach 2002).
- Explain the rationale (the 'bigger picture') for a task, as children will be more willing to put in effort on a small aspect of a skill when they can see it in context.
- Explain to children that ability alone will not ensure success, and that the need for effort says nothing about their level of talent: even the most talented athletes, for example, have to put in extraordinary effort to be successful (Martin 2002). However, the notion of simply working *harder* will not motivate most children, so you will need to explain that effort does not mean 'hard work', but rather is qualitative.

Product differentiation

Common to all children is their need to demonstrate the knowledge and skills that they have acquired. It is important that they can negotiate in which mediums and domains they will express their learning. Although early childhood curricula routinely offer this opportunity, gifted children may need some additional means of differentiation to take their product beyond the level normally achievable by other children so that it is more satisfying for them.

Tiered products

Some children will be interested in and capable of producing mature expressions of their learning; others will be at the typical early stages of drawing and other handicraft work. Projects can be excellent avenues for enrichment of content and process, as the children can pursue their interests at depth. If the children are already literate these can be presented in writing, but could also be constructions, art work, music, drama, videotaped presentations, or any medium that interests an individual child. Young children's reading and writing skills will limit their ability to record and express what they have learned, so it may be necessary to allow them to dictate stories to an adult scribe or to use a keyboard if they are able.

Use of computers

Computers allow adaptations to the learning environment, content, process, and product. They can link up isolated gifted children; provide access to more diverse, abstract and complex information; provoke children to construct and organise their knowledge; and help young children to produce written material when their fine motor skills would otherwise preclude handwriting (Berger & McIntire 1998; Knight et al. 1997; Spicker & Southern 1998).

Parent collaboration

A crucial aspect of your program for children will be collaboration with their parents. Over the past five decades, there has been a trend away from a medical model of professionals' relationships with parents which upheld that 'the specialist was always right' to a more collaborative approach to working with parents which recognises the distinctive but equally valuable expertise of both parents and educators. It is now acknowledged that parents not only have a right, but a duty, to advocate on behalf of their children and that parent–teacher communications are most positive when teachers do not interpret this as a threat to their professional status, but instead see it as an

Table 9.2 Common and differentiated features of curricula for young children

Environment	Content	Process	Product
Common elements			

• emotional safety
• structure
• high but realistic expectations
	• meaningful tasks
	• interdisciplinary content
	• integrated curriculum
		• active engagement
		• discovery-based learning
		• opportunities for choice
			• demonstration of key knowledge and skills
			  • across domains
			  • in a range of mediums

Differentiation methods			
• flexible time allowances • supplementary resources • increased flexibility • placement • grouping	• promote children's interests • tailored activities • tiered activities • curriculum compacting • early entry to school • grade skipping (full or partial)	• mediated learning • mediated sociodramatic play • thinking skills • metacognitive training • motivation	• tiered products • use of computers

opportunity to demonstrate professional accountability for their teaching in general, and for gifted provisions in particular.

It is worth keeping in mind that parents are generally accurate in their observations of children's skills: they see their children across settings and know their children well, so can advise teachers about both their aspirations and strategies that work for their child at home. Although in the past there has been a fear of involving 'over-invested' parents in their children's education, it is now clear that children are more engaged in programs that have their parents' backing (Holden 1996; Penney & Wilgosh 2000; Robinson 1990a).

Despite the myths, most parents seek a balanced education for their gifted child: they do not wish to promote intellectual skills alone (Creel & Karnes 1988). But, while most parents are confident that they can meet the needs of typical children, those whose children are gifted might want or need suggestions about how to support their young children's learning and emotional adjustment. At the same time, some also need permission not to focus exclusively on their gifted child and attend equally to other aspects of family life, such as looking after themselves as individuals, their marital relationship and any other children.

Keep in mind that, in the past, parents may have faced teachers who were indifferent at best, or hostile at worst to the needs of their gifted children (Fraser 1996; McBride 1992). Also, most will have endured an educational system that was unresponsive to their own giftedness, so they bring to their conversations with you some fears about how their child's education will proceed. Their fears can be reduced by your respectful and collaborative stance.

Conclusion

It could seem frustrating that there is no recipe for gifted education, but this should come as no surprise, given that we do not expect to offer all children with disabilities identical programs, but instead respond to their individual needs.

Curriculum differentiation measures are not employed widely in regular classes (Archambault et al. 1993; Westberg et al. 1993a, 1997). However, this neglect can be reversed when educators receive training to recognise and meet the needs of gifted children. Educators also need to be interested in this group of children, to collaborate with each other, parents and specialists and to have the support of their principals (Davis & Rimm 2004). At the same time, professionalism does not require you to know everything—just to know what you do not know and to be willing to update your knowledge. When you do so, you will be in a better position to respond to gifted children's profound need for complexity and meaning in their learning.

Suggested further reading

The following text describes the curriculum planning process for all young children, with some reference to gifted children:
MacNaughton, G. and Williams, G. 1998 *Techniques for teaching young children: choices in theory and practice* Longman, Sydney.

For a review of research on curricular modifications for gifted learners:
Rogers, K.B. 2002 *Re-forming gifted education: matching the program to the child* Great Potential Press, Scottsdale, AZ.

For extensive advice on curricular modifications for young gifted children:
Harrison, C. 2003 *Giftedness in early childhood* 3rd edn, GERRIC, Sydney.
Mares, L. and Byles, J. 1994 *One step ahead: early admission of, and school provisions for, gifted infants* Hawker Brownlow Education, Melbourne.
Morelock, M.J. and Morrison, K. 1996 *Gifted children have talents too: multidimensional programmes for the gifted in early childhood* Hawker Brownlow Education, Melbourne.
Smutny, J.F., Walker, S.Y. and Meckstroth, E.A. 1997 *Teaching young gifted children in the regular classroom: identifying, nurturing, and challenging ages 4–9* Free Spirit Publishing, Minneapolis, MN.

For curricular suggestions for school-aged gifted children, which will have to be adapted for early childhood settings:
Bailey, S., Knight, B.A. and Riley, D. 1995 *Developing children's talents: guidelines for schools* Hawker Brownlow Education, Melbourne.
Braggett, E., Day, A. and Minchin, M. 1997 *Differentiated programs for primary schools* Hawker Brownlow Education, Melbourne.
Eyre, D. 1997 *Able children in ordinary schools* David Fulton, London.
Pohl, M. 1997 *Teaching thinking skills in the primary years: a whole school approach* Hawker Brownlow Education, Melbourne.
Van Tassel-Baska, J. 1994 *Comprehensive curriculum for gifted learners* 2nd edn, Allyn & Bacon, Boston.
Winebrenner, S. 2001 *Teaching gifted kids in the regular classroom* 2nd edn, Free Spirit Press, Minneapolis, MN.

For an overview of the curriculum planning process:
Braggett, E.J. 1994 *Developing programs for gifted students: a total-school approach* Hawker Brownlow Education, Melbourne.

DISADVANTAGED

GIFTED CHILDREN ten

Giftedness is not just a product of intelligence or achievement, but is also affected by sociological distance from the centers of power and wealth. Thus, the more stigma, economic difficulties, and cultural barriers one must overcome, the more 'gifted' one needs to be to achieve in mainstream society. (Kerr & Cohn 2001: 43)

Introduction

A reformist view of education (as described in Chapter 9) recognises that gifted children whose abilities are manifested in non-traditional patterns are at risk of being overlooked within the education system. Some forms of disadvantage, such as the special challenges experienced by boys and girls separately, may be less obvious in the early childhood years but the seeds of subsequent difficulties are sown at young ages. Therefore, this is the age when educators can act to prevent the emergence of later difficulties.

Gender and giftedness

Gender makes more difference to gifted than to average learners, with gender being the single strongest influence on achievement levels (Freeman 2000). Taking females first, although much of the research on gifted girls is dated and modern girls' experiences may differ from those of their predecessors, many writers argue that the recent gains made by females are mostly in the middle and later high school years rather than in adulthood, and even then mainly in the middle classes of industrialised societies (Kerr 2000). Many young women who display exceptional skills still have to contend with greater alienation from their families, culture and sex than do boys, because high achievement—particularly in certain fields—is considered unfeminine (Kerr 2000; Noble et al. 1999). In adult occupations they may have to negotiate male-dominated domains and, unlike men, their achievement relies on their ability to balance family and career responsibilities (Noble et al. 1999). Despite diminishing gender differences in abilities, and despite gifted girls having less sex-stereotyped interests than average girls, males achieve to higher levels in their careers; this gender difference is most pronounced among the highly gifted (Callahan 1991; Lubinski et al. 1993; Randall 1997). The result is that any mature women look back with regret on lives of unrealised potential (Holahan 1996; Reis 1987).

Recognition of giftedness

Given that giftedness is often evident at an earlier age in girls than in boys, it might be expected that girls' giftedness would be more often recognised in the early years. However, the reverse is true: teachers more often identify gifted boys than girls (Reis 2002). In Lee's (2000) study, for example, two teachers with a combined total of 44 years of teaching experience claimed never to have met a gifted girl, although they had occasionally recognised gifted boys. Meanwhile, across most cultures there is a ratio of two boys to every girl identified by their parents as gifted (Freeman 2000).

On the other hand, given that boys have a higher rate of learning disabilities, more gifted boys than girls will have dual exceptionalities, which will be more often overlooked or dismissed on the grounds that 'boys will be boys'.

Pressure to conform

Throughout their schooling, gifted girls and boys are probably exposed to similar levels of peer pressure to be ordinary (albeit for different reasons), but girls are relatively disadvantaged in comparison with boys as a result of many external and internal barriers to success (Callahan et al. 1994; Davis & Rimm 2004; Freeman 1996; Kerr 1997, 2000; Lea-Wood & Clunies-Ross 1995; Leroux 1988; Macleod 2004; Randall 1997; Reis 2002; Smutny 1998; White 2000). The first has to do with *perceptions*: although teachers' perceptions of gifted girls' performances might be improving (Siegle & Reis 1998), in general teachers, parents and gifted girls themselves commonly underestimate their skills, even though girls' abilities equal or exceed those of boys throughout the school years (Marsh et al. 1988; Noble et al. 1999; Siegle & Reis 1998). Gifted girls are less willing than gifted boys to take intellectual risks, are more prone to perfectionism (that is, to have high aspirations coupled with uncertainty about their ability to attain these) and more often attribute their successes to outside forces such as luck or effort rather than ability (Baker 1996; Callahan et al. 1994; Jacobs & Weisz 1992; Kerr 1997; Lubinski et al. 1993; Randall 1997; Reis 2002; Smutny 1998).

The second cause is *sex role stereotyping*, whereby gifted girls experience social stigma and isolation if they excel over classmates. This also leads to an unwillingness to compete—especially with boys and men—perhaps because that seems 'unfeminine' or violates affiliation needs and, for example, leads to more girls than boys refusing acceleration and dropping out of gifted programs (Davis & Rimm 2004). Girls' conformity to their gender role means that they work for the approval of their parents and teachers, rather than for their own fulfilment. Being compliant and doing what is expected of them allows them to do well in their school work, but this conventionality can disadvantage them in adult life, while their docility can cause their learning disabilities to be overlooked (Davis & Rimm 2004; Kerr 1996; Kline & Short 1991; Loeb & Jay 1987). As their parents' expectations recede in importance throughout the latter school years, the impact of peers—particularly male peers—increases (Davis & Rimm 2004). In her election victory speech, South Australian politician, Dr Jane Lomax-Smith, described this commonly negative influence (adding that, fortunately, it did not apply to herself):

> Behind every successful woman
> is a man trying to get her to stop.

This male peer pressure to suppress high achievement also feeds into a third cause—namely a *'culture of romance'* whereby some girls expect to rely on a male partner and so minimise the importance of an independent career, and expect to experience success secondhand by supporting their male partners' achievements. They are willing to sacrifice their own ambitions and dreams because they feel a duty to nurture their relationships, whereas boys and men are able to have both (Kerr 1996).

Fourth is *'superwoman syndrome'*, which makes girls unwilling to focus on and excel at just one or two activities. Some writers argue that this may not diminish their life satisfaction (Delisle 1998; Lubinski et al. 1993), although it could equally be argued that their contentment with lower achievement is itself a collusion with low expectations.

These pressures result in girls' diminishing hopes, aspirations and achievements during adolescence and adulthood (Butler-Por 1993; Freeman 1996, 1998; Kerr 1996, 1997; Reis & Callahan 1989). Throughout life, their decline in self-esteem is three times greater than for boys (Davis & Rimm 2004).

Meanwhile, the pressure for boys to conform has a different basis. Whereas both gifted girls and boys typically have wide-ranging play interests, girls are allowed to be tomboyish in their preferences, but homophobic attitudes imposed on boys disallow any attraction towards 'feminine' skills or interests (Kerr & Cohn 2001). There is a 'boy code' that expects boys to adopt roles which, if anything, are even more rigid than those demanded of females. This code comprises the following four imperatives (Pollack 1998, in Kerr & Cohn 2001).

- Boys should be a 'sturdy oak': independent and stoic, which results in a boy's premature separation from his mother and tough punishment for misdemeanours in order to 'toughen him up'. The sensitivity of emotional giftedness is derided rather than being seen as an interpersonal asset.
- Boys are supposed to 'give 'em hell': to take risks and act tough. In this respect, boys are more likely than girls to clown around in class—even when doing so attracts teacher sanctions (Luftig & Nichols 1991). This can help boys' popularity with peers, but can affect their achievement levels.
- Boys must be a 'big wheel': the most powerful and dominant one. The sensitivity of many gifted boys that causes them to shun competition is at odds with this imperative.
- 'No sissy stuff': boys should never be emotional. Whereas all boys can suffer from having to conform to this code, the emotional intensity and creativity of many gifted boys make it doubly difficult for them to fit into the macho culture of their peers. They often have to hide their interests and disguise their inner selves. If they are bullied or mocked for their sensitivity, they dare not report it as that will be seen as further weakness (Kerr & Cohn 2001).

Unlike girls, whose mothers typically remain as strong role models for them, by adolescence gifted boys' fathers often seem unavailable to help them find their identity as intellectuals (Alvino 1991), while male teachers and coaches might not be able to act as mentors for fear of accusations of inappropriate intimacy (Kerr & Cohn 2001). Meanwhile, adults might encourage—even pressure—boys to pursue their talents independently, while neglecting their social skills, with the result that boys can become increasingly isolated and consequently lack social supports and friendships (Wolfle 1991). Their isolation from both peers and parents is thus absolute.

The stereotype that boys are relatively less mature than girls has recently led to an increase in holding many boys back from starting school, simply on the grounds that they *are* boys. There are two problems with this for all boys: first, there is considerable overlap in the skills and maturity of the sexes, such that many boys will be more mature than their female age mates; second, age of entry is an issue for school adjustment only when combined with specific disadvantaging circumstances such as poverty, for example (DeMeis & Stearns 1992). But this practice is doubly inappropriate for gifted boys, who will excel over most age mates, whatever their sex. This blanket practice has all the academic, social and emotional disadvantages of a failure to accelerate gifted learners. Rather than reaping social rewards, gifted boys can thereafter be deprived of intellectual peers. As Kerr and Nicpon (2003: 497) report: 'When a gifted boy has difficulty relating to his peers, it is more likely because his classmates are too young for him rather than too old for him.'

Gendered patterns of underachievement

The separate strictures on both girls and boys often cause them to suppress or disguise their giftedness in school and beyond, producing the gendered life patterns described in Box 10.1 (Kerr & Cohn 2001; Kerr & Nicpon 2003). These patterns can be similar for males and females, with the exceptions perhaps of the nonconformist and leader roles being less available to females.

Supporting high achievement for both sexes

A strong belief in self is the most important factor enabling the success of both girls and boys, providing the energy, drive and tools for high achievement (Hébert 2002). To promote this self-efficacy, both will benefit from questioning sex-based stereotypes. To give gifted children permission to challenge and attain their goals, it will not be enough to raise their aspirations: they need help to become deeply committed to their dreams (Kerr 1996; Kline & Short 1991). This begins from early childhood onwards, with the measures outlined in Box 10.2.

For boys, this will involve challenging the macho culture whereby athletic success has more status than academic achievement, encouraging boys to express their talents whether or not these lie in non-traditional domains, and giving increased recognition to boys' abilities in language skills (Siegle & Reis 1998). Boys in particular need support to develop emotional awareness of themselves and others (empathy) so they can balance their emotional and intellectual lives and make sense of their life experiences. They need to see this sensitivity as a core ingredient of a strong male identity (Hébert 2002).

Gifted children from minority cultures

The understanding that individuals' abilities are shaped by a dynamic interaction between their genetic endowment and their environment renders irrelevant the debates about apparent differences in intellectual capacities between racial groups: when children have the same opportunities to learn, one who has learned more will have done so because of more efficient learning ability. But when children have had differing opportunities, any differences in their achievement are *definitely* environmental and only *possibly* genetic as well.

There are two issues relating to the education of children from minority cultures. The first is their relative underachievement in school and beyond. To understand this requires an appreciation of a distinction between voluntary and involuntary minority groups: some families migrate voluntarily to a country in search of more opportunities, whereas involuntary minorities

Box 10.1 Gender-based life patterns

Pattern	Female	Male
Conformists: Meet others' expectations but, while outwardly successful, find their lives not as satisfying as expected.	Enter a helping profession and become a home-maker. Career takes second place to their spouse's achievements.	Have a secure and predictable life and career. Suppress their emotions to conform to the macho 'boy code'.
Popularity seekers: Hide their giftedness to be accepted by peers.	Do not pursue high-level courses. Withdraw from competition, especially with males.	Seek to be a 'regular guy' by withdrawing from academics and playing sport instead.
Players: In order to fit in, seek the approval of whoever they are with at the time, while subverting their true selves.	Social chameleons: change their nature, views and behaviour to agree with present company.	Learn to appear to be how others want them to be. Fear being found out.
Nonconformists: Realise that their eccentricities mean that they will never fit in.	Withdraw, become isolated.	If supported, will thrive creatively; if not, will be intellectual delinquents.
Closet learners: Engage in regular activities by day but read voraciously or are highly creative when alone.	Support their bosses or husbands to excel, despite themselves being the more able.	Have a sound but ordinary job and an attractive partner but only intimates know of their spiritual and creative sides.
Leaders: Evaluate their own goals and live out their own life script. Define their own life purpose.	Strive in dual careers of paid work and homemaker. Experience the glass ceiling.	Define masculinity as a blend of emotionality and strength.

Box 10.2 Measures to encourage high achievement in girls and boys

Climate

- Educate teachers, parents and psychologists about the specific educational and emotional needs of gifted girls and boys.
- Honour and encourage diversity in all its forms.
- Celebrate excellence, including in intellectual domains.
- Avoid sex-role stereotyped teaching materials and question gender stereotypes on TV, in books and with respect to toys.
- Prohibit sexual harassment and bullying in homes and schools, particularly anti-intellectual derision.

Curricular measures

- Assess young children's development to assist in planning for their individual needs.
- Introduce spatial activities early before gender stereotyping intervenes to discourage girls' engagement in these activities.
- Give girls and boys an equal share of teacher attention.
- Encourage girls in individual pursuits, rather than promoting mainly cooperative activities.
- Assign leadership roles to girls as well as boys.
- Where indicated, employ accelerative measures such as early admission to school or grade advancement.

Personal support

- Teach girls about competition and do not shelter them from failure.
- Accept assertive behaviour from girls to the same extent as from boys.
- Give girls the confidence to persevere.
- Teach girls to attribute their success to their abilities and efforts, rather than to external forces such as luck.
- Provide access to other gifted children of the same sex.
- Expose children to successful role models and same-sex mentors.
- Counsel gifted children so that they understand their own capabilities, interests and values, as it is these that should dictate their career choices, not a profession's status or others' expectations.
- By late primary school, offer career counselling to enhance children's awareness of their options. For girls, this includes awareness of the costs and benefits of the career patterns of traditional homemaker, delayed career, simultaneous career and parenting roles, and a career that is deferred until after parenting. For boys, this includes information about non-traditional male careers.

• Counsel parents to allow their daughters' and sons' natural talents to flourish, regardless of whether these are in traditional gendered domains or not.
• Teach boys that they will achieve more intimacy and fulfilment in relationships with intelligent females than with submissive nonentities.

Sources: Butler-Por 1993; Davis & Rimm 2004; Delisle 1998; Fitzgerald & Keown 1996; Freeman 1993, 1996; Jacobs & Weisz 1992; Kelly 1988; Kerr 1996, 1997, 2000; Kline & Short 1991; Lubinski et al. 1993; Macleod 2004; Reis & Callahan 1989; Smutny 1998; White 2000.

---

were brought to a country against their will (e.g. African Americans) or were invaded (as with Native Americans, Australian Aborigines and the New Zealand Māori peoples) (Borland & Wright 2000).

Individuals from voluntary minority groups have difficulties with assimilating into the dominant culture in the first and perhaps second generations, often as a result of language differences, although achieving proficiency in English does not necessarily guarantee school achievement (Reis & McCoach 2000). This tells us that discrimination is also an issue. From an early age, children who are experiencing cultural oppression are aware of the injustices in their lives, and benefit when they and those from the privileged culture challenge these (MacNaughton 2003). With respect to education, migrant parents have obviously been born and educated in their home country, so may have less understanding of the local schooling system and doubt their abilities to support their child's education; these parents may be doubly disempowered when it comes to understanding gifted provisions.

Meanwhile, the history of oppression and ongoing negative contact between involuntary minorities and the dominant culture generate repeated disadvantage and oppositional coping mechanisms, including a resistance to 'acting white' via school success (Borland & Wright 2000). For these groups, school learning is perceived not as *adding* to their lives, but as *detracting from* their own cultural values, traditions and attitudes, while effort during the school years is less likely to be rewarded in their working life. Educators therefore need to find a way of showing these children that academic achievement will be good for them, their families and their communities (Kerr & Cohn 2001).

This points to the need to promote pluralism (in contrast with assimilationism) so that children from minority cultures feel that they can preserve their own cultural heritage at the same time as acquiring the knowledge and skills that are necessary for success in the majority culture (Maker & Schiever 1989).

The second issue with respect to the education of children from minority cultures is that these children are underidentified as being gifted (Borland &

Wright 2000; Braggett 1998; Butler-Por 1993; Davis & Rimm 2004; Ford et al. 2000; Frasier 1989, 1997; Gallagher & Gallagher 1994; Maker 1996; Renzulli 1973; Richert 1987, 1997; Scott et al. 1996; Tannenbaum 1983). This is clearly inequitable, as giftedness occurs at equal rates in all cultures (Borland & Wright 1994, 2000; Casey & Quisenberry 1976).

The reduced recognition of children from minority backgrounds comes about in part because of the social disadvantage they experience. This results in these children performing less well on ability tests designed for the dominant culture because of their reduced facility in spoken or written English (Brooks 1998; Frasier 1997; Renzulli 1973; Robisheaux & Banbury 1994; Tyler-Wood & Carri 1993) and low self-expectations of success on tests, which leads to self-defeating test-taking behaviour and, in turn, lower scores (Ford 2002).

Underidentification also arises because, although all cultures accept that individuals possess advanced skills, the skills that are particularly valued differ across cultures and environments; however, teachers in general are not attuned to non-traditional signs of giftedness (Frasier 1997). Furthermore, many teachers' stereotypical low expectations of culturally and linguistically different children can become a self-fulfilling prophecy (Brooks 1998; Butler-Por 1993; Frasier 1997; Gibson 1998; Kolb & Jussim 1994; Rist 1970).

Culture-fair assessment

The 'identification by provision' approach to assessment that was introduced in Chapter 8 actually avoids many of the difficulties of overlooking gifted minorities. You might recall that, in this model, educators facilitate an enriching program for all and then observe how each child responds, particularly watching for exceptionality in the following non-traditional domains (Frasier 1993; Gibson 1998; Shaklee 1993; Shaklee & Viechnicki 1995; Torrance 1998):

- *communication* skills that are rich in imagery, while adjusting expectations for a lack of proficiency in English if it is not the children's first language (Fernández et al. 1998);
- ability in *visual or performing arts*;
- *social* skills such as responsiveness to the feelings of others or skilfulness in group activities, including leadership—although in some cultures, such as amongst the New Zealand Māori peoples, this will not always be expressed assertively as leading from the front but might instead take the form of facilitating or guiding others behind the scenes (Bevan-Brown 1999, 2004); and
- *emotional* expressiveness.

At the same time, you will observe *how* the children acquire, generate and apply their knowledge, for which they will require (Haensly & Kyong 2000):

- flexibility, creativity and imagination;
- reasoning (logical thinking) abilities;
- agency — or, in other words, an internal locus of control whereby the children perceive themselves as agents who can act on the world to produce outcomes;
- prospectivity: the ability to plan and anticipate events; and
- retrospectivity, which is the ability to make connections between present and past experience, to use remembered information to inform their present choices.

The goal is not to fit diverse students into the dominant culture's definition of giftedness, but to adjust that definition to recognise diversity. So any tests that are part of the assessment process need to be as culturally fair as possible: the Ravens Matrices might be the most readily available alternative to IQ tests, whose high verbal content and individual administration might disadvantage some minority children (Ford 2003; Patton 1992). At the same time, tests should still be included as part of a comprehensive assessment, as minority children could be overlooked if we rely only on nominations by teachers from the dominant culture or from parents who might not be aware of the indicators of gifted development.

Multicultural curricula

Teachers from the dominant culture will need professional development and multicultural experiences to help them become aware of their own cultural assumptions and biases. Particularly in the face of the traditional silencing of minorities, teachers will need to listen to students, their families and other members of a minority culture to find out how to make learning culturally meaningful and relevant for these children (Ford & Trotman 2001).

Thus self-awareness and cultural awareness are the first measures for culturally competent teaching of diverse students. Next is establishing high expectations for all students. Third is establishing a climate in which prejudice is prohibited, including adults' prejudice against children's use of dialects and their home languages (Ford 2003; Ford & Harris 2000; Ford et al. 2000; Harmon 2002). The final measure is an anti-bias curriculum, which acknowledges and celebrates differences openly and honestly. Rather than perpetuating stereotypes through a 'tourist curriculum' (Derman-Sparks & the ABC Task Force 1989) that focuses on a culture's exotic customs, the curriculum must recognise how the various cultural groups that make up a society have contributed to how it has been shaped as a collective (Ford 2003; Ford & Harris 2000; Ford et al. 2000). It must integrate multicultural perspectives and alter its basic goals, structure and content to enable all students to view issues from the perspectives of diverse groups (Ford & Harris 2000).

In terms of teaching and learning processes, although all children benefit from multisensory experiences and a blend of individual and cooperative learning, these various methods may most benefit those from minority cultures, whose learning style may rely on movement, spirituality, expressiveness and emotion to an even greater extent than in the dominant culture (Harmon 2002; Ford et al. 2000).

A final consideration is that gifted children from minority cultures may feel especially sensitive to participating in activities that mark them out from members of their own cultural group (Evans 1993). Their communal ethos means that curricular differentiation methods such as pull-out programs will be inappropriate for some students from minority cultures (Bevan-Brown 1999, 2004).

Emotional support

All children, whatever their abilities, can experience challenges as a result of their minority status, but gifted children from minority cultures are likely to be more sensitive to the injustices they experience and more likely to feel a conflict between their racial identity and high achievement in the dominant culture's terms (Ford 2002). Yet those who feel pride in their own cultural identity, as well as permission to excel in their gifted domain, will have a high self-esteem and strong achievement drive (Bevan-Brown 1999, 2004).

Children from minority cultures will need access to other gifted diverse students and to extracurricular activities that promote social interaction across groups (Ford 2002). They will need help to acquire skills for moving within and between their separate cultures, which can include using their own dialect and standard English variously across settings (Ford & Harris 2000; Ford et al. 2000; Frasier 1997). Meanwhile, although it is important to encourage excellence, educators' feedback about children's achievement must not draw attention to individual children, as this can be inappropriate within certain cultures, especially when the children are among 'outsiders' rather than their own cultural group (Bevan-Brown 1999, 2004).

Collaboration with parents can be crucial, as the most important condition for high achievement is the support the children receive, the most valuable source of which is their families. Parents are more likely to support their child's inclusion in gifted programs if they see these as culturally mixed, non-elitist and unthreatening (Davis & Rimm 2004).

Children in poverty

Children are the most likely of any age group to be living in poverty (with the elderly being the next most probable). In Australia, approximately 20 per cent of children experience poverty (with this figure being higher among Aboriginal children) (Gilding 1997); in Britain, rates for both transitory and chronic poverty are highest for those under school age, with 26 per cent of this age group living in families who earn less than half the average income (Hill & Jenkins 2001); in the United States the poverty rate is 20–30 per cent, depending on how it is calculated, which is mid-range in absolute terms but equal highest (with Russia) in relative terms among industrialised nations (Aber & Ellwood 2001).

Poverty has a significant and direct effect on young children, as that is the time when development is most vulnerable to the detrimental effects of inadequate nutrition and stimulation (Bradbury et al. 2001). Sameroff (1990), for example, reports that the rate of mild intellectual disability (or mental retardation, in U.S. terms) is eight times higher in the United States than in Sweden, which he attributes to the superior levels of support available to impoverished families in Sweden.

Furthermore, functioning under the burden of chronic poverty is linked with other risk factors that are detrimental to children—such as poor housing, limited social supports when one lives in a neighbourhood where others are equally stressed, inadequate health care, and low-quality child care and educational services (Schaffer 1998). In response, parents might neglect their children's needs as they become caught up in their own issues of survival; inadequate guidance can lead children to develop undesirable peer relationships (selecting friends who are similarly stressed or behaving in anti-social ways) (Schaffer 1998); the parents themselves might develop mental illnesses in response to their trying circumstances (or a mental illness may be the cause of their poverty); and the parents' relationship can be strained.

The restricted learning opportunities available to impoverished children will often reduce their abilities compared with more advantaged children (Kitano & Perez 1998). For this reason, it may be more suitable to compare their development to other children with similarly disadvantaging backgrounds, yielding a relative rather than an absolute measure of giftedness.

At the same time, just as we have to guard against stereotypes about children from other cultures, so too we need to be aware that knowledge of children's backgrounds can be a two-edged sword: it can help us to understand disadvantaged children's developmental patterns, but it can also cause us to lower our expectations of them (Spicker et al. 1987). Contrary to urban myths, socioeconomic status has very little impact on *individual* children's academic achievement: parents' ability to manage family crises, their encouragement of learning and the quality of their parenting skills—which are independent of family income—have most impact (Freeman 1993; Robinson et al. 2002; White 1982). Also, even when individuals are disadvantaged by their family circumstances, many are nevertheless resilient, especially when significant adults in their lives support them emotionally. These two facts together mean that educators do not need to feel helpless about the potential of children who live in poverty.

Children from impoverished backgrounds who later attend middle-class or private schools (perhaps on scholarships) can find it difficult to fit into their new social stratum and may need support to maintain contact with both strata (Freeman 1993). For the reasons already cited, such support can be unavailable from their families so educators play a crucial role in supporting these children to cross social boundaries.

Rural children

Two or three generations ago, the IQs of rural children were, on average, six points below metropolitan children's; this difference has now become negligible—in the order of only two IQ points—although there may still be a wider range of abilities within rural communities (Loehlin 2000). Gifted children in rural areas can be disadvantaged for a range of reasons, the most fundamental of which is the higher incidence of poverty and less stable employment in rural communities, factors which disadvantage rural children in the same ways that they do urban children (Colangelo et al. 2003).

Some disadvantages for rural students relate to developing their talents in the first place and some to being recognised as having advanced development and subsequently receiving suitable educational provisions. These disadvantages include the following (Bailey et al. 1995; Belcastro 2002; Colangelo et al. 2003; Knight et al. 1997; Lupowski 1984; Spicker & Southern 1998; Spicker et al. 1987).

Access

- Living in areas with a sparse population gives rural children a restricted range of social contacts, particularly with intellectual peers.
- Distance and seasonal inaccessibility can prevent children from accessing a breadth of experiences, peers and teachers.

Teacher experience and support

- Teacher turnover in rural areas is often higher than in metropolitan schools.
- There may be no teachers knowledgeable enough and available to teach gifted children in their special interest areas.
- Teachers in rural schools are more isolated from collegial support beyond the school and have fewer opportunities for further study, other than through correspondence courses.

Attitude to giftedness

- Giftedness might be discouraged in conservative communities, especially if it is seen to violate gender norms.
- Excelling at school might be discouraged if it will lead to leaving the area in order to receive a tertiary education.

Gifted provisions

- There tends to be a more limited curriculum in rural than in metropolitan schools, and teaching staff tend not to be able to specialise in curricular areas or develop new curricula in line with latest practices.
- There will probably be too few gifted children to justify the provision of a gifted program in a rural school, and perhaps some resistance to innovation that will make it difficult to initiate such programs.
- In rural areas, resources such as educational spending, libraries and school support personnel may be scant.

Nevertheless, rural students have the advantages of small class sizes, mixed-age classes, close acquaintance with their teachers and high levels of community participation, all of which are key components of successful gifted education (Colangelo et al. 2003). They may be able to develop independent skills and learn at their own rate (Lupowski 1984), and may have dedicated parents on hand to assist with their education (Bailey et al. 1995; Spicker & Southern 1998). Rural living can offer a range of hands-on experiences that are not as readily available in metropolitan areas, and can create the need for small groupings of able children, thus facilitating the development of a tailor-made program to suit their needs.

Meanwhile, computers can connect rural children electronically with other gifted students, even when they cannot physically meet, and can give them access to databases to support their research (Knight et al. 1997; Spicker & Southern 1998). Computers can also allow rural teachers to form relationships with distant colleagues, thus permitting an exchange of expertise to enrich their programs (Spicker et al. 1987).

Therefore, to facilitate the development of skills by rural children, teachers will need to ensure that these students have access to computers and are literate in their use from a young age (Spicker & Southern 1998). Teaching at a distance can be as effective as face-to-face instruction when computer technology can be harnessed appropriately to the task (Belcastro 2001).

Conclusion

Linda Silverman once said that gifted individuals often feel that they have 'sealed orders' and that their life's mission is to find out what those orders comprise. Neither females nor males will be satisfied if they act out others' ambitions for them, but instead need to follow their own script.

Meanwhile, poverty and other socially and educationally disadvantaging conditions are often cumulative: a female from a minority culture is that much more distant from the dominant male culture than a middle-class girl, for example. For disadvantaged children, more so than for the privileged, exceptional achievement requires the five Ds of extraordinary drive, determination, direction, dedication and discipline.

In tune with a transformist view of education, Kitano (1991) highlights that, even if equal educational attainment were achieved across the various cultural groups in our societies, this nevertheless might not result in equity in life: discrimination outside of school can still limit the attainments of individuals from minority cultures. Therefore, we must ask ourselves whether a multicultural education should be directed at effecting social change as well as reorganising curricula. As Kitano (1991: 14) states: 'The goal must be to produce citizens who, through thoughtful reflection and critical analysis, recognize social injustice and work towards a more equitable society.'

Suggested further reading

For further reading on gifted girls I recommend:
Freeman, J. 1996 *Highly able girls and boys* Department for Education and Employment, London.
Kerr, B.A. 1996 *Smart girls two: a new psychology of girls, women and giftedness* Hawker Brownlow Education, Melbourne.
Rimm, S. 2003 *See Jane win for girls: a smart girl's guide to success* Free Spirit Press, Minneapolis, MN.
Smutny, J.F. 1998 *Gifted girls* Phi Delta Kappa Educational Foundation, Bloomington, IN.

For further reading on gifted boys:
Kerr, B.A. and Cohn, S.J. 2001 *Smart boys: talent, manhood, and the search for meaning* Great Potential Press Scottsdale, AZ.

For further reading on multicultural education:
Although not referring specifically to gifted learners, any multicultural education for gifted children must be embedded within an anti-bias program for all children, so I recommend:
Dau, E. ed. 2001 *The anti-bias approach in early childhood* 2nd edn, Pearson Education Australia, Sydney.

GIFTED CHILDREN

WITH LEARNING
DISABILITIES
eleven

Rejection by others, labelling, lowered teacher expectations, and the sense of being different combine to make gifted children with disabilities feel less capable and of less worth than other children. (Davis & Rimm 2004: 391)

Introduction

Given that many disabling conditions are unrelated to giftedness, it should not be surprising that some children have both. It is thought that around 5–10 per cent of gifted children—that is, somewhere between one in 200 and one in 400 children—could also have a learning disability (Dix & Schafer 1996). This can include sensory impairments, sensory integration difficulties, physical disability or specific learning difficulties. Some of these disabilities will be apparent at a very young age, while others such as specific learning disabilities and Asperger syndrome tend not to show up until the early school years.

The reverse statistic is that approximately 2–5 per cent of children with disabilities may also be gifted (Johnson et al. 1997; Whitmore 1981; Yewchuk & Lupart 2000). These children's giftedness is often obscured by their disability, and so is seldom identified (Karnes 1979).

Specific learning disabilities

Children with specific learning disabilities are the most commonly studied group of gifted-disabled children, with dyslexia (reading difficulties) and dysgraphia (writing difficulties) the most widely known. The possibility that

 180

giftedness could coexist with these learning disabilities was first recognised in 1937 by Samuel Orton, who found that a group of dyslexic children spanned the full range of general intellectual abilities (Weill 1987). But it was not until 1963 that Kirk coined the term 'learning disabilities' to describe learning difficulties which have no apparent cause and are inconsistent with children's other skills (Baum et al. 1991; Montgomery 1996).

A learning disability is thought to come about because of information-processing deficiencies (Baum et al. 1991; Cruickshank 1977), resulting in problems with expressing or communicating ideas in written or verbal form or impoverished perception, organisation, sequencing, comprehension and memory of information (Gunderson et al. 1987; Whitmore & Maker 1985; Wingenbach 1998). The children will often display ineffective learning strategies, including brief attention span, disruptive behaviour and overactivity (Baum et al. 1991; Wingenbach 1998).

Their wide spread of abilities can leave these children frustrated and confused, their parents exasperated, and their teachers feeling helpless (Fall & Nolan 1993). This often worsens as they grow older, as the discrepancy widens between their expected and actual academic performances (Weinfeld et al. 2002).

The children's high abilities can often mask their difficulties, so a comprehensive assessment is necessary. This should, among other measures, include an IQ test, as uneven score profiles on these tests are a good indicator of dual exceptionalities. A learning difficulty can be indicated by a 20-point difference between the verbal and performance IQs; low Arithmetic and Digit Span scores on the WISC-IV (except with mathematically gifted children); discrepancies of greater than two standard deviations between upper and lower subtest scores; succeeding on harder items while failing easier ones; or a pattern of high spatial scores and low sequential scores (Brown 1984; Davis & Rimm 2004; Kokot 2003; Silverman 2003; Smith et al. 1977).

Strictly speaking, for a score to signify a disability, it should fall within the disabled range (below two standard deviations from the mean), but children's giftedness can raise their scores towards the average; similarly, to be considered gifted, scores should fall two standard deviations above the mean, but a disability can lower these to nearer the average. So there is a case for employing the gifted-learning disabled label even when the children's weaker skills are near the average, as long as the discrepancy between their lower and upper scores is marked, because subtest score fluctuations are common within the gifted population.

Academic difficulties cannot show up until the children are given academic tasks, which means that learning disabilities tend not to be recognised before the early to middle primary school years. Once of this age, there are three types of gifted learning disabled children (Baum 1989; Baum et al. 1991; Ellston 1993; Gunderson et al. 1987; Rivera et al. 1995; Toll 1993).

- The first are *subtle gifted learning disabled* children, whose giftedness is recognised but whose disorganised work habits cause others to think of them as unmotivated or lazy. These children's learning disabilities are unrecognised altogether or are noticed much later than is the case for less able children.
- The second group of *recognised learning disabled* children are identified as having learning disabilities but not as being gifted, as their disability impairs their performances. They may receive remedial services, but their special talents and interests are overlooked. At school they may display disruptive behaviour and achieve at low levels but may employ their creative talents at home, when they are allowed to produce work in other than written form, or when they are taught non-traditionally (Baum et al. 1991; Ellston 1993).
- The third group is the *hidden gifted learning disabled* children, whose dual exceptionalities both go unrecognised because their abilities compensate for their learning problems and their learning problems obscure their gifts. This is especially true for girls, whose learning disabilities tend to be identified later than those of boys (Dole 2000), and when children's gifted abilities and disabilities are both in academic areas (Brody & Mills 1997). Because these children invest high levels of energy in compensating for their learning difficulties, they are able to achieve at age level. The results are that their overall abilities are thought to be average, while the effort required to hide or overcome their learning problems takes its toll emotionally. Fatigue from the extra effort required can impair their concentration span. Their skills often surface when given creative projects to do, or when they are working in their area of greatest talent (Toll 1993). This may be the largest group of gifted learning disabled children and, while all three groups are educationally disadvantaged, these children whose gifts and disabilities both go unrecognised are most at risk educationally (Rivera et al. 1995).

It is important to recognise when children's disability impairs their achievement in areas that they value highly, as their difficulties in these domains will have most impact on their self-esteem (Whitmore & Maker 1985). Their self-esteem is vulnerable because they will be aware that they do not understand without knowing why, but sensing that they are not stupid (Swesson 1994). Many are frustrated that they cannot make their brain or body do as directed (Brody & Mills 1997). Box 11.1 lists these and other specific characteristics frequently displayed by gifted children with learning disabilities. Some of these are similar to gifted children's characteristics, some equate to the traits of children with learning disabilities and some are unique to children with both exceptionalities.

Box 11.1 Characteristics of gifted children with specific learning disabilities

Gifted learning disabled children have some intellectual skills within the gifted range but also some academic skills below age level.

Academic performance

- strengths or expertise in at least one specific academic subject;
- very able at mathematics, but poor in language/arts or vice versa;
- difficulties with spelling or handwriting;
- speaking vocabulary exceeds written expression.

Learning style

- understand and discover patterns and connections between concepts;
- unusual and active imagination;
- highly creative;
- excel at tasks requiring abstract thinking, analysis and problem solving;
- deep commitment to and highly productive in activities outside of school;
- wide range of interests;
- difficulty with simple tasks, but competent at more sophisticated activities;
- sophisticated sense of humour.

Intellectual skills: auditory-sequential giftedness

- exceptional comprehension;
- superior memory and general knowledge;
- extensive vocabulary;
- good communication skills;
- grasp metaphors, satire and analogies.

Intellectual skills: visual-spatial giftedness

- keen visual memory;
- capable at puzzles and mazes;
- exceptional ability in geometry and science;
- difficulty with computation but capable of higher-level mathematical reasoning;
- can articulate the goal of tasks but cannot complete the sequence of steps needed for completion;
- ability to grasp broad concepts at once, rather than 'step by step';
- inattentive to verbal instruction;
- poor spelling;
- difficulty with phonics;
- difficulty with rote memorisation.

Emotional signs

- fragile self-esteem;
- feel academically inept;
- generalise minor academic failures to feelings of overall inadequacy;
- unrealistically high or low self-expectations;
- are confused about their abilities;
- report feeling different from others;
- strong anxiety or fear of failure in academic tasks;
- do not achieve well under pressure—e.g. on timed tasks;
- sensitive to criticism of their work, even constructive criticism;
- experience intense frustration;
- poor social skills with children and adults.

Behaviours

- disruptive in class;
- often off-task;
- disorganised, especially when unmotivated;
- impulsive and act out without thinking about the consequences;
- offer creative excuses to avoid difficult tasks;
- often aggressive;
- may be withdrawn.

Sources: Baum 1988; Baum & Owen 1988; Fall & Nolan 1993; Fetzer 2000; Gunderson et al. 1987; Kitano 1986; Rivera et al. 1995; Silverman 1989a; Sturgess 2004; Vespi & Yewchuk 1992; Yewchuk & Lupart 2000.

Central auditory processing disorder

Children who suffer recurrent ear infections (otitis media) in their first two years of life are often found later to have central auditory processing difficulties (Silverman 2003): they do not learn to pay attention to and process language because their fluctuating hearing impairment means that sometimes they cannot hear, even when they listen. Central auditory processing problems and hearing difficulties can be difficult to detect in gifted children because they will often compensate for their fluctuating hearing such that their language development will proceed as expected (Silverman 2003).

These children will often have accompanying deficits in sequential processing because the predictable sequence of language gives extensive practice at processing sequential information. Therefore, their learning style often resembles that of visual-spatial learners but with *deficits* in auditory-sequential processing, rather than merely a *preference* for holistic learning.

Sensory integration difficulties

The second most common disability—after language impairments—is sensory integration (SI) difficulties. Children with SI difficulties have problems filtering out irrelevant sensory information and making sense of relevant input. They literally have problems *integrating* the information that they are receiving through the seven senses of hearing, vision, touch, taste, smell, the vestibular (the balance mechanism in the inner ear), and the proprioceptive sense (which provides information from our joints about our body position). Some children over-react to stimuli and become alarmed or too alert; some under-react; and some do both at various times or across different sensory modalities.

Gifted children are often described in similar terms to those who over-react to sensory input. Specifically, some gifted children:

- are overly alert;
- are sensitive to their clothing: they require labels to be removed from their clothes, socks to be worn inside-out so that the seam does not irritate their toes; or dislike particular clothing textures;
- become overwhelmed readily, as if already besieged by the amount of information that they are having to deal with and so cannot cope with one more challenge;
- are overly sensitive to temperature or pain;
- are bothered by high levels of noise, movement and/or light;
- avoid certain tastes, textures or temperatures of foods, or eat only certain foods;
- avoid getting messy.

Given that sensory integration difficulties are common across the ability spectrum, they may be similarly prevalent in the gifted population. So it could be that those children who display the above features do so not because of their giftedness but because they also have accompanying sensory integration difficulties, particularly over-sensitivity. In that case, sensory integration therapy from a specialist occupational therapist will be useful, while in the preschool or school setting it will be necessary to help the children to settle their nervous systems, using rhythmical linear movement (as with swinging, or jumping forwards and backwards over a line, rope or on a trampoline); giving deep pressure massage; having the children perform heavy work activities such as wheeling a laden wheelbarrow or sweeping; placing a wheat bag on their laps during quiet activities; or using earplugs or headphones for those who over-react to auditory input (Neihart 2000; Soden 2002a, 2002b).

The autism spectrum disorders

The autism spectrum of disorders is characterised by severe language and social impairments in combination with sensory integration difficulties. Around 75 per cent of children with autism also have an intellectual disability (which is known as mental retardation in the United States), with 40 per cent recording IQs below 50 (Howard et al. 2001). Unlike most children with autism, those with Asperger syndrome acquire language at around the usual age, although as a result of their impaired social perceptiveness their language use can be pedantic or formal, and non-verbal behaviours such as eye contact can be disturbed (Mauk et al. 1997). Many have high levels of anxiety.

A rare few children with autism will be intellectually gifted. These children face a particular challenge in that, because of their disability, many will be educated in remedial programs alongside those with intellectual disabilities, while those with Asperger syndrome are likely to receive little educational support because of their relatively high levels of functioning (Neihart 2000). Those in regular classes are likely to be ostracised by their peers because of their rigid or hyperactive behaviour. If detachment from others is a feature of their disability, they might not feel this isolation, but those who are more socially aware could sense their disconnectedness very keenly (Cash 1999; Neihart 2000).

The attention deficit disorders

There are two main types of attention deficit disorders: ADHD, which comprises inattentiveness *and* hyperactivity (verbal and/or physical); and ADD, which involves inattentiveness only. The terms are relatively new labels for a condition that was first identified a hundred years ago and which has variously been described as hyperactivity, minimal brain dysfunction and hyperkinesis (Anastopoulos & Barkley 1992).

Sometimes, children's giftedness is mistaken for ADHD, because many gifted children *are* restless, imaginative but inattentive daydreamers with high levels of physical or verbal energy and are likely to be disruptive when under-stimulated (Davis & Rimm 2004; Mendaglio 1995a; Silverman 1998b; Webb & Latimer 1997). Yet the two conditions can be distinguished on the dimensions listed in Box 11.2.

One view of the attention deficit disorders is that, at heart, they entail impulsiveness—that is, poor self-regulatory mechanisms (Anastopoulos & Barkley 1992). This is an aspect of metacognitive functioning, at which gifted children typically excel. Therefore it seems impossible for children to have both conditions, as they are the opposite of each other. However, although some children's knowledge acquisition and information processing skills may be unimpaired (because deficits in these are probably incompatible with giftedness), their output or performance could be affected

Box 11.2 Distinctions between giftedness and ADHD

Giftedness	ADHD
Attention skills	
Able to focus.	Difficulty getting started on tasks because of inattention to instructions, forgetting instructions or disorganisation.
Can sustain attention when interested in a task.	Difficulty staying on task, with editing their efforts and completing tasks.
Prefer novel tasks with higher-order challenges, but can attend to routine tasks.	Cannot attend to routine tasks.
If visually gifted, will be inattentive to auditory input only.	Will be inattentive to most stimuli.
Will be off-task mainly when the activity is below their ability level.	Have difficulties concentrating in most settings (except computer games and TV).
In their drive to achieve, gifted children may be *unwilling* to postpone their agendas to focus on adult-directed activities.	May not be *able* to control their attention, even with adult guidance.
Academic performance	
Gifted children often *dislike* handwriting because their hands cannot move as quickly as their minds.	Likely to have accompanying learning disabilities, such as poor phonic awareness, visual-motor difficulties affecting their hand-writing, and problems with rote memory.
Produce consistently high performances when they like their teacher and are being challenged intellectually.	Performances vary in quality.
Seek cognitive and creative stimulation such as with daydreaming.	Seek sensory (especially visual) and physical stimulation.

Giftedness	ADHD
Activity levels	
Activity levels are focused and directed, although not always towards those activities selected by adults.	Activity levels are excessive, task-irrelevant and developmentally inappropriate pervasively across settings.
Love to talk or move.	Cannot stop moving or talking.
Relationships	
Have poor peer relationships if they lack intellectual peers.	Have poor peer relationships as a result of their high rates of verbal and physical aggression towards others.
In heterogeneous groups, gifted learners often prefer to work alone as that is more efficient for them.	Often prefer to work with others. However, they are often off-task and overly sociable, excitable and bossy as they have difficulty managing the social processes of group work.

Sources: Flint 2001; Leroux & Levitt-Perlman 2000; Yewchuk & Lupart 2000; Zentall et al. 2001.

(Kaufmann & Castellanos 2000): they might have difficulty organising their resources efficiently and consistently, with the result that their work output is below that of even averagely achieving classmates.

A second view of giftedness upholds that it requires a strong working memory—the ability to weigh up many pieces of data at once or, in colloquial terms, to 'keep many balls in the air' simultaneously. One view is that, while gifted children will have superior working memory capacity, it is possible for ADHD to disorganise their thinking, which in turn leads to the information processing and emotional regulation difficulties characteristic of ADHD (Zentall et al. 2001).

A third possibility is that some children are physically unwell, which in turn is affecting their brain functioning in ways that mimic ADHD. I have found three categories of such children. The first comprises those who have extended family members with obesity or mature-onset diabetes. These children have been shown to produce too much insulin, causing their blood sugar levels to drop too low for optimal brain function. MRI scans have shown that the area of the brain that starts to underperform when deprived of fuel is the prefrontal lobes, which are responsible for impulse control (Blum & Mercugliano 1997). This group of children could be characterised as carbohydrate addicts, and their symptoms of ADHD improve with a diet with equal proportions of proteins and carbohydrates at each meal. (Any modification to children's diet should, of course, be medically supervised.)

A second group is made up of those with a personal or family history of allergic conditions such as asthma, eczema or migraines. These children often have quite severe symptoms of ADHD and seem the most likely to experience food intolerances (Goldstein 1995). There are three classes of foods to which they can be sensitive: first, whole foods such as dairy products, eggs, wheat, corn, cereals and caffeine (in chocolate, coke, tea and coffee); second, artificial additives such as colourings, flavourings and preservatives; and third, naturally occurring chemicals such as sugars, salicylates, amines, MSG, sulphites, benzoates, nitrates and sorbates (Dengate 2004). Children with food sensitivities can often improve with naturopathic treatment and diets that eliminate their specific trigger foods (again, under medical supervision).

A third group of unwell children consists of those who have had a viral infection, particularly one of the herpes family of viruses, which includes herpes simplex (which causes cold sores), cytomegalovirus (which is related to viral meningitis), Epstein-Barr virus (which causes glandular fever) and chicken pox (which later leads to shingles). These viruses can remain dormant in the body but, although clinically inactive according to standard medical tests, nevertheless can affect both the immune and nervous systems, the latter causing a range of neurological symptoms including intellectual, emotional and behavioural problems. The children often have morbid thoughts, sad or angry emotional outbursts, and disruptive behaviours. This means that any children—gifted, average or otherwise—can show the signs of ADHD as a result of a physical illness. At this stage, orthodox medical treatments are seldom effective as the illness is subclinical, but I am finding some success with a naturopathic treatment known as bioresonance therapy, as it can both detect and treat reactions to foods, chemicals or viruses. Although evidence about such naturopathic treatments is scant, we cannot ask parents to do nothing while the evidence is amassing, as by then their children would be adults.

Thus it does indeed seem possible that children can have both giftedness and ADHD. Children with both conditions tend to be less mature emotionally than purely gifted children and to underachieve academically. In these cases, their ADHD symptoms are likely to be overlooked because their skills allow them to camouflage their difficulties (Kaufmann & Castellanos 2000). If their dual exceptionality is not recognised, their teachers can find them a frustrating group to teach because they seem so capable and yet appear to be intentionally unproductive. A focus on their talents and interests, however, along with specific instruction in how to structure their approach to tasks, can improve their attention skills and ability to persist in their weaker areas (Zentall et al. 2001).

Gifted underachievers

In essence, underachievement means that children are seen to be achieving academically below their abilities or 'potential', as indicated by their scores on the likes of IQ tests. A pattern of underachievement might show up in avoidance of school tasks, particularly rote learning; displaying poor organisational skills; and applying themselves inconsistently to school work; while displaying superior comprehension and retention, sophisticated abstract reasoning skills and active imagination when interested (Butler-Por 1993; Davis & Rimm 2004; Diaz 1998; Dowdall & Colangelo 1982; Fine & Pitts 1980; Hishinuma 1996; Hishinuma & Tadaki 1996; Moltzen 2004b; Whitmore 1980).

However, the concept of underachievement is beset with three problems: how to assess ability in the first place; how to judge performances; and how to establish that the two are discrepant enough to warrant concern (Peters et al. 2000).

Taking each in turn, there is no sure way to assess potential. Errors of measurement in test scores might inflate our expectations of students; low test ceilings mean that children's achievements could be declining, but this is not noticed because their scores are still at the top of the scale; low achievement on tests by children from minority cultures could mean that their potential is underestimated so their underachievement is overlooked (Reis & McCoach 2000). Furthermore, the notion of a discrepancy between IQ and academic performance overlooks the fact that not everyone who is intellectually gifted will also be academically gifted, as there are more ways to be intelligent than in reading, writing and maths.

The second issue is that a diagnosis of underachievement is subjective: it is in the eye of the beholder (Schultz 2002a). Teachers are likely to perceive nonconformist behaviour more negatively when displayed by a gifted learner than if it were displayed by a less able student, and consequently award gifted children lower grades, resulting in an apparent discrepancy between their grades and their scores on standardised tests (Kolb & Jussim 1994). Some will thus have been mislabelled as underachievers, while others will then conform to their teachers' low expectations of them and indeed underachieve (Kolb & Jussim 1994). Still others will appear to be underachieving in school when they have undiagnosed learning difficulties. The pattern of behaviours listed in Box 11.1—including disruptiveness in school—is common to both. Detailed assessment is therefore essential so that children's learning difficulties are not overlooked.

Third, there is no way to quantify how large the discrepancy between ability and performance must be to cause concern, or for how long the pattern must persist (Peters et al. 2000; Reis & McCoach 2000). Particularly when the comparison is IQ scores, if students have been inattentive in school for some years, that will lower both their school grades and their test scores in the present so discrepancies might be apparent only in comparison to earlier test results.

As to the commonly cited causes of underachievement, it is clear that ability does not automatically imply high achievement, as many factors contribute to under-performance at school (Baker et al. 1998; Baum et al. 1994, 1995; Butler-Por 1993; Diaz 1998; Dowdall & Colangelo 1982; Hébert 2001; Martin 2002; Moltzen 2004b; Peters et al. 2000; Reis & McCoach 2000; Rimm 2003a; Siegle & McCoach 2002). The first class of these is *personal* factors, which include: children's emotional difficulties such as anxiety and low self-esteem; a fear of failure leading to avoidance of risk and procrastination; dysfunctional perfectionism; confused or unrealistic aspirations; an external locus of control; poor organisation; and inability to employ unstructured time wisely. Even these factors are not universally endorsed as contributing to underachievement, however: some studies have found underachievers' internal locus of control and self-esteem to be equal to those of other gifted students (Davis & Connell 1985; McCoach & Siegle 2003).

Second, *family* factors have been implicated in underachievement, including family disorganisation; parents' mixed messages about the value of achievement; lack of respect for school; excessive pressures to excel—especially in comparison with highly achieving siblings; and lack of emotional support for the children.

Third, *school* factors that discourage students' effort include their lack of trust in their academic environment; poor relationships with teachers; lack of success at school; an emphasis on conformity rather than creativity; and finding school meaningless (Siegle & McCoach 2002). Unstimulating curricula can allow students to be successful without effort or perseverance, causing them to find it difficult to apply themselves when challenged. Undiagnosed learning difficulties have also been cited, as have mismatches between teaching methods and students' preferred learning styles, and rigid teaching practices that do not accommodate students' individuality (Rimm 2003a).

Next, *social* factors such as peer group pressure are often held responsible. Although peer groups are diverse, in general peers support high but not outstanding achievement (Brown & Steinberg 1990). On the other hand, pressure to be as successful as highly achieving peers can be equally destructive (Hébert 2001).

Finally, *environmental* factors such as poverty and after-hours employment affect students' ability to apply themselves at school. Social pressures on minority cultural members and girls in particular can lower their achievement level (Peters et al. 2000).

Hébert (2001) discovered that these factors interact, whereby a low-quality academic curriculum and poor relationships with teachers lead to apathy which, in turn, causes young people to succumb to negative environmental and family influences. It must also be emphasised that the direction of causality has not been proven: for example, family dysfunction appears to result from, rather than cause, underachievement, while students might select unsuccessful peers so they can underachieve with impunity, rather than the peers instigating the underachievement (Reis & McCoach 2000).

In highlighting personal and family causes, the above list reflects an orthodox view of underachievement, based on a notion that underachievers are defective and need repair (Schultz 2002a). This view is particularly problematic during the early years, when children surely cannot be held to account for failing to 'meet their potential' or for not applying themselves adequately to their 'work'. Although it might appear that young children are 'wasting their time' with activities they have already mastered, it is important to remember that learning occurs in spurts and plateaus, with periods of consolidation essential before children can acquire new knowledge or skills. (Naturally, for gifted learners, this consolidation phase might be briefer than for average learners.) Young children need a broad base of competence before they can make the leap to the next level of skill: the pyramid with its wide base is a more stable structure than the skyscraper with its narrow foundation.

The view of underachievement as deviance also represents a misunderstanding of motivation by framing it as a facet of individuals' personalities while ignoring the context in which they are being asked to work and the tasks to which they are expected to apply themselves. I agree with Bill Glasser (1998), who says that all individuals are motivated—to meet their needs (which were described in Part II of this book). If they are not motivated to do school work, this is simply because it is not meeting their needs. In that case, the solution is to frame a curriculum that *will* satisfy the children's needs.

Third, underachievement is not the same as being non-productive (Freeman 1995a). Some children do not perform scholastically, but instead channel their energies into extracurricular activities or areas of special interest, where their productivity is both excellent and personally rewarding (Richert 1991, in Piirto 1999; Whitmore 1986). These selective learners tend to be self-confident people who realise that there is more to life than intellectual pursuits, so balance their academic striving with other demands and interests. If they feel personally fulfilled by their choices, others should not criticise them for failing to reach the expected heights of academic output (Delisle 1994b). This is really a conflict in values about what is worth learning, and it is debatable whether adults have the right to impose their values on young people (Reis & McCoach 2000).

On the other hand, underachievement can be imposed on even the very young by an intellectually unstimulating program. The early years of education are, self-evidently, children's first introduction to schooling—so it is crucial that, in these early years, children's programs are responsive to who they are and how they learn, and thereby communicate that they are accepted as gifted learners. Adequate intellectual challenge, with active selection of and engagement in topics of interest, and a supportive climate will avoid involuntary underachievement being imposed by an unchallenging curriculum (Reis & McCoach 2000; Schultz 2002b).

In her study of exceptionally gifted children, Gross (2004) details a range of behaviours and emotions that can signal when children are deeply frustrated with their schooling. These include tantrums, aggression, a loss of enthusiasm for learning, a sullenness that mimics depression, hopelessness, disdain towards adults, and myriad psychosomatic illnesses. Perhaps such signs differentiate voluntary non-producers from children on whom under-achievement is being imposed.

Applying the 'underachieving' label in these circumstances is unfortunate because it focuses blame on 'troublesome' gifted children and burdens them with the sole responsibility of reversing their 'academic neglect' (Delisle 1994b). It is hurtful and disrespectful, kicking children when they are down and when they are already well aware that their performances are disappointing the important people in their lives. And it distracts us from the realisation that their underachievement is being imposed on them and that we need to adjust their educational program so that it respects and reflects their skills and motivates engagement by offering meaningful challenge (Delisle 1994a, 1994b; Moltzen 1996b; Seeley 1993).

Programming for gifted children with learning difficulties

Educational programs for children with learning difficulties must focus on their gifts as well as their processing deficits, as this will help them to believe in themselves (Baum et al. 1989; Ellston 1993; Wingenbach 1998). Children receiving only remedial programs have lower self-esteem than those whose programs also focus on their strengths (Fetzer 2000; Nielsen & Mortorff-Albert 1989). Meanwhile, they are more likely to put in effort in their weaker domains when their strengths are being addressed (Weinfeld et al. 2002).

Collaboration

The most important feature of programs for children with dual exceptionalities is collaboration between teachers, specialists, parents and (probably beyond the early childhood years) the children themselves. Parents in particular can be a valuable resource as, when their child's disability has been recognised for some time, many will already be familiar with individual education plans and feel comfortable about making active contributions to their child's education. On the other hand, many parents will be confused by the puzzling array of their child's skills and may need guidance from educators to understand and support their child (Fall & Nolan 1993).

Emotional needs

The emotional needs of children with dual exceptionalities must be met before any improvement in their performances can be achieved (Dole 2000). This means that they will need support in the following ways (Butler-

Por 1993; Clasen & Clasen 1995; Ellston 1993; Fall & Nolan 1993; Hishinuma 1993; Kitano 1986; Montgomery 1996; Swesson 1994; Vespi & Yewchuk 1992; Whitmore 1981; Whitmore & Maker 1985).

- Develop a warm relationship with underfunctioning children so that they know that you are interested in them as individuals, not just for what they can achieve.
- Help children to recognise that they are gifted and to understand its implications for them. They will need to accept both their talents and their weaknesses—that is, to develop some comfort with a realistic self-concept.
- Guide the children to have realistic expectations for themselves. A cooperative rather than competitive setting will encourage these children not to shun any task where they will not be perfect.
- Give them experience of genuine success at meaningful tasks, so that their opinion of their abilities improves.
- Encourage them to be independent in age-appropriate ways.
- Assist them to find ways to express their frustration and confusion appropriately.
- Guide them to act less impulsively when under stress.
- Teach the children to value learning by displaying your passion for knowledge, communicating your own interest in their efforts, and making learning a pleasure by incorporating their interests.

Social skills

As is the case for all gifted children, developing accepting relationships with other children who value achievement is crucial. Some children will need help to reflect on their social behaviour and its effects on the other children's willingness to play with them, while others may need help in negotiating social situations, as they might blame other children for their feelings of isolation or react aggressively to feeling out of place socially (Kitano 1986).

Academic assessment

The existence of gifted children with disabilities reinforces the message emphasised in Chapter 8 that we must assess comprehensively, across time and settings and using a range of measures including parental reports and prolonged observation (Karnes 1979). Any tests that are part of this process should be conducted by child specialists who have experience in both disabilities *and* giftedness so that they can recognise the separate influences of both on children's performances (Yewchuk & Lupart 2000).

The aims of assessment are to identify the appropriate *level* of learning for each child so that the program can provide appropriate levels of challenge while minimising stress, and to identify children's preferred learning style so you can employ that teaching style as much as possible. Kokot

(2003) also advises that educators look out for which type of stimuli distract individual children, which tasks demand most energy and so fatigue the children most quickly (e.g. handwriting), and what environmental changes improve their learning.

Curriculum differentiation

The program for gifted children with learning difficulties should provide *complexity* and *challenge* to nurture their strengths and maintain the rigor and high standards appropriate for gifted learners, with organisational *structure* and *support* to help the children circumvent their learning difficulties (Kaufmann & Castellanos 2000; Weinfeld et al. 2002). Specifically, these children will need the following educational measures, individually tailored to their particular combination of strengths and difficulties (Baum 1984, 1988, 1989; Baum & Owen 1988; Baum et al. 1989, 1994, 1995; Brody & Mills 1997; Butler-Por 1993; Clements et al. 1994; Davis & Rimm 2004; Dix & Schafer 1996; Dole 2000; Fetzer 2000; Fox 1984; Heacox 1991; Hishinuma 1993; Miller 1991; Montgomery 1996; Patrick 1990; Rimm 1986, 1987; Silverman 1989a, 2003; Sturgess 2004; Toll 1993; Wees 1993; Weinfeld et al. 2002; Whitmore 1981, 1986; Whitmore & Maker 1985; Wingenbach 1998; Yewchuk & Lupart 2000).

School climate

- Provide a nurturing environment that not only recognises but also honours diversity and individual differences (Bernal 1989).
- Model high achievement but do not pressure children to perform (Freeman 1993).
- Encourage children to take safe intellectual risks and to learn that neither failure nor success is a threat.
- Empower students to advocate for the adjustments they need in order to be successful academically.

Teacher variables

As a result of their history of failure, children with dual exceptionalities will be in particular need of warm and accepting relationships with teachers who encourage creativity and tolerate nonconformity. Training in the combination of giftedness and learning disabilities can help teachers establish appropriate (not too high and not too low) expectations of these children's performances.

Curricular content

When children have fallen behind others academically, curricular enrichment measures may fail to meet their needs unless they are also given remedial help to expand their knowledge and develop learning strategies (Borland & Wright 1994). Single-subject acceleration might be appropriate in some cases, but is unlikely to be effective if, for example, the children have reading difficulties which impair their access to the advanced curriculum.

- Tap into children's interests. Using these as a vehicle for teaching allows children to learn in their preferred style, produce in their favourite mode, and concentrate on their areas of strength. This is fundamental to motivating them to learn, particularly as they will have experienced so much previous failure (Baum et al. 1994, 1995; Clements et al. 1994).
- Teach learning skills such as perseverance, organisation, research skills, goal setting, critical thinking, problem solving, memory strategies and note taking. Such strategies can assist children to achieve in their weak domain.

Teaching and learning processes

To maximise engagement, goal setting, self-direction and problem solving, the curriculum needs to be inquiry-based with a focus on abstract thinking (Weinfeld et al. 2002).

- Give children choices about and control over their own learning.
- Particularly for visual learners, keep instructions brief and concise, and write as well as speak them. Use diagrams and expect to have to repeat instructions more often than usual.
- Explain the rationale for a task—that is, explain what the students will learn from engaging in the activity. If they can see the bigger picture, they will often see the point of focusing on one aspect of it.
- Allow children to observe others before having to attempt new tasks.
- To ground their abstract understanding in reality, provide hands-on and visual experiences and minimise rote and repetitious learning.
- Use assistive technologies that allow students to circumvent their specific learning difficulties. Calculators, computers, graphic organisers and visual charts can all help the children to become self-sufficient in their learning. While all children with disabilities benefit from such technological assistance, it helps gifted children in particular by allowing them to move ahead at a pace their giftedness demands.
- Remember that gifted children often learn concepts while neglecting the details; while not allowing them to avoid necessary detail, give them opportunities to explore global concepts as well (Roeper 1995a).
- Recommend some outside activities, where the children can exercise their talents in a safe setting. Passion for and commitment to hobbies translates into improved self-esteem and performance at school.

Products

- Allow the children to complete projects that call on their creative abilities and to present products in a medium (e.g. orally or with photographs) that avoids their problems with written expression. Alternatives might include using computers, scribes or tape recorders to circumvent handwriting and spelling difficulties.
- Ensure that they have sufficient time to generate these products, as accuracy is more important than speed.

Conclusion

Gifted children with learning difficulties are not easy to identify, as their disabilities can obscure their gifts and their gifts can compensate for and thus hide their disabilities. However, awareness of the possibility of dual exceptionalities increases the chances that these children will be recognised.

A promising finding is that children whose gifts and disabilities are recognised and addressed in early childhood maintain their improved talents over time (Johnson et al. 1997). Baum and colleagues (1994, 1995) use the metaphor of a prism: when light enters the prism, it is split into beautiful colours and progresses in a new direction. Likewise, when children with dual exceptionalities are presented with a program that meets their emotional, social and educational needs, their performances both change direction and take on a new quality.

Suggested further reading

Baum, S., Owen, S.V. and Dixon, J. 1991 *To be gifted and learning disabled: from identification to practical intervention strategies* Hawker Brownlow Education, Melbourne.

Davis, G.A. and Rimm, S.B. 2004 *Education of the gifted and talented* 5th edn, Allyn & Bacon, Boston, MA.

Chapter 7 ('Helping the underfunctioning able') of the following text provides a useful overview:
Montgomery, D. 1996 *Educating the able* Cassell, London.

Websites

Virtual School for the Gifted: www.vsg.edu.au
Linda Silverman's site, which discusses visual-spatial learners, among other topics, is: www.gifteddevelopment.com

For information on food intolerances: www.fedupwithfoodadditives.info
For information about bioresonance treatment: www.regumed.de

FORMULATING A
POLICY ABOUT
GIFTED LEARNERS

twelve

Provision for talented children [has] to be entrenched at the school level so that if an individual teacher transfer[s], the program [can] still continue. (Forster 2002: 82)

Introduction

In general, policies describe what services you will offer and how you will deliver these. Your centre will have many policies governing its operations; the purpose of this chapter is to describe what a policy for advanced—that is, gifted—learners could comprise.

The first step of developing a policy for meeting the needs of advanced learners is to acknowledge that gifted children do exist in every location, and that some of these will have needs that are not being met within the regular program. This signals that there will be a need for gifted provisions and hence for a policy to guide these.

Benefits of formal policies

Written policies have many benefits for educators, parents and children. First among these is that policies help to heighten awareness of specific issues—in this case, the needs of children with advanced development—and to signal the commitment of staff to attending to these needs (Freeman 1995c). Other advantages include the following (Farmer 1995; Stonehouse 1991).

- Policies offer children, staff and parents safeguards and clear expectations of their roles, rights and responsibilities.
- Policy development allows staff to plan how to act rather than having to make hasty decisions in response to a problem that has already arisen.
- The procedures laid out in a policy document can guide action when a difference of opinion occurs among or between staff, families and management.
- Written guidelines help to ensure that decisions about practice are consistent across time and fair to all stakeholders.
- Written documentation helps with familiarising new staff and parents with the philosophy and workings of the program.
- Written policies assist in evaluation and accountability.

By far the most important advantage, however, comes not from the existence of a policy document, but from the process of formulating it. This process gives staff and parents the opportunity to clarify their views and priorities and to do so collaboratively (Stonehouse 1991). This means that you simply cannot import the policy of another centre or school, as it is the process of clarifying your assumptions and goals that makes a policy powerful, while imported policies may be irrelevant to your particular setting.

Components of a policy

Your policy could comprise: a description of your mandate; a definition of giftedness; your philosophy; your mission or goals; a theoretical rationale that will guide practices; and a set of procedures for meeting the needs of gifted learners, including a method for evaluating the effects of your program.

Mandate

The purpose of gifted provisions or programs is to meet the needs of children who are presently not being catered for by the regular program. Any policy for achieving this will need to be framed within the guidelines imposed by any federal or state legislation or the policy of your governing body concerning both gifted education and the wider curriculum.

Definition

You will need to begin by proffering a definition of advanced learners, as that will be the basis for your decisions about identification and programming (Delisle & Lewis 2003). Your definition will need to draw attention to the fact that not all gifted learners will be high achievers: slow-to-warm-up children and those with educationally disadvantaging circumstances or dual exceptionalities are just a few of those whose giftedness can be disguised.

Your definition will need to take a stand on whether you seek to include only a few exceptional children within your definition (a conservative definition) or to encompass a larger proportion of children (a liberal stance) — see Chapter 2. If you believe that children can be gifted in any developmental domain, you will need to examine whether all of these are the core business of education and so should all be fostered, or whether you consider that your main task is to focus on intellectual giftedness (Borland 1989).

Philosophy

Your philosophy section will detail *why* a focus on gifted learners is necessary, and in which ways gifted provisions would be consistent with your mandate (Borland 1989). It could, for example, comprise a simple statement about your respect for all children and their diversity. It will also need to describe whether your efforts are guided by a national resources rationale; a goal of helping children to reach their potential; or a special education model of responding to children's additional needs — see Chapter 7.

Mission (goals)

This section details your purpose in providing for gifted children — that is, your educational goals for them. These will need to be clearly written and feasible and should incorporate both educational and social-emotional goals (Carter & Hamilton 1985). You will also need to discriminate outcomes, which detail what children will be able to do, from process goals such as the provision of inservice training, which is a means to an end rather than an end in itself (Borland 1989). At young ages, improved academic achievement is unlikely to be a central goal; instead, you might aim to enhance the children's engagement, employment of thinking and emotional dispositions and satisfaction with peer relationships — as it is these aspects that are most impaired by unchallenging programs.

Your goal statement must specify what benefits the gifted children will gain that are not relevant for all learners, and what the gifted provisions will achieve that a regular program could not (Borland 2003). The goals must be measurable, so vague language such as 'striving for excellence' is to be avoided, as it communicates nothing to parents and does not imply day-to-day practices for educators.

Theory

Your theoretical base will need to be comprehensive — that is, it should help you to understand gifted children's needs and give you a sound body of information about appropriate curricular measures to cater for these. When selecting a guiding theory, you will need to consider whether its assumptions and practices are effective, ethical and consistent with your views about regular education and pedagogy.

Practices

Forster (2002) reports that it is not safe to assume that awareness of giftedness alone will result in action. So the practices section of your policy document will describe which procedures are to be used by whom in order to achieve your goals. This will incorporate descriptions of your assessment methods and which forms of grouping, acceleration and enrichment you might use.

Your specific curriculum differentiation measures will need to be described here as well. These must be clearly articulated and represent a planned and integrated approach to the curriculum, rather than just offering busy or trivial activities to keep advanced children out of trouble. The measures chosen must be aimed at providing appropriate challenge for advanced learners in a range of domains.

As you detail your intended practices, you will need to ensure that these are consistent with your mandate, philosophy, mission and theory. Espoused practices cannot merely be a wish list but must be feasible in terms of the skills needed by staff, the resource and time commitment required of staff and parents, and manageable within the constraints imposed by your context.

Methods for ensuring continuity of commitment to gifted provisions will also need to be considered. One approach could be to appoint one staff member to be responsible for overseeing this aspect of your program.

Professional development for staff

Your policy will need to detail specific procedures for supporting staff, such as provision of a staff resource library and giving access to professional training in giftedness.

Partnership with parents

Given the pervasive myth that 'all parents think their child is gifted', it could be important for parents' self-confidence to include a statement about your desire to work in partnership with them in meeting their child's exceptional needs, and your faith in their ability to support their gifted child.

Referral to consultants

Clear and uncomplicated procedures for gaining access to advisers is crucial for both staff and parents. So it would be useful to include in your policy a statement about how staff and parents can use consultants, to whom to refer children and families, and in which circumstances children might be referred.

Special issues

In describing your practices you might want to cover methods of identifying advanced development in non-traditional domains or in children who are experiencing poverty or other disadvantaging circumstances. You might mention other 'high-risk' groups such as gifted girls and boys separately, as well as some methods for preventing children's underachievement and for catering for children with learning difficulties that accompany their gifted-ness.

Finally, you might want to describe how you plan to advocate for the needs of gifted children in their next educational setting and how to execute the transition to school, especially in cases of early entry.

Evaluation

In order to make improvements in your provisions for gifted children, you will need an ongoing review of your measures. So the final section of your policy document will need to detail when and how such an evaluation will be conducted, and who will be responsible.

Evaluation necessarily involves a judgment, but one that examines the educational merit of the program rather than its political worth as a selling feature. It can also describe the strengths and weakness of programs, detailing to what extent goals are being achieved and negative collateral outcomes are being avoided (Borland 2003).

Given that programs for gifted children must fit their unique context and that, therefore, your goals will be individually tailored for your setting, your evaluation will be specific to your centre (Carter & Hamilton 1985). Four aspects can be examined: resources (inputs), processes, outcomes and the format of your evaluation report (Davis & Rimm 2004; Reid 2004).

In terms of *resources*, the key question to consider is whether your gifted provisions make efficient and ethical use of the time of staff, parents and children and of the available funding. You will also need to consider whether staff have sufficient resources, such as a library and access to consultants, and adequate facilities for delivering the provisions as originally planned.

Evaluation of *processes* spans assessment methods, teacher training, teaching methods and parent involvement. A key question will be whether these activities are being enacted as originally conceived. Are they being offered regularly? Are some being overlooked?

When considering *outcome* measures, there are two aspects: the effects of the program on the target children, and the effects on other stakeholders. Taking each in turn, you will need to detail how you will judge whether the outcomes are congruent with what you set out to accomplish—that is, your original goals.

Given that the children are young, much of your assessment of outcomes will be based on your own observations of their learning of significant content, skills and dispositions, and on their parents' feedback. The most basic test of the success of your provisions will be the contentment and physical and social engagement of the children (Bryant 1987; Montessori, in Delisle & Lewis 2003).

Part of your assessment of outcomes will be whether there are children for whom the program is more or less successful than others—for example, you might want to take special note of the effects of the program on gifted children from minority cultures. A second aspect is whether there are other, important, unanticipated outcomes for gifted children and others. It is not enough that the program does what it sets out to do if, in so doing, it harms others—for example, by leading to neglect of children with learning difficulties or creating resentment in the parents of children not targeted by your gifted provisions.

Finally, planning for the evaluation of your program needs to consider how and to whom evaluation information will be reported. The formality of your evaluation report will depend on its audience: parents, teaching staff, school board or your funding body (such as state or federal governments). Each of these stakeholders will need differing levels of detail, with parents wanting information only about outcomes for their individual child but all others requiring an evaluation of inputs, processes and outcomes for all the target children (Davis & Rimm 2004).

Although evaluation might seem burdensome, it can be professionally fulfilling to be able to demonstrate to yourself—if to no one else—that what you are doing is effective. Reflecting on your practice can only enhance your confidence in what you do, which in turn will empower you to advocate for gifted children. And, as Borland (2003) states, trying to improve a program that has not been evaluated is even more daunting: it is difficult to reach a target if you do not know where it is.

Conclusion

Although formulating policy is time-consuming, the process gives all participants the opportunity to clarify their values and to become clear about day-to-day practice. It can be an educational process for all those involved in framing a policy, and can ensure that actions based on it receive wide-based support.

Suggested further reading

For an overview of the policies in use in Australia, I recommend:
Wilson, P. 1996 *Challenges and changes in policy and thinking in gifted education in Australia* Hawker Brownlow Education, Melbourne.

For information on gifted education policies in New Zealand:
McAlpine, D. and Moltzen, R. (eds) 2004 *Gifted and talented: New Zealand perspectives* 2nd edn, Kanuka Grove Press, Palmerston North.

For an international perspective, you could consult:
Heller, K.A., Mönks, F.J., Sternberg, R.J. and Subotnik, R.F. (eds) 2000 *International handbook of giftedness and talent* 2nd edn, Elsevier, Oxford.

For detail on framing a gifted policy:
Borland, J.H. 1989 *Planning and implementing programs for the gifted* Teachers College Press, New York.
Delisle, J. and Lewis, B.A. 2003 *The survival guide for teachers of gifted kids* Free Spirit, Minneapolis.

PARENTING GIFTED CHILDREN
thirteen

When we are willing to explore the social and emotional needs of the gifted from their viewpoint, we are most effective in leading them to thrive and survive the challenges that accompany high potential. (Galbraith 1985: 18, in Kunkel et al. 1992: 10)

Introduction

As a parent, the information that your child is gifted can be a good news–bad news split: the good news is that your child is gifted . . . the bad news is that your child is gifted. Although there is a common misconception that all parents want their child to be gifted, it can be a mixed blessing. This is because uncertainty and questions immediately follow, such as: What does this mean for our child? What does it mean for us, both personally (as adults who were probably gifted children ourselves) and as parents? What about our child's siblings? What do we do now? These questions relate to the impact both on you personally and as a parent, and can be most confronting during the early childhood years when you are first learning how to parent (particularly a first or only child) and first coming to grips with your child's additional needs.

Personal implications for parents

Your responses to your child's giftedness will depend, in part, on your values about giftedness, your experiences of how giftedness was handled in your family of origin, what you have believed about your own abilities throughout your life and your own schooling history (Solow 2001).

Values about giftedness

Your own values will affect how you respond to your child's abilities. You might be tempted to discount your children's talents in intellectual fields, preferring that they develop emotional skills, relationship or 'people' skills, or well-rounded abilities rather than excelling in one domain. Or you might want your children to fit in with the majority rather than being seen to be 'elitist'. While these are valid goals, it is a mistake to regard them as incompatible with fostering intellectual giftedness.

Giftedness in your family of origin

Over and over again I have spoken with parents who are deeply concerned for their gifted child's welfare on the grounds that a gifted uncle, sister or brother fared badly in school or later life. Emotional problems that could have had any number of causes have been attributed by family folklore to that family member's giftedness. This often leads parents to want to minimise their child's skills. Some will use statements such as: 'It's all very well to be clever, but you have to have common sense' or the modern equivalent: 'Emotional intelligence is more important than intellectual intelligence'. Both comments demean the children's abilities and imply that these are incompatible with real-world skills, when in fact emotional and intellectual abilities go hand in hand. And denying your child's talent could, paradoxically, be the same strategy used in your family of origin—which may have contributed to the difficulties of the now-troubled relative.

Your own family history can provoke other issues that can unconsciously be imposed on the next generation of gifted children. Giftedness could have led to favouritism of a sibling by your own parents, or your own abilities might have been overlooked, leading naturally to resentment of the whole concept of giftedness. You might see your gifted parents or yourself as having underachieved in life and are determined not to let that happen to your own child. This can lead to the syndrome of helicopter parents, who hover over their children's every action, trying to ensure that it reflects their true abilities. This over-involvement can itself create the very problems you were trying to prevent.

Beliefs about your own abilities

The diagnosis of giftedness in your child is likely to lead to some soul searching about yourself. It probably means that you are gifted too, as giftedness needs facilitating genes. This spectre often provokes some profound reactions in parents.

The first reaction is denial: some parents insist that, despite their child's exceptional skills, they are not gifted themselves. A few may be right about this, but the odds are against it. If you believe that you are not gifted, it can cause you to doubt whether you can supply what your child needs. In fact, you could be guided (but not dictated to) by information about giftedness and your knowledge about what might have been useful for you. You can, indeed, trust your own instincts about your child.

For others, identification of their child's giftedness forces them to come to terms with their own. I have found that the parents of children with both gifts and learning disabilities have the most profound reaction. Because both conditions run in families, the fathers in particular are likely also to have had dual exceptionalities but, if they received any help at all at school, it was special education. They came out of school thinking of themselves as disabled, not gifted. When confronted with the realisation that their pattern of skills closely matches their child's, they often feel sad and angry at the loss of self-esteem they have endured as a result of their deficits having been highlighted and their giftedness going unnoticed.

Some have always been aware that they were different and had no explanation—other than that there was something wrong with them, rather than that they were highly able. There can be a grieving process for the sad and confused child they once were, with regret that they did not know that giftedness was behind these feelings.

Meanwhile, if you have been aware for most of your life that you were a gifted child, you might be especially sensitive to the challenges that might lie ahead for your own gifted child, particularly if your schooling was traumatic.

Your schooling history

Discussion about your child's atypical educational needs may also force you to come to terms with your own unsatisfactory education: if your experience was negative, it could generate extra fears for your child—some of which may not be warranted, given that your experiences occurred a generation ago and may no longer be relevant (Damiani 1997).

Parenting issues

As described in previous chapters, gifted children can be 'high maintenance' people. Their atypical needs mean that they do not slot neatly into the education system; their asynchronous (uneven) development means that they function at various levels across domains and time; and their nonconformity challenges parental authority. And, whereas parents of children with disabilities often receive some empathy and support from other parents, the concerns of parents of gifted children are often ignored, so you find yourself isolated from others.

Your parenting role

My belief about our role as parents is not to impose our own ambitions on our children, but to help them become who they need to be in life. Our job is to help them discover and then fulfil their personal mission. As the poet Kahlil Gibran states, we can strive to be like our children but cannot compel them to be like us, and we can give them our love but cannot impose our thoughts on them, as their strong moral development means that they will need to establish their own codes for living.

Effects of labelling

As I see it, the main disadvantage of labelling children as gifted is that the term itself implies that the children are so extraordinary that some parents feel that they must do something equally extraordinary to ensure that their child's 'potential' is not wasted (Colangelo & Brower 1987; Fisher 1981; Hackney 1981). This pressure can mean that the family becomes organised around the gifted child's 'specialness', to the detriment of other aspects of family functioning (Colangelo 2003; Hackney 1981).

Some researchers have argued that labelling children as gifted causes them to be less well adjusted, less socially accepted by classmates and more anxious about meeting high expectations (Cornell 1989; Freeman 2000). Clearly, imposing inflated expectations on children in response to the 'gifted' label will be unhealthy for them. However, usually children are assessed and subsequently labelled in response to parents' prior concerns about some aspect of their emotional, social or academic adjustment. So it is these prior difficulties, not the label itself, which give rise to later adjustment problems.

Given that children are already aware that they are different, and are likely to explain this in terms either that there is something wrong with them or with everyone else, it seems beneficial to explain the real reason for their differences, even if this entails a label. This was confirmed in a study of adolescents in which three-quarters of the participants had been well aware that they were different and identification or labelling merely confirmed that (Manaster et al. 1994). Few had to struggle with coming to terms with their own giftedness as a result of being labelled, as the label merely explained and confirmed their experience. And, if labelling results in educational provisions that meet their needs, its effects are positive (Hershey & Oliver 1988; Ring & Shaughnessy 1993).

Gifted children's emotional adjustment

Most parents just want their children to be happy. There is no reason to think this is less likely for the gifted—and, indeed, the research reported in Part II suggests that, on the whole, gifted individuals are well adjusted. I often describe that children's emotional maturity falls between their actual and mental age, but nearer the latter. Their intellectual skills do not pull their emotional maturity all the way up to their mental age, as they simply have not been alive long enough to have sufficient life experience, but it still exceeds their chronological age, as illustrated in Figure 13.1.

Specific concerns such as perfectionism can be dealt with by keeping children's self-esteem intact with informative feedback (see Chapter 4), and

Figure 13.1 Emotional maturity of gifted children

by demonstrating a tolerant attitude to your own mistakes: children believe what you do about your imperfections, rather than what you say about theirs.

A second key is to teach children an internal locus of control and to attribute outcomes to their own actions rather than to factors that are outside their control. This was discussed in Chapter 6.

Third, teach children to delay gratification. It is the ability to put in effort now for some longer-term gain that distinguishes successful from unsuccessful individuals of equal ability (Goleman 1994).

If your child is having emotional difficulties, do not be too quick to dismiss these as if they were an inevitable result of being gifted. It is more likely that the child is reacting to life's normal challenges, such as family upsets or bullying at school. If you believe that your children's emotional difficulties are being caused by their giftedness, you might think that there is nothing you can do to help, with the result that they remain troubled (Freeman 1991, 1994, 1997).

Sibling adjustment

The identification of one of your children as gifted raises three issues for your parenting: how to support siblings with average skill levels; how to ensure that differently gifted children are not overlooked; and how to manage a family of individuals, each of whom may be gifted in different ways.

First, with regard to the effect of the gifted label on the other siblings' feelings about themselves, some studies show that the siblings who are not identified as gifted can experience low self-esteem, poor emotional adjustment, heightened anxiety and increased competitiveness as a result of having a brother or sister who has been labelled as gifted. Younger siblings of a gifted child might resent having such a hard act to follow (Grenier 1985), while older siblings can be embarrassed that a younger gifted brother or sister is surpassing them (Keirouz 1990). Even so, Silverman (1997) points out that only 20 per cent of siblings evidence adjustment difficulties, and that in many cases these are due to the failure to identify them as gifted. Meanwhile, an age gap in excess of three years between siblings can reduce tensions between them, although this is not something you can adjust after the fact.

In terms of sibling relationships, some studies have found that siblings of average development express more positive feelings about family relationships than do the gifted children themselves (Chamrad et al. 1995; Colangelo & Brower 1987; Keirouz 1990). Ultimately, how you treat the children strongly influences how they feel about themselves and each other, so the following measures can be useful (Chamrad et al. 1995; Cornell & Grossberg 1986; Davis & Rimm 2004; Grenier 1985; Keirouz 1990).

- Be honest about differences in siblings' abilities, as the children will already have noticed.
- Do not favour—or allow relatives and friends to give preferential treatment to—the gifted child.
- On the other hand, if a gifted child requires more resources, it is not equitable to deny them these on the grounds that the other children do not require them also: fairness lies in meeting the specific needs of each child.
- Do not allow a verbally precocious child to taunt, boss around or manipulate you or his or her siblings.
- Encourage siblings to develop different interests from one another so they are not directly competing with each other.
- Do not draw comparisons between the grades or performances of your children, as this will heighten competition between them.
- Do not try to placate those with average skills that they have 'common sense' or are good people, as this unwittingly tells the gifted child that he or she does not have these qualities, which is a put-down.

Grade skipping can pose a challenge for siblings. It can be particularly awkward when one child of twins is judged to need acceleration, when a younger sibling would enter an older sibling's class if grade skipped, or when only one of two equally able siblings needs grade skipping because although one's needs are being met, those of the other are not. With delicate handling, however, each of these situations can usually be explained so that one child is not penalised by a sibling's sensibilities.

This leads to the second issue between siblings: how to ensure that we do not overlook a child whose giftedness differs from a sibling's. Verbally gifted children might call attention to themselves, and parents can come to define high verbal ability as giftedness while a sibling with, say, spatial abilities, is thought not to be gifted. To ensure that you do not fall into this trap, I advise that if you are having one child in the family tested, test them all.

The third issue is that, while some family difficulties can come about because of a single gifted child, they can also arise because *all* family members are more or less gifted and more or less emotionally intense. This can mean that a gifted child's emotional outbursts spark off and are added to by reactions of other family members (Silverman 1997). When all siblings are gifted, this can also heighten rivalry between them. I once tested three siblings who were all gifted, but differently: one was highly creative and academically able; one was evenly able across all academic skills; and one had extreme peaks and more average abilities in some tasks—but their IQ scores were almost identical. So, to minimise competition between the children, I used the analogy of a traffic roundabout: vehicles can arrive on the same roundabout via different roads . . . and children can arrive at the same score by different routes.

Behavioural issues

Children who achieve at high levels are typically curious, with a hunger to learn and a strong need to control (Freeman 2000). Although these traits foster high achievement, they can simultaneously create conflict with authoritarian disciplinarians at home or school. Combined with advanced verbal skills, many gifted children can negotiate seemingly endlessly, to the intense frustration of parents trying to ensure compliance.

It *can* be confusing to know what to expect of children who perform at advanced levels one minute then revert to age level the next. (Linda Silverman once said that gifted children should have a light installed on their forehead that could flash 'I'm being the eight-year-old now . . . I'm back to being four now'.) The uncertainty can lead either to indulging children's excessive demands or thoughtless behaviour on the grounds of their gifted-ness (Fisher 1981; Keirouz 1990; Sapon-Shevin 1987), or expecting too much of them in the belief that they 'should know better' (Colangelo 2003; Colangelo & Assouline 2000).

In Chapter 6, I reported that rewards and punishments often provoke the very disruptive behaviours that adults are trying to correct. My own research which concludes this (Porter 1999) is supported by prior studies showing that when mothers exercise restrictive control over their children, the children become defiant, uncooperative, withdrawn, anxious, unhappy, hostile when frustrated, and unwilling to persist at tasks (Baumrind, 1967, 1971; Crockenberg & Litman, 1990). The conclusion is that authoritative parenting—that is, acting as a leader rather than a boss—avoids power struggles over children's behaviour and teaches self-discipline.

A second behavioural issue is that, by late primary (elementary) school, gifted children might develop disrespect for their teachers in the belief that they are smarter than their teachers. This is true inasmuch as their thinking skills do exceed those of most adults. However, to encourage a healthy level of respect for adults, you can use a computer analogy which states that their teachers' software (or means of data processing) can be equivalent to the gifted child's but they know more (have more data) to process. So the children still have something to learn from their educators.

A third behavioural issue is gifted children's advanced awareness of adult concerns. I refer you to Chapter 7 for a discussion on how to help children to grow down when they are adopting responsibility for issues before they have the power to solve them.

Gender issues

The separate issues for gifted girls and boys were discussed in Chapter 10. As a reminder, the measures recommended there were to teach children a strong sense of self by supporting even non-traditional interests; teaching an internal locus of control; fostering a climate of intellectualism by modelling high achievement and prohibiting anti-intellectual taunting between siblings; and exposing children of both sexes to same-sex gifted peers and mentors (which includes you, their parents).

Visual-spatial (or holistic) learners

If you are an auditory-sequential learner, you might find yourself somewhat confused by your visual-spatial son or daughter. These children tend not to be able to follow long sequences of instruction; when distressed, they cannot be calmed by verbal explanations; and they find it difficult to change tack when they have a fixed plan of action in their minds. Some tips for more harmonious relationships include the following.

- Give instructions in visual language. Rather than: 'Get your pyjamas and a book from your room' try: 'Picture your room . . . Can you see where your pyjamas are at the moment? . . . Okay, get them.' If your child can handle a second instruction, add in the instruction to retrieve the book; otherwise, deliver that directive later, once part one is completed.
- Sometimes the children have a fixed picture that they need, say, to complete their model aeroplane, but this conflicts with your imperative that they get ready for school. In such situations, do not force them to abandon their picture entirely but instead instruct them to 'change channels' in their head—just as they change channels on TV—to shift attention to another picture, knowing that they can return to their own picture at another time.
- Take photos of the tasks they need to do each morning: breakfast, toothbrush, hairbrush, clothes, the made bed, and so on, and put these on a chart which the children can independently check to remind themselves of what they need to be doing.
- For tasks that are best done in steps, remind them to use analytical and sequential thinking. Ask things such as: 'Where are you going to start? . . . What will you do next? . . . Is that working? . . . Are you finished?' Most visual-spatial learners *can* perform sequences but, because they are more efficient at learning holistically, do not think to use a sequential strategy even when that would be most effective.

Issues with other parents and the community

Some of your most difficult moments can occur when talking to other parents whose children are not gifted learners (Hall 1994). When exchanging stories about your children, you might feel that you have to hold back for fear of appearing to brag (Fisher 1981), as other parents can be unsympathetic to the notion that a gifted child could be experiencing any difficulties (Hall 1994). Yet the quality of your support network both increases your own confidence as a parent and allows you to exchange information with other parents, while also having a measurable impact on children's cognitive and social development because a wide parental network exposes children to a wide range of adult and child contacts (Melson et al. 1993). For this reason, it can be useful to get in touch with your local Gifted and Talented Children's Association and meet with other parents of gifted children. This can normalise what you are experiencing, provide information about solutions to common issues, reduce your own isolation and give you some emotional support (Moon et al. 1997; Webb 1993).

Schooling options

Wherever you live, there will probably be four schooling options available to you: public, elite private schools, small independent (often religious) schools and, for want of a better word, the 'alternative' schools. Home schooling is also an option for some.

For gifted children, no one schooling system is necessarily superior to another. Instead, you need to find a match between your child's particular needs and the practices of a school. The elite private schools are well resourced and typically have strong academic programs. This will be ideal for children who are academically gifted but may not be as suitable for those who are emotionally gifted. The pressure to excel academically and the competitive social context of some elite schools can be detrimental to emotionally sensitive children—and boys in particular. At the same time, these schools tend to attract more able children so, amongst a bright peer group, a gifted child can often be catered for routinely within the classroom without the need for special pull-out programs with their social stigma and disconnectedness with the regular curriculum.

In comparison, public schools have a strong tradition of catering for the full range of children across the ability spectrum and all walks of life. These schools therefore often have mechanisms for responding to atypical needs so, in this respect, can be well suited to catering for gifted learners, especially those with dual exceptionalities. On the other hand, the peer group may not be as able as is found in an elite private institution. By the beginning of secondary school (at age thirteen), public school classes will typically have a range of ability levels spanning at least from ten to sixteen years. This is a very broad range of abilities to teach to, and can result in the relative neglect of the more able cohort within a class.

The smaller parochial schools tend to be underresourced, and as a result offer few opportunities for their staff to access professional development. This reduces the likelihood that these schools will have a core of teachers with extensive knowledge of gifted education. If small in size, these schools can be nurturing for emotionally sensitive children; on the other hand, if a school is too small, there is a reduced chance statistically that your child will be able to locate a similarly gifted peer with whom to develop a friendship.

The last option is the 'alternative' schools. The very liberal schools might be too unstructured for children who like to be clear about expectations, while being ideal for those who resist restrictions; while Montessori education can be suited to children who like structure. A Steiner (also known as Waldorf) education might, on the face of it, seem to be the opposite of what gifted children need, in that formal instruction in literacy skills starts later in these schools, which can frustrate academically gifted children. On the other hand, the emotional meaning embedded in a Steiner curriculum can be ideal for emotionally and creatively gifted children. Again, size can be a factor in these schools, as is the case with the smaller religious schools.

Single-sex schools can encourage gifted girls to select courses that they otherwise might not, and to adopt leadership positions—although this might not translate into adult life in mixed-sex settings. Academically, single-sex schools seem to favour high achievement, but perhaps academic skills are not the only requisite for success in adult life: getting along with the other 50 per cent of the population is also a crucial skill to learn and practise throughout life.

This leaves home schooling. This, of course, is a big commitment and not one that everyone is in a position financially or otherwise to fulfil. It can also come at some cost to the children's socialisation with peers. I wonder if withdrawing them from school might tell them that the world is a dangerous place and that they are too fragile to cope with it. The lack of separation between parent and child could also deprive children of the many small steps needed to gain full independence as adults.

As mothers are almost always their children's home school instructor, I also wonder at the message this gives about women sacrificing themselves for others. And sometimes I am concerned that home schooling is almost imposed on some children because of their parents' own negative reactions to school, rather than their child's actual difficulties.

These hesitations aside, home schooling can be the only option when schools cannot or will not provide what gifted children need, and when negotiations with schools have broken down. In some locations, tutors see small groups of children for each academic subject, augmented by parent instruction and other extracurricular activities. This can be the best of both worlds, offering some expert instruction as well as social interaction with others.

Selecting a school

When choosing a school, the match between your child's individual needs and school practices is the prime consideration. To gauge that, your first step is to interview the principal. Ask about the school's policy on gifted education, whether it has accepted children for early entry to school or allowed them to skip grades because of their giftedness, whether it has a gifted education coordinator and specific gifted programs. Be very cautious if you receive in answer any of the following slogans in response to your report that your child is gifted:

- *All parents think their child is gifted.* Substitute the word *disabled* in this sentence, and you will recognise that a principal would never say 'Every parent thinks her child has a disability'.
- *Every child in this school is gifted.* This signals that the principal knows next to nothing about giftedness and has few plans to find out.
- *We will make our own assessment once your child starts school.* Naturally educators will engage in ongoing assessment of children; that the principal thinks this statement needs making suggests an attempt to pull rank, to dismiss your own assessment—and even an IQ report—as less accurate than teachers' own assessments. Anyone with any background in education of the gifted knows this to be a fallacy.
- *We strive for excellence here.* Given that no school's slogan is 'We strive for mediocrity', this statement is meaningless unless backed up by specific programs that cater for gifted and other atypical learners.
- The above slogan is often followed up with *So we don't believe there is any need for specific gifted provisions.* Substitute the word *special* for *gifted* in this sentence and then reflect on whether principals would feel quite as comfortable saying: 'Every child in our school has a disability so we don't find any need for individualised special education.'
- *We do not accelerate gifted students because we are concerned for them as a whole person and for their emotional and social needs.* This is an attempt to justify a lack of appropriate provision for gifted learners. The fact that the principal does not appreciate that intellectual and emotional giftedness are linked signals that he or she knows very little about gifted children.

The next step is to interview your child's likely class teacher. Like the principal, this person does not need to have extensive knowledge of giftedness, but should at least not be misinformed and should be interested in finding out more—which, among other things, will entail respecting you as a valuable source of information.

Third, if the school has a nominated gifted education coordinator, interview that teacher about the specific programs that the school offers. Enquire into that person's qualifications for the position and whether he or she is allocated some specific time to coordinate gifted provisions or whether it is a nominal responsibility that is tacked on to an already full workload. Ask how the children are selected to participate in gifted programs, and how gifted provisions are coordinated with the children's regular curriculum—that is, are the activities just add-ons or are they integrated into the child's wider program.

Be specific in your questions about these gifted provisions. Some schools offer only an hour or two a week of extension, and sometimes then only by an older peer or a willing parent. This is seldom enough in terms of time or expertise to satisfy the thirst of gifted students.

Fourth, check that the school has a staff library containing texts on gifted education. This can tell you whether there is a culture of inquisitiveness within the school that impels teachers to continue to perfect their craft. The job of professionals is not to know everything, but to know what they do not know and be willing to find out. If there is no staff library or there are no books in it on gifted education, this casts doubts on how much they can know, given that there are no resources to inform them.

Next, I believe that the role of schools is to teach children *how* to think. Children who are nonconformist or independent thinkers are likely to resist being told *what* to think, particularly if they are coerced to go against their own moral values. This can cause them to come into conflict with the ideology of the school, so matching the school's ethos with the children's values is crucial.

The last consideration is personal: your own schooling history. Apparently only 20 per cent of children like school, 60 per cent tolerate it and 20 per cent loathe it. I suspect that gifted children (who often grow into the parents of gifted children) are over-represented in the group who dislike school. This means that you might be carrying some emotional baggage left over from your own schooling experiences. Although you cannot impose this on your children, neither can you expect yourself to take your children every day to a setting which causes you to feel sad for them. So you will have to choose a schooling system where you feel safe: your children will pick up on your vibes and feel comfortable there also. So listen to your instincts, without indulging your own emotions.

Advocating for gifted children within educational settings

Most parents want to be able to slot their child into the education system at the age of five or six years and pick the child up some thirteen years later, with only the usual transitions along the way. This is not as likely for gifted children. As is often the case for children with disabilities, many parents of gifted children mourn the loss of the 'normal' child, whose needs could be catered for routinely within the education system (Silverman 1997).

There is often a need to advocate for children at every year level, which raises the spectre of having to be a pushy parent and to cope with conflict with school personnel. Many parents achieve special educational provisions only when they instigate them, and have to spend a great deal of energy just trying to make sure that their children are actually learning something at school (Fraser 2004).

Conflict between parents and teachers can arise when the two of you do not agree on the necessity for gifted provisions (Moon 2003). In the face of disillusionment, you might react by continually pressuring teachers, by providing all enrichment as extra curricular activities (which is a strain on both your time and resources), or withdrawing from contact with your child's teachers and complaining instead (Colangelo 2003; Colangelo & Assouline 2000). As none of these responses is ideal, cooperation can be enhanced when you can employ the following strategies.

- State clearly and repeatedly that you do not want a *better* education for your gifted child—just a *developmentally appropriate* one, as is any child's right.
- Recognise that teachers want the same things that you do: for children to be contented in school and to feel positively about learning and about themselves as learners.
- Recognise that teachers are often uncertain about gifted education, just as you are. Like you, they too feel alone in their efforts, hampered by a lack of training in gifted education and by bureaucratic constraints on best practice (Chyriwsky & Kennard 1997; Hall 1994).
- Maintain realistic expectations of teachers. Even when individual teachers have the skills to provide for your child's needs, they are working within the constraints of large classes and the various needs of many children.
- Go directly to your child's teacher with any complaints and speak to the principal only if that fails, as going to superiors first is disrespectful and will only make teachers defensive (Penney & Wilgosh 2000).
- Make an appointment for a teacher conference, rather than detaining your child's teacher on the run. Teachers are likely to feel pressured if expected to come up with suggestions without prior warning or when they have an impending commitment elsewhere.
- Set a specific goal for your meeting, perhaps having just one priority measure that you would like enacted at school (Smutny 2001).
- Become well versed in gifted education so that you can counter any myths your child's teacher puts forward as an argument against gifted provisions (Diezmann et al. 2001).
- Comment on the positive things that are happening at school for your child.

- Document your child's exceptional achievements, as teachers might not see these in their setting, for reasons given in Chapter 8.

Information required by gifted children

Throughout their life, gifted children will need some reassurance that 'they are not abnormal, they are not weird, and they are not alone' (Davis & Rimm 2004: 426). They will need to develop healthy emotions and attitudes to themselves and others, to understand and accept their own strengths and limitations, and to practise strategies to cope with life's challenges (Hickson 1992).

Information about brains

Children will need to know that they are gifted so they can understand why they feel different from others. I begin by asking the children whether they have ever sat in a shopping centre watching people passing by. They might have noticed that, even though every face is made up of the same ingredients — two eyes, a nose, mouth, chin — no two people look alike. So it is with brains. They all have a front part which is in charge of their thinking, a back part which works their bodies, the left half controlling language, and the right in charge of music and visual thinking. (This description is an oversimplification, of course.) Despite the fact that everyone's brain has the same parts or ingredients, all brains work differently.

Next, I describe to the children that their brain is a machine for learning, going on to say that, just as some children can run more quickly, so too some children can learn more quickly than others. Their brain is one of those that can learn more quickly than usual. This is exciting because they can find lots of different things that interest them . . . but they still have to stay in charge of their brains. No matter how good their family car is — it might be a BMW — it still needs someone to steer it; it cannot drive itself. In the same way, no matter how good a brain is, it still needs someone to be in command of it.

Rather than making children self-satisfied or smug, this type of information merely confirms what the children already know about themselves (Riley 1997). It allows them to enjoy their deeper understandings and not to feel at fault when other people do not share these. And, given that they will have noticed the differences between themselves and others, telling them the facts replaces what may otherwise be inaccurate explanations for the dissimilarities.

Understanding giftedness

Some children view giftedness from an 'entity' perspective, as if giftedness is a 'thing' that you either have or you don't and which means that learning does not require effort. If they have to work at something, this view continues, this must mean they are not talented—so they come to avoid activities in which they cannot become instant experts. Instead, children need to regard giftedness from an 'incremental' perspective which recognises that ability flows from effort and that putting in work will both produce results and be more fun for themselves (Robinson 1996). Thus it will be useful for gifted children to learn that:

Effort will surpass talent when talent makes no effort.

At the same time, you will find it difficult to sell working 'hard', so instead will have to talk of working smarter, while not expecting children to be at peak performance all the time.

Understanding normality

Gifted children need to hear that they are still normal. Although a statistical rarity, psychologically they have the same needs (for self-esteem, autonomy and to belong) as everyone else. In fact, they are both normal and abnormal at the same time. This is like having fillings in your teeth: as most people have fillings, it is statistically normal; however, as teeth do not erupt already filled, having fillings is medically abnormal.

Friendships

It is crucial that gifted young children's experiences of feeling 'out of step' with children of their own age are validated by the important people in their lives. They need to hear that what they feel is okay and that they can trust their perceptions (LeVine & Kitano 1998).

They might need to accept that one cost of being gifted is a certain degree of alienation from others (LeVine & Kitano 1998). Conforming and being 'normal'—that is, the same as everyone else—is not an option for them. It might be tempting to protect them from feeling isolated by rationalising that they are different from others 'in a better way', but this could alienate them still further (Hackney 1981). Instead, you can help them to understand that no one has more than one or two friends at a time, and that that their selectivity with friendships and self-sufficiency can be beneficial.

You must also keep in mind that, while children's giftedness makes them different in some ways from average learners, they also share many characteristics in common with all others and so, while you must be your children's advocate, you also need to guide them to build bridges to others (Roeper 1995b).

Romantic relationships

Throughout their childhoods, sex and sexuality need to be an open topic and children should never be teased or chided for having or not having friends of the other sex. Girls need to learn that they must be active in their choice of partner: it is not difficult to find a man willing to have a mate, and they do not have to be grateful if a man finds them attractive. The real challenge is to find a man worthy of them and a relationship that fosters the personal growth of both partners.

For their part, boys need to be taught that they will achieve more intimacy and fulfilment in relationships with intelligent females than with 'trophy wives' or submissive nonentities. If for no other reason than for their own emotional satisfaction, they will need to anticipate adopting child care-taking duties alongside their intelligent wives.

Verbally bright, emotionally aware, mature young people can find that they are a magnet for unsolicited romantic advances. Being popular with potential sexual partners might seem to be the type of problem that every adolescent wants to have, but unwanted attention can be embarrassing, so young people in this position will need your guidance about how to decline unwelcome advances tactfully.

As for their own sexuality, although their sexual orientation will emerge during adolescence, children as young as five or six can already have some awareness of their sexual preferences (Peterson & Rischar 2000), so exposing them early to homophobic attitudes could set them up for self-denigration later in life if they then find they are lesbian or gay. More than most, gifted homosexuals may feel a responsibility to be perfect and, as a result of their giftedness, may have a smaller social network from whom to seek acceptance and will have a restricted pool of gifted homosexual partners to support them and help them mature socially and sexually (Peterson & Rischar 2000). As a result, these young people can be intensely isolated by the social imperative to hide both their giftedness and their homosexuality (Cohn 2002). Yet their advanced moral reasoning can mean that they become distressed at having to 'live a lie', so will need your support to discuss their sexual identity: a positive relationship with your children will mean that you will both come to accept who they are.

Career guidance

Gifted children begin to consider their career options earlier than other children—often during primary (or elementary) school. Because of their high accomplishments, they often set themselves career goals that require lengthy academic preparation (Moon et al. 1997). This makes career guidance an important counselling need from the late primary school years onwards.

Rather than abiding by the maxim that 'You are what you do', gifted young men and women have the luxury of abilities that enable them, when they are willing to rise to the challenge, to 'Do what you are'. This means that individuals need to select careers that reflect their abilities, interests and values, rather than status or salary.

It has been assumed that it can be difficult for gifted individuals to select one career because they are capable and interested in many fields. This has been termed multipotentiality. However, when ability tests offer adequate challenge, peaks and troughs do show up in most gifted people's ability profiles, while most do in fact have focused interests (Achter et al. 1997; Milgram & Hong 1999).

A more common problem for the gifted is having to select a career when they feel compelled to make the perfect choice, or are trying to meet their own or others' high expectations. You can help with this by making sure that your children are not under pressure to satisfy your expectations, but are free to take the risks necessary to find their own meaning and purpose in their career path (Greene 2002).

One clue about your children's career choice is to look at their hobbies, as many adults end up working at what they chose to do in their spare time during adolescence (Colangelo & Assouline 2000; Milgram & Hong 1999). Still others get their ideas from their parents' line of work. However, this can take careful handling, particularly when both the parent and child are highly achieving in the same field and are of the same sex, as it can be difficult for the offspring to get out of the shadow of the parent and establish individuality (Kerr & Cohn 2001).

Whatever children choose to do, it is important not to make them feel obliged to 'meet their potential', as if their exceptional abilities are some gift that they have received for which they are beholden. They must fulfil their own mission in life, which might not be entirely clear to them at the outset.

Also, when children have a specific field of talent, we should not pressure them to be 'well-rounded', but instead allow them to pursue their passions (Kerr & Cohn 2001). As with so many aspects of parenting, this of course must be a question of balance. I attempt to achieve this by, in consultation with their parents, advising young children that no one expects them to 'do their best' at something they dislike, but just to do enough work at it so it does not block their ability to use the skills they *do* value. For example, children who are fascinated by creative writing need to practise their spelling just enough so that stopping to think how to spell a word does not constantly interrupt the flow of their creative ideas; children who want to be scientists need to practise handwriting or keyboarding skills just enough that they can record scientific facts that interest them.

Conclusion

Parents of gifted children are often characterised as pushing their 'star' children to feed their own egos; teaching their children to act as if they are superior to others; bragging about their gifted children; comparing their children to others; and being overprotective at the same time as making their children into premature adults (Silverman 1997). The reality, however, is that most gifted children have parents who are also gifted and who have excellent problem-solving skills and healthy personal adjustments. These adult skills in turn feed the family's overall healthy interaction patterns (Chamrad & Robinson 1986; Silverman 1997).

Suggested further reading

Smutny, J.F. 2001 *Stand up for your gifted child: how to make the most of kids' strengths at school and at home* Free Spirit, Minneapolis.

For information on counselling gifted children and their families:
Silverman, L.K. ed. 1993 *Counselling the gifted and talented* Love Publishing, Denver, CO.

For detailed information on and evidence about the options for gifted provisions in schools, see:
Rogers, K.B. 2002 *Re-forming gifted education: matching the program to the child* Great Potential Press, Scottsdale, AZ.

For general parenting skills:
Faber, A. and Mazlish, E. 1999 *How to talk so kids will listen and listen so kids will talk* Avon, New York.
Porter, L. 2005 *Children are people too: a guide for parents to children's behaviour* 4th edn, East Street Publications, Adelaide.

BIBLIOGRAPHY

Aber, J.L. and Ellwood, D.T. 2001 'Thinking about children in time' in *The dynamics of poverty in industrialised countries* eds B. Bradbury, S.P. Jenkins & J. Micklewright, Cambridge University Press, Cambridge, pp. 281–300.

Ablard, K.E. 1997 'Self-perceptions and needs as a function of type of academic ability and gender' *Roeper Review* vol. 20, no. 2, pp. 110–16.

Ackerman, C.M. 1997 'Identifying gifted adolescents using personality characteristics: Dabrowski's overexcitabilities' *Roeper Review* vol. 19 no. 4, pp. 229–36.

Achter, J.A., Benbow, C.P. and Lubinski, D. 1997 'Rethinking multipotentiality among the intellectually gifted: a critical review and recommendations' *Gifted Child Quarterly* vol. 41, no. 1, pp. 5–13.

Adderholdt-Elliot, M. 1992 *Perfectionism: what's bad about being too good* Hawker Brownlow Education, Melbourne.

Albert, R.S. and Runco, M.A. 1986 'The achievement of eminence: a model based on a longitudinal study of exceptionally gifted boys and their families' in *Conceptions of giftedness* eds R.J. Sternberg & J.E. Davidson, Cambridge University Press, Cambridge, pp. 332–57.

Allan, S.D. 1991 'Ability-grouping research reviews: what do they say about grouping and the gifted?' *Educational Leadership* vol. 48, no. 6, pp. 60–5.

Alvino, J. 1991 'An investigation into the needs of gifted boys' *Roeper Review* vol. 13, no. 4, pp. 174–80.

Amabile, T.M. 1990 'Within you, without you: the social psychology of creativity, and beyond' in *Theories of creativity* eds M. Runco & R.S. Albert, Pitzer College, Claremont, CA, pp. 61–91.

Anastopoulos, A.D. and Barkley, R.A. 1992 'Attention deficit-hyperactivity disorder' in *Handbook of clinical child psychology* 2nd edn, eds C.E. Walker & M.C. Roberts, John Wiley and Sons, New York, pp. 413–30.

Anderson, M. 1992 *Intelligence and development: a cognitive theory* Blackwell, London.

Archambault, F.X. Jr, Westberg, K.L., Brown, S.W., Hallmark, B.W., Zhang, W. and Emmons, C.L. 1993 'Classroom practices used with gifted third and fourth grade students' *Journal for the Education of the Gifted* vol. 16, no. 2, pp. 103–19.

Asher, S.R. 1983 'Social competence and peer status: recent advances and future directions' *Child Development* vol. 54, pp. 1427–34.

Asher, S.R. and Parker, J.G. 1989 'Significance of peer relationship problems in childhood' in *Social competence in developmental perspective* eds B.H. Schneider, G. Attili, J. Nadel and R.P. Weissberg, Kluwer Academic Publishers, Dordrecht, pp. 5–23.

Asher, S.R. and Renshaw, P.D. 1981 'Children without friends: social knowledge and social-skill training' in *The development of children's friendships* eds S.R. Asher and J.M. Gottman, Cambridge University Press, Cambridge, pp. 273–96.

Austin, A.B. and Draper, D.C. 1981 'Peer relationships of the academically gifted: a review' *Gifted Child Quarterly* vol. 25, no. 3, pp. 129–33.

Bailey, D.B. and Harbin, G.L. 1980 'Nondiscriminatory evaluation' *Exceptional Children* vol. 46, no. 8, pp. 590–6.

Bailey, D.B. and Wolery, M. 1992 *Teaching infants and preschoolers with handicaps* 2nd edn, Merrill, Columbus, OH.

Bailey, S. 1993 'Acceleration: an introduction' in *Gifted children need help?: a guide for parents and teachers* ed. D. Farmer, New South Wales Association for Gifted and Talented Children Inc., Sydney, pp. 117–9.

—— 1997 'Acceleration as an option for talented students' in *Parents as lifelong teachers of the gifted* eds B.A. Knight & S. Bailey, Hawker Brownlow Education, Melbourne, pp. 43–50.

—— 1998 'Missionary zeal and surviving in the meantime' Eminent Australian address to the 7th National conference of the Australian Association for the Education of the Gifted June 1998, Hobart.

Bailey, S., Knight, B.A. and Riley, D. 1995 *Developing children's talents: guidelines for schools* Hawker Brownlow Education, Melbourne.

Baker, J.A. 1996 'Everyday stressors of academically gifted adolescents' *The Journal of Secondary Gifted Education* vol. 7, pp. 356–68.

Baker, J.A., Bridger, R. and Evans, K. 1998 'Models of underachievement among gifted preadolescents: the role of personal, family, and school factors' *Gifted Child Quarterly* vol. 42, no. 1, pp. 5–15.

Balson, M. 1992 *Understanding classroom behaviour* 3rd edn, ACER, Melbourne.

Bandura, A. 1986 *Social foundations of thought and action* Prentice Hall, Englewood Cliffs, NJ.

Barbour, N.B. 1992 'Early childhood gifted education: a collaborative perspective' *Journal for the Education of the Gifted* vol. 15, no. 2, pp. 145–62.

Barclay, K. and Benelli, C. 1994 'Are labels determining practice? Programming for preschool gifted children' *Childhood Education* vol. 70, no. 3, pp. 133–6.

Baska, L.K. 1989 'Characteristics and needs of the gifted' in *Excellence in educating the gifted* eds J. Feldhusen, J. Van Tassel-Baska and K. Seeley, Love Publishing, Denver, CO, pp. 15–28.

Baum, S. 1984 'Meeting the needs of learning disabled gifted students' *Roeper Review* vol. 7, no. 1, pp. 16–19.

—— 1988 'An enrichment program for gifted learning disabled students' *Gifted Child Quarterly* vol. 32, no. 1, pp. 226–30.

—— 1989 'Gifted but learning disabled: a puzzling paradox' *Preventing School Failure* vol. 34, no. 1, pp. 11–14.

Baum, S. and Owen, S.V. 1988 'High ability/learning disabled students: how are they different' *Gifted Child Quarterly* vol. 32, no. 3, pp. 321–6.

Baum, S., Emerick, L.J., Herman, G.N. and Dixon, J. 1989 'Identification, programs and enrichment strategies for gifted learning disabled youth' *Roeper Review* vol. 12, no. 1, pp. 48–53.

Baum, S., Owen, S.V. and Dixon, J. 1991 *To be gifted and learning disabled: from identification to practical intervention strategies* Hawker Brownlow Education, Melbourne.

Baum, S., Renzulli, J.S. and Hébert, T.P. 1994 'Reversing underachievement: stories of success' *Educational Leadership* vol. 52, no. 3, pp. 48–53.

—— 1995 'Reversing underachievement: creative productivity as a systematic intervention' *Gifted Child Quarterly* vol. 39, no. 4, pp. 224–35.

Baumrind, D. 1967 'Child care practices anteceding three patterns of preschool behavior' *Genetic Psychology Monographs* vol. 75, pp. 43–88.

—— 1971 'Current patterns of parental authority' *Developmental Psychology Monographs* vol. 4, no. 1, pp. 1–103.

Bay-Hinitz, A.K., Peterson, R.F. and Quilitch, R. 1994 'Cooperative games: a way to modify aggressive and cooperative behaviors in young children' *Journal of Applied Behavior Analysis* vol. 27, no. 3, pp. 435–46.

Bayley, R. 2002 'Thinking skills in the early years' *Gifted Education International* vol. 16, no. 3, pp. 248–60.

Beaty, J.J. 2002 *Observing development of the young child* 5th edn, Merrill Prentice Hall, Upper Saddle River, NJ.

Belcastro, F.P. 1987 'Elementary pull-out program for the intellectually gifted—boon or bane?' *Roeper Review* vol. 9, no. 4, pp. 208–12.

—— 2002 'Electronic technology and its use with rural gifted students' *Roeper Review* vol. 25, no. 1, pp. 14–16.

Belgrad, S.F. 1998 'Creating the most enabling environment for young gifted children' in *The young gifted child: potential and promise, an anthology* ed. J.F. Smutny, Hampton Press, Cresskill, NJ, pp. 369–79.

Ben Ari, R. and Rich, Y. 1992 'Meeting the educational needs of all students in the heterogeneous class' in *To be young and gifted* eds P.S. Klein and A.J. Tannenbaum, Ablex, Norwood, NJ, pp. 348–78.

Benbow, C.P. 1991 'Meeting the needs of gifted students through use of acceleration' in *Handbook of special education: research and practice* eds M.C. Wang, M.C. Reynolds and H.J. Walberg, Pergamon Press, Oxford, pp. 23–36.

—— 1992 'Challenging the gifted: grouping and acceleration' *Gifted Child Quarterly* vol. 3, no. 2, p. 59.

Berger, S.L. and McIntire, J. 1998 'Technology-based instruction for young gifted children' in *The young gifted child: potential and promise, an anthology* ed. J.F. Smutny, Hampton Press, Cresskill, NJ, pp. 535–46.

Bernal, E.M. 1989 '"Pluralism and power"—dare we reform education of the gifted along these lines?' in *Critical issues in gifted education: defensible programs for cultural and ethnic minorities* eds C.J. Maker & S.W. Schiever, Pro-Ed, Austin, TX, pp. 34–6.

Bevan-Brown, J. 1999 'Special abilities: a Māori perspective, implications for catering for gifted children from minority cultures' *Gifted Education International* vol. 14, no. 1, pp. 86–96.

—— 2004 'Gifted and talented Māori learners' in *Gifted and talented: New Zealand perspectives* 2nd edn, eds D. McAlpine and R. Moltzen, Kanuka Grove Press, Palmerston North, pp. 171–97.

Bland, L.C., Sowa, C.J., and Callahan, C.M. 1994 'Overview of resilience in gifted children' *Roeper Review* vol. 17, no. 2, pp. 77–80.

Blum, N.J. and Mercugliano, M. 1997 'Attention-deficit/hyperactivity disorder' in *Children with disabilities* 4th edn, ed. M.L. Batshaw, MacLennan and Petty, Sydney, pp. 449–70.

Bondurant-Utz, J.A. and Luciano, L.B. 1994 'Norm-based assessment: determination of eligibility' in *A practical guide to infant and preschool assessment in special education* eds J.A. Bondurant-Utz and L.B. Luciano, Allyn & Bacon, Boston, MA, pp. 151–9.

Borkowski, J.G. and Peck, V.A. 1986 'Causes and consequences of metamemory in gifted children' in *Conceptions of giftedness* eds R.J. Sternberg and J.E. Davidson, Cambridge University Press, Cambridge, pp. 182–200.

Borland, J.H. 1978 'Teacher identification of the gifted: a new look' *Journal for the Education of the Gifted* vol. 2, no. 1, pp. 22–32.

—— 1986 'IQ tests: throwing out the bathwater, saving the baby' *Roeper Review* vol. 8, no. 3, pp. 163–7.

—— 1989 *Planning and implementing programs for the gifted* Teachers College, Columbia University, New York.

—— 1990 'Postpositivist inquiry: implications of the "new philosophy of science" for the field of education of the gifted' *Gifted Child Quarterly* vol. 34, no. 4, pp. 161–7.

—— 1996a 'Book review: Playing favorites: gifted education and the disruption of community' *Roeper Review* vol. 18, no. 4, pp. 309–11.

—— 1996b 'Gifted education and the threat of irrelevance' *Journal for the Education of the Gifted* vol. 19, no. 2, pp. 129–47.

—— 2003 'Evaluating gifted programs: a broader perspective' in *Handbook of gifted education* 2nd edn, eds N. Colangelo and G.A. Davis, Allyn & Bacon, Boston, MA, pp. 293–307.

Borland, J.H. and Wright, L. 1994 'Identifying young, potentially gifted economically disadvantaged students' *Gifted Child Quarterly* vol. 38, no. 4, pp. 164–71.

—— 2000 'Identifying and educating poor and under-represented gifted students' in *International handbook of giftedness and talent* 2nd edn, eds K.A. Heller, F.J. Mönks, R.J. Sternberg and R.F. Subotnik, Pergamon, Oxford, pp. 587–94.

Bouchet, N. and Falk, R.F. 2001 'The relationship among giftedness, gender, and over-excitability' *Gifted Child Quarterly* vol. 45, no. 4, pp. 260–7.

Bradbury, B., Jenkins, S.P. and Micklewright, J. 2001 'Beyond the snapshot: a dynamic view of child poverty' in *The dynamics of poverty in industrialised countries* eds B. Bradbury, S.P. Jenkins and J. Micklewright, Cambridge University Press, Cambridge, pp. 1–23.

Braggett, E.J. 1992 *Pathways for accelerated learners* Hawker Brownlow Education, Melbourne.

—— 1993 'Acceleration: what, why, how and when?' *Gifted children need help?: A guide for parents and teachers* ed. D. Farmer, New South Wales Association for Gifted and Talented Children Inc., Sydney, pp. 120–6.

—— 1994 *Developing programs for gifted students: a total-school approach* Hawker Brownlow, Melbourne.

—— 1997 'A developmental concept of giftedness: implications for the regular classroom' *Gifted Education International* vol. 12, no. 2, pp. 64–71.

—— 1998 'Gifted and talented children' in *Educating children with special needs* 3rd edn, eds A. Ashman and J. Elkins, Prentice Hall, Sydney, pp. 229–81.

Braggett, E., Day, A. and Minchin, M. 1997 *Differentiated programs for primary schools* Hawker Brownlow Education, Melbourne.

Briggs, F. and McVeity, M. 2000 *Teaching children to protect themselves* Allen & Unwin, Sydney.

Brody, L.E. and Benbow, C.P. 1986 'Social and emotional adjustment of adolescents extremely talented in verbal or mathematical reasoning' *Journal of Youth and Adolescence* vol. 15, no. 6, pp. 1–18.

Brody, L.E. and Mills, C.J. 1997 'Gifted children with learning disabilities: a review of the issues' *Journal of Learning Disabilities* vol. 30, no. 3, pp. 282–96.

Brody, N. 2000 'History of theories and measurements of intelligence' in *Handbook of intelligence* ed. R.J. Sternberg, Cambridge University Press, Cambridge, pp. 16–33.

Bromfield, R. 1994 'Fast talkers: verbally precocious youth present challenges for parents and teachers' *Gifted Child Today* vol. 17, no. 2, pp. 32–3.

Brooks, P.R. 1998 'Targeting potentially talented and gifted minority students for academic achievement' in *The young gifted child: potential and promise, an anthology* ed. J.F. Smutny, Hampton Press, Cresskill, NJ, pp. 113–46.

Brounstein, P.J., Holahan, W. and Dreyden, J. 1991 'Change in self-concept and attributional styles among academically gifted adolescents' *Journal of Applied Social Psychology* vol. 21, no. 3, pp. 198–218.

Brown, B.B. and Steinberg, L. 1990 'Academic achievement and social acceptance' *The Education Digest* vol. 55, no. 7, pp. 57–60.

Brown, P.M., Remine, M.D., Prescott, S.J. and Rickards, F.W. 2000 'Social interactions of preschoolers with and without impaired hearing in integrated kindergarten' *Journal of Early Intervention* vol. 23, no. 3, pp. 200–11.

Brown, S.W. 1984 'The use of WISC-R subtest scatter in the identification of intellectually gifted handicapped children: an inappropriate task?' *Roeper Review* vol. 7, no. 1, pp. 20–3.

Bryant, M.A. 1987 'Meeting the needs of gifted first grade children in a heterogeneous classroom' *Roeper Review* vol. 9, no. 4, pp. 214–16.

Buescher, T.M. 1985 'A framework for understanding the social and emotional development of gifted and talented adolescents' *Roeper Review* vol. 8, no. 1, pp. 10–15.

Burns, J.M., Mathews, F.N. and Mason, A. 1990 'Essential steps in screening and identifying preschool gifted children' *Gifted Child Quarterly* vol. 34, no. 3, pp. 102–7.

Burns, R.B. 1982 *Self-concept development and education* Holt, Rhinehart & Winston, London.

Burton-Szabo, S. 1996 'Gifted classes for gifted students?: absolutely' *Gifted Child Today* vol. 19, no. 1, pp. 12–15, 50.

Butler-Por, N. 1993 'Underachieving gifted students' in *International handbook of research and development of giftedness and talent* eds K.A. Heller, F.J. Mönks and A.H. Passow, Pergamon, Oxford, pp. 649–68.

Cahan, S. and Gejman, A. 1993 'Constancy of IQ scores among gifted children' *Roeper Review* vol. 15, no. 3, pp. 140–3.

Callahan, C.M. 1991 'An update on gifted females' *Journal for the Education of the Gifted* vol. 14, no. 2, pp. 284–311.

—— 1996 'A critical self-study of gifted education: healthy practice, necessary evil, or sedition?' *Journal for the Education of the Gifted* vol. 19, no. 2, pp. 148–63.

Callahan, C.M., Cunningham, C.M. and Plucker, J.A. 1994 'Foundations for the future: the socio-emotional development of gifted, adolescent women' *Roeper Review* vol. 17, no. 2, pp. 99–105.

Cameron, J. and Pierce, W.D. 1994 'Reinforcement, reward, and intrinsic motivation: a meta-analysis' *Review of Educational Research* vol. 64, no. 3, pp. 363–423.

—— 1996 'The debate about rewards and intrinsic motivation: protests and accusations do not alter the results' *Review of Educational Research* vol. 66, no. 1, pp. 39–51.

Carr, M., Alexander, J. and Schwanenflugel, P. 1996 'Where gifted children do and do not excel on metacognitive tasks' *Roeper Review* vol. 18, no. 3, pp. 212–17.

Carr, M. and Borkowski, J.G. 1987 'Metamemory in gifted children' *Gifted Child Quarterly* vol. 31, no. 1, pp. 40–44.

Carrington, N. 1993 'Australian adolescent attitudes towards academic brilliance' *The Australasian Journal of Gifted Education* vol. 2, no. 2, pp. 10–15.

Carrington, N.G. and Bailey, S.B. 2000 'How do preservice teachers view gifted students?: evidence from a NSW study' *The Australasian Journal of Gifted Education* vol. 9, no. 1, pp. 18–22.

Carter, K.R. 1986 'Evaluating the consequences of participating in a gifted pullout program' *Journal for the Education of the Gifted* vol. 9, no. 4, pp. 265–75.

Carter, K.R. and Hamilton, W. 1985 'Formative evaluation of gifted programs: a process and a model' *Gifted Child Quarterly* vol. 29, no. 1, pp. 5–11.

Casey, J.P. and Quisenberry, N.L. 1976 'A review of the research related to giftedness in early childhood education' in *Gifted children: looking to their future* eds J. Gibson and P. Chennells, Latimer, London, pp. 88–113.

Cash, A.B. 1999 'A profile of gifted individuals with autism: the twice-exceptional learner' *Roeper Review* vol. 22, no. 1, pp. 22–7.

Cathcart, R. 1996 'Educational provisions: an overview' in *Gifted and talented: New Zealand perspectives* eds D. McAlpine and R. Moltzen, ERDC Press, Palmerston North, pp. 121–38.

Chamrad, D.L. and Robinson, N.M. 1986 'Parenting the intellectually gifted preschool child' *Topics in Early Childhood Special Education* vol. 6, no. 1, pp. 74–87.

Chamrad, D.L., Robinson, N.M. and Janos, P.M. 1995 'Consequences of having a gifted sibling: myths and realities' *Gifted Child Quarterly* vol. 39, no. 3, pp. 135–45.

Chan, L.K.S. 1988 'The perceived competence of intellectually talented students' *Gifted Child Quarterly* vol. 32, no. 3, pp. 310–14.

—— 1996 'Motivational orientations and metacognitive abilities of intellectually gifted students' *Gifted Child Quarterly* vol. 40, no. 4, pp. 184–94.

Chapman, J.W. and McAlpine, D.D. 1988 'Students' perceptions of ability' *Gifted Child Quarterly* vol. 32, no. 1, pp. 222–5.

Cheng, P-W. 1993 'Metacognition and giftedness: the state of the relationship' *Gifted Child Quarterly* vol. 37, no. 3, pp. 105–12.

Chitwood, D.G. 1986 'Guiding parents seeking testing' *Roeper Review* vol. 8, no. 3, pp. 177–9.

Christie, W. 1995 'Let their minds stretch: flexibility of options for gifted learners: a practitioner's perspective' *Gifted and Talented International* vol. 10, no. 2, pp. 61–6.

Chyriwsky, M. and Kennard, R. 1997 'Attitudes to able children: a survey of mathematics teachers in English secondary schools' *High Ability Studies* vol. 8, no. 1, pp. 47–59.

Ciha, T.E., Harris, B., Hoffman, C. and Porter, M.W. 1974 'Parents as identifiers of giftedness: ignored but accurate' *Gifted Child Quarterly* vol. 18, no. 3, pp. 191–5.

Clarizio, H.F. and Mehrens, W.A. 1985 'Psychometric limitations of Guilford's structure-of-intellect model for identification and programming for the gifted' *Gifted Child Quarterly* vol. 29, no. 3, pp. 113–20.

Clark, B. 2002 *Growing up gifted: developing the potential of children at home and at school* 6th edn, Merrill Prentice Hall, Upper Saddle River, NJ.

Clasen, D.R. and Clasen, R.E. 1995 'Underachievement of highly able students and peer society' *Gifted and Talented International* vol. 10, no. 2, pp. 67–76.

Clements, C., Lundell, F. and Hishinuma, E.S. 1994 'Serving the gifted dyslexic and gifted at risk' *Gifted Child Today* vol. 17, no. 4, pp. 12–14, 16–17, 36–7.

Cohen, L.M. 1989 'Understanding the interests and themes of the very young gifted child' *Gifted Child Today* vol. 12, no. 4, pp. 6–9.

—— 1998 'Facilitating the interest themes of young bright children' in *The young gifted child: potential and promise, an anthology* ed. J.F. Smutny, Hampton Press, Cresskill, NJ, pp. 317–39.

Cohen, R., Duncan, M. and Cohen, S.L. 1994 'Classroom peer relations of children participating in a pull-out enrichment program' *Gifted Child Quarterly* vol. 38, no. 1, pp. 33–7.

Cohen, R.J., Montague, P., Nathanson, L.S. and Swerdlik, M.E. 1988 *Psychological testing: an introduction to tests and measurement* Mayfield, Mountain View, CA.

Cohn, S.J. 2002 'Gifted students who are gay, lesbian, or bisexual' in *Social and emotional development of gifted children: what do we know?* eds M. Neihart, S.M. Reis, N.M. Robinson and S.M. Moon, National Association for Gifted Children, Washington, DC, pp. 145–53.

Colangelo, N. 2003 'Counseling gifted students' in *Handbook of gifted education* 3rd edn, eds N. Colangelo and G.A. Davis, Allyn & Bacon, Boston, MA, pp. 373–87.

Colangelo, N. and Assouline, S.G. 2000 'Counseling gifted students' in *International handbook of giftedness and talent* 2nd edn, eds K.A. Heller, F.J. Mönks, R.J. Sternberg and R.F. Subotnik, Pergamon, Oxford, pp. 595–607.

Colangelo, N., Assouline, S.G., Baldus, C.M. and New, J.K. 2003 'Gifted education in rural schools' in *Handbook of gifted education* 3rd edn, eds N. Colangelo and G.A. Davis, Allyn & Bacon, Boston, MA, pp. 572–81.

Colangelo, N. and Brower, P. 1987 'Labeling gifted youngsters: long-term impact on families' *Gifted Child Quarterly* vol. 31, no. 2, pp. 75–8.

Colangelo, N. and Davis, G.A. (eds) 2003 *Handbook of gifted education* 3rd edn, Allyn & Bacon, Boston, MA.

Coleman, L.J. 1994 'Portfolio assessment: a key to identifying hidden talents and empowering teachers of young children' *Gifted Child Quarterly* vol. 38, no. 2, pp. 65–9.

—— 1995 'The power of specialized educational environments in the development of giftedness: the need for research on social context' *Gifted Child Quarterly* vol. 39, no. 3, pp. 171–6.

Coleman, L.J. and Cross, T.L. 1988 'Is being gifted a social handicap?' *Journal for the Education of the Gifted* vol. 11, no. 4, pp. 41–56.

Coleman, J.M. and Fults, B.A. 1982 'Self-concept and the gifted classroom: the role of social comparison' *Gifted Child Quarterly* vol. 26, no. 3, pp. 116–20.

Compas, B.E. 1987 'Coping with stress during childhood and adolescence' *Psychological Bulletin* vol. 101, no. 3, pp. 393–403.

Cooper, C.S. and McEvoy, M.A. 1996 'Group friendship activities: an easy way to develop the social skills of young children' *Teaching Exceptional Children* vol. 28, no. 3, pp. 67–9.

Cornell, D.G. 1989 'Child adjustment and parent use of the term "gifted"' *Gifted Child Quarterly* vol. 33, no. 2, pp. 59–64.

Cornell, D.G. and Grossberg, I.N. 1986 'Siblings of children in gifted programs' *Journal for the Education of the Gifted* vol. 9, no. 4, pp. 253–64.

Cornell, D.G., Delcourt, M.A.B., Bland, L.C., Goldberg, M.D. and Oram, G. 1994 'Low incidence of behavior problems among elementary school students in gifted programs' *Journal for the Education of the Gifted* vol. 18, no. 1, pp. 4–19.

Corrigan, S.Z. 1994 'For the sake of the children' *Gifted Child Today* vol. 17, no. 2, pp. 22–23, 30, 41.

Cramond, B. and Martin, C.E. 1987 'Inservice and preservice teachers' attitudes toward the academically brilliant' *Gifted Child Quarterly* vol. 31, no. 1, pp. 15–19.

Craven, R.G. and Marsh, H.W. 1997 'Threats to gifted and talented students' self-concepts in the big pond: research results and educational implications' *The Australasian Journal of Gifted Education* vol. 6, no. 2, pp. 7–17.

Creel, C.S. and Karnes, F.A. 1988 'Parental expectancies and young gifted children' *Roeper Review* vol. 11, no. 1, pp. 48–50.

Crockenberg, S. and Litman, C. 1990 'Autonomy as competence in 2-year-olds: maternal correlates of child defiance, compliance, and self-assertion' *Developmental Psychology* vol. 26, no. 6, pp. 961–71.

Cropley, A. 1997 'Creativity: a bundle of paradoxes' *Gifted and Talented International* vol. 12, no. 1, pp. 8–14.

—— 2000 'Defining and measuring creativity: are creativity tests worth using?' *Roeper Review* vol. 23, no. 2 pp. 72–9.

Cross, T.L., Coleman, L.J. and Stewart, R.A. 1992 'The social cognition of gifted adolescents: an exploration of the stigma of giftedness paradigm' *Roeper Review* vol. 16, no. 1, pp. 37–40.

Cross, T.L., Coleman, L.J. and Terhaar-Yonkers, M. 1991 'The social cognition of gifted adolescents in schools: managing the stigma of giftedness' *Journal for the Education of the Gifted* vol. 15, no. 1, pp. 44–55.

Cruickshank, W.M. 1977 'Myths and realities in learning disabilities' *Journal of Learning Disabilities* vol. 10, no. 1, pp. 51–8.

Csikszentmihályi, M. 1991 'Commentary' *Human Development* vol. 34, pp. 32–4.

Curry, N.E. and Johnson, C.N. 1990 *Beyond self-esteem: developing a genuine sense of human value* National Association for the Education of Young Children, Washington, DC.

Czeschlik, T. and Rost, D.H. 1994 'Socio-emotional adjustment in elementary school boys and girls: does giftedness make a difference?' *Roeper Review* vol. 16, no. 4, pp. 294–7.

Dahlberg, G., Moss, P. and Pence, A. 1999 *Beyond quality in early childhood education and care: postmodern perspectives* RoutledgeFalmer, London.

Damiani, V.B. 1997 'Young gifted children in research and practice: the need for early childhood programs' *Gifted Child Today* vol. 20, no. 3, pp. 18–23.

Dau, E. ed. 2001 *The anti-bias approach in early childhood* 2nd edn, Pearson Education Australia, Sydney.

Dauber, S.L. and Benbow, C P. 1990 'Aspects of personality and peer relations of extremely talented adolescents' *Gifted Child Quarterly* vol. 34, no. 1, pp. 10–14.

Davis, G.A. and Rimm, S.B. 2004 *Education of the gifted and talented* 5th edn, Pearson Allyn & Bacon, Boston, MA.

Davis, H.B. and Connell, J.P. 1985 'The effect of aptitude and achievement status on the self-system' *Gifted Child Quarterly* vol. 29, no. 3, pp. 131–6.

Delisle, J.R. 1992 *Guiding the social and emotional development of gifted youth* Longman, New York.

—— 1994a 'The top ten statements that should never again be made by advocates of gifted children' *Gifted Child Today* vol. 17, no. 2, pp. 34–5, 42.

—— 1994b 'Dealing with the stereotype of underachievement' *Gifted Child Today* vol. 17, no. 6, pp. 20–1.

—— 1994c 'The inclusion movement is here—good . . . it's about time' *Gifted Child Today* vol. 17, no. 4, pp. 30–1.

—— 1998 'Gifted girls: who's limiting whom?' *Gifted Child Today* vol. 21, no. 4, pp. 20–1.

Delisle, J. and Galbraith, J. 2002 *When gifted kids don't have all the answers: how to meet their social and emotional needs* Free Spirit Press, Minneapolis, MN.

Delisle, J. and Lewis, B.A. 2003 *The survival guide for teachers of gifted kids* Free Spirit, Minneapolis, MN.

DeMeis, J.L. and Stearns, E.S. 1992 'Relationship of school entrance age to academic and social performance' *Journal of Educational Research* vol. 86, no. 1, pp. 20–7.

Dengate, S. 2004 *Fed up with ADHD* Random House, Sydney.

Denton, C. and Postlethwaite, K. 1984 'A study of the effectiveness of teacher-based identification of pupils with high ability in the secondary school' *Gifted Education International* vol. 2, no. 2, pp. 100–6.

Derevensky, J. and Coleman, E.B. 1989 'Gifted children's fears' *Gifted Child Quarterly* vol. 33, no. 2, pp. 65–8.

Derman-Sparks, L. and the ABC Task Force 1989 *Anti-bias curriculum: tools for empowering young children* National Association for the Education of Young Children, Washington, DC.

Diaz, E.I. 1998 'Perceived factors influencing the academic underachievement of talented students of Puerto Rican descent' *Gifted Child Quarterly* vol. 42, no. 2, pp. 105–22.

Diezmann, C.M., Watters, J.J. and Fox, K. 2001 'Early entry to school in Australia: rhetoric, research and reality' *The Australasian Journal of Gifted Education* vol. 10, no. 2, pp. 5–18.

Dix, J. and Schafer, S. 1996 'From paradox to performance: practical strategies for identifying and teaching GT/LD students' *Gifted Child Today* vol. 19, no. 1, pp. 22–4, 28–9.

Dixon, D.N. and Scheckel, J.R. 1996 'Gifted adolescent suicide: the empirical base' *The Journal of Secondary Gifted Education* vol. 7, pp. 386–92.

Dole, S. 2000 'The implications of the risk and resilience literature for gifted students with learning disabilities' *Roeper Review* vol. 23, no. 2, pp. 91–6.

Dowdall, C.B. and Colangelo, N. 1982 'Underachieving gifted students: review and implications' *Gifted Child Quarterly* vol. 26, no. 4, pp. 179–84.

Dowling, M. 2002 'Developing potential in the early years' *Gifted Education International* vol. 16, no. 3, pp. 241–7.

Eales, C. and de Paoli, W. 1991 'Early entry and advanced placement of talented students in primary and secondary schools' *Gifted Education International* vol. 7, no. 3, pp. 140–4.

Ebert, E.S. 1994 'The cognitive spiral: creative thinking and cognitive processing' *Journal of Creative Behavior* vol. 28, no. 4, pp. 275–90.

Eisenberger, R. and Armeli, S. 1997 'Can salient reward increase creative performance without reducing intrinsic creative interest?' *Journal of Personality and Social Psychology* vol. 72, no. 3, pp. 652–63.

Elkind, D. 1988 'Acceleration' *Young Children* vol. 43, no. 4, p. 2.

Ellston, T. 1993 'Gifted and learning disabled: a paradox?' *Gifted Child Today* vol. 16, no. 1, pp. 17–19.

Evans, K. 1993 'Multicultural counseling' in *Counseling the gifted and talented* ed. L.K. Silverman, Love Publishing, Denver, CO, pp. 277–90.

Eyre, D. 1997 *Able children in ordinary schools* David Fulton, London.

Eysenck, H.J. 1986 'The biological basis of intelligence' in *Giftedness: a continuing worldwide challenge* eds K.K. Urban, H. Wagner and W. Wieczerkowski, Trillium Press, New York, pp. 97–114.

Faber, A. and Mazlish, E. 1999 *How to talk so kids will listen and listen so kids will talk* Avon, New York.

Fall, J. and Nolan, L. 1993 'A paradox of exceptionalities' *Gifted Child Today* vol. 16, no. 1, pp. 46–9.

Farmer, S. 1995 *Policy development in early childhood services* Community Child Care Cooperative Ltd, Sydney.

Fatouros, C. 1986 'Early identification of gifted children is crucial . . . but how should we go about it?' *Gifted Education International* vol. 4, no. 1, pp. 24–8.

Feldhusen, J.F. 1985 'The teacher of gifted students' *Gifted Education International* vol. 3, no. 2, pp. 87–93.

—— 1986 'A conception of giftedness' in *Conceptions of giftedness* eds R.J. Sternberg & J.E. Davidson, Cambridge University Press, Cambridge, pp. 112–27.

—— 1989 'Synthesis of research on gifted youths' *Educational Leadership* vol. 46, no. 6, pp. 6–11.

—— 1997 'Educating teachers for work with talented youth' in *Handbook of gifted education* 2nd edn, eds N. Colangelo and G.A. Davis, Allyn & Bacon, Boston, MA, pp. 547–52.

Feldhusen, J.F. and Baska, L.K. 1989 'Identification and assessment of the gifted' in *Excellence in educating the gifted* eds J. Feldhusen, J. Van Tassel-Baska and K. Seeley, Love Publishing, Denver, CO, pp. 85–102.

Feldhusen, J.F., Dai, D.Y. and Clinkenbeard, P.R. 2000 'Dimensions of competitive and cooperative learning among gifted learners' *Journal for the Education of the Gifted* vol. 23, no. 3, pp. 328–42.

Feldhusen, J.F. and Nimlos-Hippen, A.L. 1992 'An exploratory study of self concepts and depression among the gifted' *Gifted Education International* vol. 8, no. 3, pp. 136–8.

Feldhusen, J.F., Proctor, T.B. and Black, K.N. 1986 'Guidelines for grade advancement of precocious children' *Roeper Review* vol. 9, no. 1, pp. 25–7.

Feldhusen, J.F., Sayler, M.F., Nielson, M.E. and Kolloff, P.B. 1990 'Self-concepts of gifted children in enrichment programs' *Journal for the Education of the Gifted* vol. 13, no. 4, pp. 380–7.

Feldhusen, J.F., Van Winkle, L. and Ehle, D.A. 1996 'Is it acceleration or simply appropriate instruction for precocious youth?' *Teaching Exceptional Children* vol. 28, no. 3, pp. 48–51.

Feldman, D.H. 1984 'A follow-up of subjects scoring above 180 IQ in Terman's "Genetic studies of genius"' *Exceptional Children* vol. 50, no. 6, pp. 518–23.

—— 1993 'Child prodigies: a distinctive form of giftedness' *Gifted Child Quarterly* vol. 37, no. 4, pp. 188–93.

Fernández, A.T., Gay, L.R., Lucky, L.F. and Gavilán, M.R. 1998 'Teacher perceptions of gifted Hispanic and limited English proficiency students' *Journal for the Education of the Gifted* vol. 21, no. 3, pp. 335–51.

Fetzer, E.A. 2000 'The gifted/learning disabled child: a guide for teachers and parents' *Gifted Child Today* vol. 23, no. 4, pp. 44–50.

Fiedler, E.D., Lange, R.E. and Winebrenner, S. 1993 'In search of reality: unraveling the myths about tracking, ability grouping and the gifted' *Roeper Review* vol. 16, no. 1, pp. 4–7.

Field, T. 1991 'Quality infant day-care and grade school behavior and performance' *Child Development* vol. 62, no. 4, pp. 863–70.

Fine, M.J. and Pitts, R. 1980 'Intervention with underachieving gifted children: rationale and strategies' *Gifted Child Quarterly* vol. 24, no. 2, pp. 51–5.

Fisher, E. 1981 'The effect of labeling on gifted children and their families' *Roeper Review* vol. 3, no. 3, pp. 49–51.

Flint, L. 2001 'Challenges of identifying and serving gifted children with ADHD' *Teaching Exceptional Children* vol. 33, no. 4, pp. 62–9.

Ford, D.Y. 2002 'Racial identity among gifted African American students' in *Social and emotional development of gifted children: what do we know?* eds M. Neihart, S.M. Reis, N.M. Robinson and S.M. Moon, National Association for Gifted Children, Washington, DC, pp. 155–63.

—— 2003 'Equity and excellence: culturally diverse students in gifted education' in *Handbook of gifted education* 3rd edn, eds N. Colangelo and G.A. Davis, Allyn & Bacon, Boston, MA, pp. 506–20.

Ford, D.Y. and Harris, J.J. III 2000 'A framework for infusing multicultural curriculum into gifted education' *Roeper Review* vol. 23, no. 1, pp. 4–10.

Ford, D.Y., Howard, T.C., Harris, J.J. III and Tyson, C.A. 2000 'Creating culturally responsive classrooms for gifted African American students' *Journal for the Education of the Gifted* vol. 23, no. 4, pp. 397–427.

Ford, D.Y., Russo, C.J. and Harris, J.J. III 1993 'The quest for equity in gifted education' *Gifted Child Today* vol. 16, no. 6, pp. 8–11.

Ford, D.Y. and Trotman, M.F. 2001 'Teachers of gifted students: suggested multicultural characteristics and competencies' *Roeper Review* vol. 23, no. 4, pp. 235–9.

Ford, M.A. 1989 'Students' perceptions of affective issues impacting the social emotional development and school performance of gifted/talented youngsters' *Roeper Review* vol. 11, no. 3, pp. 131–4.

Forster, J. 2002 'The reality of opportunities for gifted and talented students' in *The gifted enigma: a collection of articles* eds W. Vialle and J. Geake, Hawker Brownlow, Melbourne, pp. 74–90.

Fowler, W., Ogston, K., Roberts-Fiati, G. and Swenson, A. 1995 'Patterns of giftedness and high competence in high school students educationally enriched during infancy: variation across educational racial/ethnic backgrounds' *Gifted and Talented International* vol. 10, no. 1, pp. 31–6.

Fox, L.H. 1984 'The learning-disabled gifted child' *Learning Disabilities* vol. 8, no. 10, pp. 117–28.

Fraser, N. 2004 'Parenting' in *Gifted and talented: New Zealand perspectives* 2nd edn, eds D. McAlpine and R. Moltzen, Kanuka Grove Press, Palmerston North, pp. 501–21.

Fraser, S. and Gestwicki, C. 2002 *Authentic childhood: exploring Reggio Emilia in the classroom* Delmar, Albany, NY.

Frasier, M.M. 1989 'Poor and minority students can be gifted too!' *Educational Leadership* vol. 46, no. 6, pp. 16–18.

—— 1993 'Issues, problems and programs in nurturing the disadvantaged and culturally different talented' in *International handbook of research and development of giftedness and talent* eds K.A. Heller, F.J. Mönks and A.H. Passow, Pergamon, Oxford, pp. 685–92.

—— 1997 'Gifted minority students: reframing approaches to their identification and education' in *Handbook of gifted education* 2nd edn, eds N. Colangelo and G.A. Davis, Allyn & Bacon, Boston, MA, pp. 498–515.

Freeman, J. 1983 'Emotional problems of the gifted child' *Journal of Child Psychology and Psychiatry and Related Disciplines* vol. 24, no. 3, pp. 481–5.

—— 1991 *Gifted children growing up* Cassell, London.

—— 1993 'Parents and families in nurturing giftedness and talent' in *International handbook of research and development of giftedness and talent* eds K.A. Heller, F.J. Mönks and A.H. Passow, Pergamon, Oxford, pp. 669–84.

—— 1994 'Some emotional aspects of being gifted' *Journal for the Education of the Gifted* vol. 17, no. 2, pp. 180–97.

—— 1995a 'Review of current thinking on the development of talent' in *Actualizing talent: a lifelong challenge* eds J. Freeman, P. Span & H. Wagner, Cassell, London.

—— 1995b 'Annotation: recent studies of giftedness in children' *Journal of Child Psychology and Psychiatry* vol. 36, no. 4, pp. 531–47.

—— 1995c 'Toward a policy for actualizing talent' in *Actualizing talent: a lifelong challenge* eds J. Freeman, P. Span and H, Wagner, Cassell, London, pp. 174–92.

—— 1996 *Highly able girls and boys* Department for Education and Employment, London.

—— 1997 'The emotional development of the highly able' *European Journal of Psychology of Education* vol. 12, no. 4, pp. 479–93.

—— 1998 *Educating the very able: current international research* Office for Standards in Education, London.

—— 2000 'Families: the essential context for gifts and talents' in *International handbook of giftedness and talent* 2nd edn, eds K.A. Heller, F.J. Mönks, R.J. Sternberg and R.F. Subotnik, Pergamon, Oxford, pp. 573–85.

Fuchs-Beauchamp, K.D., Karnes, M.B. and Johnson, L.J. 1993 'Creativity and intelligence in preschoolers' *Gifted Child Quarterly* vol. 37, no. 3, pp. 113–17.

Gagné, F. 1995 'From giftedness to talent: A developmental model and its impact on the language of the field' *Roeper Review* vol. 18, no. 2, pp. 103–11.

—— 1997 'Critique of Morelock's (1996) definitions of giftedness and talent' *Roeper Review* vol. 20, no. 2, pp. 76–85.

—— 2003 'Transforming gifts into talents: the DMGT as a developmental theory' in *Handbook of gifted education* 3rd edn, eds N. Colangelo and G.A. Davis, Allyn & Bacon, Boston, MA, pp. 60–74.

Galbraith, J. 1985 'The eight great gripes of gifted kids: responding to special needs' *Roeper Review* vol. 8, no. 1, pp. 15–18.

Gallagher, J.J. 1988 'National agenda for educating gifted students: statement of priorities' *Exceptional Children* vol. 55, no. 2, pp. 107–14.

—— 1991 'Educational reform, values, and gifted students' *Gifted Child Quarterly* vol. 35, no. 1, pp. 12–19.

—— 1996 'A critique of critiques of gifted education' *Journal for the Education of the Gifted* vol. 19, no. 2, pp. 234–49.

—— 2000 'Unthinkable thoughts: education of gifted students' *Gifted Child Quarterly* vol. 44, no. 1, pp. 5–12.

Gallagher, J.J. and Gallagher, S.A. 1994 *Teaching the gifted child* 4th edn, Allyn & Bacon, Boston, MA.

Gallagher, J.J. and Moss, J.W. 1963 'New concepts of intelligence and their effect on exceptional children' *Exceptional Children* vol. 30, no. 1, pp. 1–5.

Gallucci, N.T. 1988 'Emotional adjustment of gifted children' *Gifted Child Quarterly* vol. 32, no. 2, pp. 273–6.

Gallucci, N.T., Middleton, G. and Kline, A. 1999a 'Intellectually superior children and behavior problems and competence' *Roeper Review* vol. 22, no. 1, pp. 18–21.

—— 1999b 'The independence of creative potential and behavior disorders in gifted children' *Gifted Child Quarterly* vol. 43, no. 4, pp. 194–203.

Gamoran, A. 1992 'Is ability grouping equitable?' *Educational Leadership* vol. 50, no. 2, pp. 11–17.

Gardner, H. 1983 *Frames of mind: the theory of multiple intelligences* Basic Books, New York.

—— 1997 'Six afterthoughts: comments on "Varieties of intellectual talent"' *Journal of Creative Behavior* vol. 31, no. 2, pp. 120–4.

—— 1999 *Intelligence reframed: multiple intelligences for the 21st century* Basic Books, New York.

Garland, A.F. and Zigler, E. 1999 'Emotional and behavioral problems among highly intellectually gifted youth' *Roeper Review* vol. 22, no. 1, pp. 41–4.

Gartrell, D. 2003 *A guidance approach for the encouraging classroom* 3rd edn, Delmar, New York.

Geake, J. 1997 'Thinking as evolution in the brain: implications for giftedness' *The Australasian Journal of Gifted Education* vol. 6, no. 1, pp. 27–33.

Gear, G.H. 1976 'Accuracy of teacher judgement in identifying intellectually gifted children: a review of the literature' *Gifted Child Quarterly* vol. 20, pp. 478–90.

—— 1978 'Effects of training in teachers' accuracy in identifying gifted children' *Gifted Child Quarterly* vol. 22, no. 1, pp. 90–7.

Gibson, K. 1998 'A promising approach for identifying gifted Aboriginal students in Australia' *Gifted Education International* vol. 13, no. 1, pp. 73–88.

Gilding, M. 1997 *Australian families: a comparative perspective* Longman, South Melbourne.

Gillman, J. and Hansen, H. 1987 'Gifted education in Minnesota kindergartens' *Roeper Review* vol. 9, no. 4, pp. 212–4.

Glasser, W. 1986 *Control theory in the classroom* Harper and Row, New York.

—— 1998 *The quality school: managing students without coercion* rev edn, Harper Perennial, New York.

Goldstein, S. 1995 'Attention deficit hyperactivity disorder' in *Understanding and managing children's classroom behavior* ed. S. Goldstein, John Wiley & Sons, New York, pp. 56–78.

Goleman, D. 1994 *Emotional intelligence* Bantam Books, New York.

Gordon, T. 1970 *Parent effectiveness training* Plume, New York.

—— 1974 *Teacher effectiveness training* Peter H. Wyden, New York.

Gottfredson, L. 2003 'The science and politics of intelligence in gifted education' in *Handbook of gifted education*, 3rd edn, eds N. Colangelo and G.A. Davis, Allyn & Bacon, Boston, MA, pp 24–40.

Gould, S. J. 1981 *The mismeasure of man* W.W. Norton, New York.

Grant, B.A. and Piechowski, M.M. 1999 'Theories and the good: toward child-centered gifted education' *Gifted Child Quarterly* vol. 43, no. 1, pp. 4–12.

Greene, M.J. 2002 'Career counseling for gifted and talented students' in *Social and emotional development of gifted children: what do we know?* eds M. Neihart, S.M. Reis, N.M. Robinson and S.M. Moon, National Association for Gifted Children, Washington, DC, pp. 223–35.

Grenier, M.E. 1985 'Gifted children and other siblings' *Gifted Child Quarterly* vol. 29, no. 4, pp. 164–7.

Gridley, B.E. 2002 'In search of an elegant solution: reanalysis of Plucker, Callahan, and Tomchin, with respects to Pyryt and Plucker' *Gifted Child Quarterly* vol. 46, no. 3, pp. 224–34.

Grinder, R.E. 1985 'The gifted in our midst: by their divine deeds, neuroses, and mental test scores we have known them' in *The gifted and talented: developmental perspectives* eds F.D. Horowitz and M. O'Brien, American Psychological Association, Washington, DC, pp. 5–36.

Gross, M.U.M. 1992 'The use of radical acceleration in cases of extreme intellectual precocity' *Gifted Child Quarterly* vol. 36, no. 2, pp. 91–9.

—— 1993a 'Nurturing the talents of exceptionally gifted individuals' in *International handbook of research and development of giftedness and talent* eds K.A. Heller, F.J. Mönks and A.H. Passow, Pergamon, Oxford, pp. 473–90.

—— 1993b 'The use of radical acceleration in cases of extreme intellectual precocity' *Gifted children need help?: a guide for parents and teachers* ed. D. Farmer, New South Wales Association for Gifted and Talented Children Inc., Sydney, pp. 127–42.

—— 1996 'The pursuit of excellence or the search for intimacy: the forced-choice dilemma for gifted youth' in *Gifted children: the challenge continues: a guide for parents and teachers* eds A. Jacob and G. Barnsley, New South Wales Association for Gifted and Talented Children, Sydney, pp. 111–20.

—— 1997 'How ability grouping turns big fish into little fish—or does it? Of optical illusions and optimal environments' *The Australasian Journal of Gifted Education* vol. 6, no. 2, pp. 18–30.

—— 1998 'Fishing for the facts: a response to Craven and Marsh (1998)' *The Australasian Journal of Gifted Education* vol. 7, no. 1, pp. 16–28.

—— 1999 'Small poppies: highly gifted children in the early years' *Roeper Review* vol. 21, no. 3, pp. 207–14.

—— 2004 *Exceptionally gifted children* 2nd edn, London, RoutledgeFalmer.

Gross, M.U.M. and Start, K.B. 1990 '"Not waving, but drowning": the exceptionally gifted child in Australia' *The challenges of excellence: a vision splendid: selected papers from the 8th world conference on gifted and talented children* eds S. Bailey, E. Braggett and M. Robinson, Australian Association for the Education of the Gifted and Talented, Wagga Wagga, NSW, pp. 25–36.

Grossberg, I.N. and Cornell, D.G. 1988 'Relationship between personality adjustment and high intelligence: Terman versus Hollingworth' *Exceptional Children* vol. 55, no. 3, pp. 266–72.

Gruber, H.E. 1986 'The self-construction of the extraordinary' in *Conceptions of giftedness* eds R.J. Sternberg and J.E. Davidson, Cambridge University Press, Cambridge, pp. 247–63.

Guilford, A.M., Scheuerle, J. and Shonburn, S. 1981 'Aspects of language development in the gifted' *Gifted Child Quarterly* vol. 25, no. 4, pp. 159–63.

Guilford, J.P. 1959 'Three faces of intellect' *American Psychologist* vol. 14, no. 8, pp. 469–79.

—— 1988 'Some changes in the structure-of-intellect model' *Educational and Psychological Measurement* vol. 48, pp. 1–4.

Gunderson, C.W., Maesch, C., and Rees, J.W. 1987 'The gifted/learning disabled student' *Gifted Child Quarterly* vol. 31, no. 4, pp. 158–60.

Guskin, S.L., Peng, C.J. and Majd-Jabbari, M. 1988 'Teachers' perceptions of giftedness' *Gifted Child Quarterly* vol. 32, no. 1, pp. 216–21.

Gust, K. 1997 'Is the literature on social and emotional needs empirically based?' *Gifted Child Today* vol. 20, no. 3, pp. 12–13.

Gust-Brey, K. and Cross, T. 1999 'An examination of the literature base on the suicidal behaviors of gifted students' *Roeper Review* vol. 22, no. 1, pp. 28–35.

Hackney, H. 1981 'The gifted child, the family, and the school' *Gifted Child Quarterly* vol. 25, no. 2, pp. 51–4.

Hadaway, N. and Marek-Schroer, M.F. 1992 'Multidimensional assessment of the gifted minority student' *Roeper Review* vol. 15, no. 2, pp. 73–7.

Haensly, P.A. and Kyung, S.L. 2000 'Gifted potential and emerging abilities in young children: as influenced by diverse backgrounds' *Gifted Education International* vol. 14, no. 2, pp. 133–50.

Haensly, P.A. and Reynolds, C.R. 1989 'Creativity and intelligence' in *Handbook of creativity* eds J.A. Glover, R.R. Ronning and C.R. Reynolds, Plenum Press, New York, pp. 111–32.

Haensly, P.A., Reynolds, C.R. and Nash, W R. 1986 'Giftedness: coalescence, context, conflict, and commitment' in *Conceptions of giftedness* eds R.J. Sternberg and J.E. Davidson, Cambridge University Press, Cambridge, pp. 128–48,

Hall, E.G. 1993 'Educating preschool gifted children' *Gifted Child Today* vol. 16, no. 3, pp. 24–7.

Hall, J.M. 1994 'Schooling concerns of gifted children' *Gifted* August, pp. 7–10.

Hallinan, M.T. 1990 'The effects of ability grouping in secondary schools: a response to Slavin's best-evidence synthesis' *Review of Educational Research* vol. 60, no. 3, pp. 501–4.

Han, K-S. and Marvin, C. 2002 'Multiple creativities: investigating domain-specificity of creativity in young children' *Gifted Child Quarterly* vol. 46, no. 2, pp. 98–109.

Hannah, C.L. and Shore, B.M. 1995 'Metacognition and high intellectual ability: insights from the study of learning-disabled gifted students' *Gifted Child Quarterly* vol. 39, no. 2, pp. 95–109.

Hansen, J.B. and Feldhusen, J.F. 1994 'Comparison of trained and untrained teachers of gifted students' *Gifted Child Quarterly* vol. 38, no. 3, pp. 115–21.

Hansen, J.B. and Linden, K.W. 1990 'Selecting instruments for identifying gifted and talented students' *Roeper Review* vol. 13, no. 1, pp. 10–15.

Harmon, D. 2002 'They won't teach me: the voices of gifted African American inner-city students' *Roeper Review* vol. 24, no. 2, pp. 68–75.

Harrison, C. 2003 *Giftedness in early childhood* 3rd edn, GERRIC, Sydney.

Harrison, C. and Tegel, K. 1999 'Play and the gifted child' in *Child's play: revisiting play in early childhood settings* ed. E. Dau, MacLennan and Petty, Sydney, pp. 97–110.

Harslett, M. 1996 'The concept of giftedness from an Aboriginal cultural perspective' *Gifted Education International* vol. 11, no. 2, pp. 100–6.

Hartup, W.W. 1979 'Peer relations and social competence' in *Social competence in children* eds M.W. Kent and J.E. Rolf, University Press of New England, Hanover, NH, pp. 150–70.

Hastorf, A.H. 1997 'Lewis Terman's longitudinal study of the intellectually gifted: early research, recent investigations and the future' *Gifted and Talented International* vol. 12, no. 1, pp. 3–7.

Hay, I. 1993 'Motivation, self-perception and gifted students' *Gifted Education International* vol. 9, no. 1, pp. 16–21.

Hayes, M.L. and Sloat, R.S. 1989 'Gifted students at risk for suicide' *Roeper Review* vol. 12, no. 2, pp. 102–7.

Heacox, D. 1991 *Up from under-achievement: how teachers, students and parents can work together to promote student success* Hawker Brownlow Education, Melbourne.

Hébert, T.P. 2001 ' "If I had a notebook, I know things would change": bright under-achieving young men in urban classrooms' *Gifted Child Quarterly* vol. 45, no. 3, pp. 174–94.

—— 2002 'Gifted males' in *Social and emotional development of gifted children: what do we know?* eds M. Neihart, S.M. Reis, N.M. Robinson and S.M. Moon, National Association for Gifted Children, Washington, DC, pp. 137–44.

Heinbokel, A. 1997 'Acceleration through grade skipping in Germany' *High Ability Studies* vol. 8, no. 1, pp. 61–77.

Heller, K.A., Mönks, F.J., Sternberg, R.J. and Subotnik, R.F. eds 2000 *International handbook of giftedness and talent* 2nd edn, Pergamon, Oxford.

Hensel, N.H. 1990 'Developing leadership and prosocial behaviours in young gifted children' in *The challenges of excellence: a vision splendid: selected papers from the 8th world conference on gifted and talented children* eds S. Bailey, E. Braggett and M. Robinson, Australian Association for the Education of the Gifted and Talented, Wagga Wagga, NSW, pp. 392–98.

Hensel, N.H. 1991 'Social leadership skills in young children' *Roeper Review* vol. 14, no. 1, pp. 4–6.

Hershey, M. and Oliver, E. 1988 'The effects of the label gifted on students identified for special programs' vol. 11, no. 1, pp. 33–4.

Hertzog, N.B. 1998 'Open-ended activities: differentiation through learner responses' *Gifted Child Quarterly* vol. 42, no. 4, pp. 212–27.

Hess, L.L. 1994 'Life, liberty and the pursuit of perfection' *Gifted Child Today* vol. 17, no. 3, pp. 28–31.

Hickson, J. 1992 'A framework for guidance and counseling of the gifted in a school setting' *Gifted Education International* vol. 8, no. 2, pp. 93–103.

Hill, M.S. and Jenkins, S.P. 2001 'Poverty among British children: chronic or transitory?' in *The dynamics of child poverty in industrialised countries* eds B. Bradbury, S.P. Jenkins and J. Micklewright, Cambridge University Press, Cambridge, pp. 174–95.

Hishinuma, E.S. 1993 'Counseling gifted/at risk and gifted/dyslexic youngsters' *Gifted Child Today* vol. 16, no. 1, pp. 30–3.

—— 1996 'Motivating the gifted underachiever: implementing reward menus and behavioral contracts within an integrated approach' *Gifted Child Today* vol. 19, no. 4, pp. 30–6, 43–8.

Hishinuma, E. and Tadaki, S. 1996 'Addressing diversity of the gifted/at risk: characteristics for identification' *Gifted Child Today* vol. 19, no. 5, pp. 20–5, 28–9, 45, 50.

Hodge, K. 2004 *Issues in the identification of giftedness in young children* Unpublished doctoral thesis, Macquarie University, Sydney.

Hoge, R.D. and McSheffrey, R. 1991 'An investigation of self-concept in gifted children' *Exceptional Children* vol. 57, no. 3, pp. 238–45.

Hoge, R.D. and Renzulli, J.S. 1993 'Exploring the link between giftedness and self-concept' *Review of Educational Research* vol. 63, no. 4, pp. 449–65.

Holahan, C.K. 1996 'Lifetime achievement among the Terman gifted women' *Gifted and Talented International* vol. 11, no. 2, pp. 65–71.

Holden, B. 1996 'Educational provisions: early childhood' in *Gifted and talented: New Zealand perspectives* eds D. McAlpine and R. Moltzen, ERDC Press, Palmerston North, pp. 139–58.

Hooper, S.R. and Edmondson, R. 1998 'Assessment of young children: standards, stages and approaches' in *Young children with special needs* 3rd edn, eds W. Umansky and S.R. Hooper, Merrill, Upper Saddle River, NJ, pp. 340–71.

Horowitz, F.D. 1987 'A developmental view of giftedness' *Gifted Child Quarterly* vol. 31, no. 4, pp. 165–8.

—— 1992 'A developmental view on the early identification of the gifted' in *To be young and gifted* eds P.S. Klein and A.J. Tannenbaum, Ablex, Norwood, NJ, pp. 73–93.

Howard, V.F., Williams, B.F., Port, P.D. and Lepper, C. 2001 *Very young children with special needs: a formative approach for the 21st century* 2nd edn, Merrill Prentice Hall, Upper Saddle River, NJ.

Howard-Hamilton, M. and Franks, B.A. 1995 'Gifted adolescents: psychological behaviors, values and developmental implications' *Roeper Review* vol. 17, no. 3, pp. 186–91.

Hunsaker, S.L., Finley, V.S. and Frank, E.L. 1997 'An analysis of teacher nominations and student performance in gifted programs' *Gifted Child Quarterly* vol. 41, no. 2, pp. 19–24.

Irvine, D. 1987 'What research doesn't show about gifted dropouts' *Educational Leadership* vol. 44, no. 6, pp. 79–80.

—— 1991 'Gifted education without a state mandate: the importance of vigorous advocacy' *Gifted Child Quarterly* vol. 35, no. 4, pp. 196–9.

Ivory, J.J. and McCollum J.A. 1999 'Effects of social and isolate toys on social play in an inclusive setting' *The Journal of Special Education* vol. 32, no. 4, pp. 238–43.

Jackson, N.E. 1992 'Precocious reading of English: origins, structure, and predictive significance' in *To be young and gifted* eds P.S. Klein and A.J. Tannenbaum, Ablex, Norwood, NJ, pp. 171–203.

Jackson, N.E. and Butterfield, E.C. 1986 'A conception of giftedness designed to promote research' in *Conceptions of giftedness* eds R.J. Sternberg and J.E. Davidson, Cambridge University Press, Cambridge, pp. 151–81.

Jacobs, J.C. 1971 'Effectiveness of teacher and parent identification of gifted children as a function of school level' *Psychology in the Schools* vol. 8, no. 2, pp. 140–2.

Jacobs, J.E. and Weisz, V. 1992 'Gender stereotypes: implications for gifted education' *Roeper Review* vol. 16, no. 3, pp. 152–5.

Janos, P.M. 1987 'A fifty-year follow-up of Terman's youngest college students and IQ-matched agemates' *Gifted Child Quarterly* vol. 31, no. 2, pp. 55–8.

Janos, P.M., Marwood, K.A. and Robinson, N.M. 1985 'Friendship patterns in highly intelligent children' *Roeper Review* vol. 8, no. 1, pp. 46–53.

Janos, P.M. and Robinson, N.M. 1985 'Psychosocial development in intellectually gifted children' in *The gifted and talented: developmental perspectives* eds F.D. Horowitz and M. O'Brien, American Psychological Association, Washington, DC, pp. 149–96.

Jenkins-Friedman, R. 1982 'Myth: cosmetic use of multiple selection criteria!' *Gifted Child Quarterly* vol. 26, no. 1, pp. 24–6.

Jenkins-Friedman, R. and Murphy, D.L. 1988 'The Mary Poppins effect: relationships between gifted students' self-concept and adjustment' *Roeper Review* vol. 11, no. 1, pp. 26–30.

Johnsen, S., Ryser, G. and Dougherty, E. 1993 'The validity of product portfolios in the identification of gifted students' *Gifted International* vol. 8, no. 1, pp. 43–7.

Johnson, D.W. and Johnson, R.T. 1991 *Learning together and alone* 3rd edn, Allyn & Bacon, Boston, MA.

Johnson, L.J., Karnes, M.B. and Carr, V.W. 1997 'Providing services to children with gifts and disabilities: a critical need' in *Handbook of gifted education* 2nd edn, eds N. Colangelo and G.A. Davis, Allyn & Bacon, Boston, MA, pp. 516–27.

Jones, K. and Day, J.D. 1996 'Cognitive similarities between academically and socially gifted students' *Roeper Review* vol. 18, no. 4, pp. 270–3.

Jones, V.F. and Jones, L.S. 2001 *Comprehensive classroom management: creating communities of support and solving problems* 6th edn, Allyn & Bacon, Boston, MA.

Joswig, H. and Tuchow, A. 1996 'On the social self-concept of exceptionally gifted pupils' *Gifted and Talented International* vol. 11, no. 2, pp. 76–9.

Joyce, B.R. 1991 'Common misconceptions about cooperative learning and gifted students: a response to Allan' *Educational Leadership* vol. 48, no. 6, pp. 72–4.

Kail, R. 2000 'Speed of information processing: developmental change and links to intelligence' *Journal of School Psychology* vol. 38, no. 1, pp. 51–61.

Kammer, P.P. 1986 'Attribution for academic successes and failures of students participating and not participating in programs for the gifted' *Journal for the Education of the Gifted* vol. 9, no. 2, pp. 123–31.

Kanevsky, L. 1992 'The learning game' in *To be young and gifted* eds P.S. Klein and A.J. Tannenbaum, Ablex, Norwood, NJ, pp. 204–41.

—— 1994 'A comparative study of children's learning in the zone of proximal development' *European Journal for High Ability* vol. 5, pp. 163–75.

Kaplan, J.S. and Carter, J. 1995 *Beyond behavior modification: a cognitive-behavioral approach to behavior management in the school* 3rd edn, Pro-Ed, Austin, TX.

Karnes, F.A. and Wherry, J.N. 1981 'Self-concepts of gifted students as measured by the Piers–Harris children's self-concept scale' *Psychological Reports* vol. 49, no. 1, pp. 903–6.

Karnes, M.B. 1979 'Young handicapped children can be gifted and talented' *Journal for the Education of the Gifted* vol. 2, no. 3, pp. 157–72.

Karnes, M.B. and Johnson, L.J. 1991 'The preschool/primary gifted child' *Journal for the Education of the Gifted* vol. 14, no. 3, pp. 267–83.

Karnes, M.B., Shwedel, A.M. and Kemp, P.B. 1985 'Preschool: programming for the young gifted child: maximizing the potential of the young gifted child' *Roeper Review* vol. 7, no. 4, pp. 204–9.

Katz, L. 1995 *Talks with teachers of young children* Ablex, Norwood, NJ.

Katz, L.G. and Chard, S.C. 1989 *Engaging children's minds: the project approach* Ablex, Norwood, NJ.

Kaufman, A.S. 1992 'Evaluation of the WISC-III and WPPSI-R for gifted children' *Roeper Review* vol. 14, no. 3, pp. 154–8.

Kaufman, A.S. and Harrison, P.L. 1986 'Intelligence tests and gifted assessment: what are the positives?' *Roeper Review* vol. 8, no. 3, pp. 154–9.

Kaufmann, F.A. and Castellanos, F.X. 2000 'Attention-deficit/hyperactivity disorder in gifted students' in *International handbook of giftedness and talent* 2nd edn, eds K.A. Heller, F.J. Mönks, R.J. Sternberg and R.F. Subotnik, Pergamon, Oxford, pp. 621–32.

Keirouz, K.S. 1990 'Concerns of parents of gifted children: a research review' *Gifted Child Quarterly* vol. 34, no. 2, pp. 56–63.

Kelly, A. 1988 'Gender differences in teacher–pupil interactions: a meta-analytic view' *Research in Education* vol. 39, pp. 1–23.

Kelly, K.R. and Colangelo, N. 1984 'Academic and social self-concepts of gifted, general, and special students' *Exceptional Children* vol. 50, no. 6, pp. 551–4.

Kelly, K.R. and Moon, S.M. 1998 'Personal and social talents' *Phi Delta Kappan* vol. 79, no. 10, pp. 743–6.

Kerr, B.A. 1996 *Smart girls two: a new psychology of girls, women and giftedness* Hawker Brownlow Education, Melbourne.

—— 1997 'Developing talents in girls and young women' in *Handbook of gifted education* 2nd edn, eds N. Colangelo and G.A. Davis, Allyn & Bacon, Boston, MA, pp. 483–97.

—— 2000 'Guiding gifted girls and young women' in *International handbook of giftedness and talent* 2nd edn, eds K.A. Heller, F.J. Mönks, R.J. Sternberg and R.F. Subotnik, Pergamon, Oxford, pp. 649–57.

Kerr, B.A. and Cohn, S.J. 2001 *Smart boys: talent, manhood, and the search for meaning* Great Potential Press, Scottsdale, AZ.

Kerr, B., Colangelo, N. and Gaeth, J. 1988 'Gifted adolescents' attitudes towards their giftedness' *Gifted Child Quarterly* vol. 32, no. 2, pp. 245–7.

Kerr, B.A. and Nicpon, M.F. 2003 'Gender and giftedness' in *Handbook of gifted education* 3rd edn, eds N. Colangelo and G.A. Davis, Allyn & Bacon, Boston, MA, pp. 493–505.

Khatena, J. 1992 *Gifted: challenge and response for education* F.E. Peacock, Chicago, IL.

Kingore, B. 1995 'Portfolios for young children' *Understanding Our Gifted* vol. 7, no. 3, pp. 1, 10–13.

Kitano, M. 1982 'Young gifted children: strategies for preschool teachers' *Young Children* vol. 37, no. 4, pp. 14–24.

—— 1985 'Ethnography of a preschool for the gifted: what gifted young children actually do' *Gifted Child Quarterly* vol. 29, no. 2, pp. 67–71.

—— 1986 'Counseling gifted preschoolers' *Gifted Child Today* vol. 9, no. 4, pp. 20–25.

—— 1990a 'A developmental model for identifying and serving young gifted children' *Early Child Development and Care* vol. 63, pp. 19–31.

—— 1990b 'Intellectual abilities and psychological intensities in young children: implications for the gifted' *Roeper Review* vol. 13, no. 1, pp. 5–10.

—— 1991 'A multicultural educational perspective on serving the culturally diverse gifted' *Journal for the Education of the Gifted* vol. 15, no. 1, pp. 4–19.

Kitano, M. and Perez, R.I. 1998 'Developing the potential of young gifted children from low-income and culturally and linguistically diverse backgrounds' in *The young gifted child: potential and promise, an anthology* ed. J.F. Smutny, Hampton Press, Cresskill, NJ, pp. 119–32.

Klein, A.G. and Zehms, D. 1996 'Self-concept and gifted girls: a cross sectional study o intellectually gifted females in grades 3, 5, 8' *Roeper Review* vol. 19, no. 1, pp. 30–4.

Klein, P.S. 1992 'Mediating the cognitive, social, and aesthetic development of precocious young children' in *To be young and gifted* eds P.S. Klein and A.J. Tannenbaum, Ablex, Norwood, NJ, pp. 245–77.

Kline, B.E. and Meckstroth, E.A. 1985 'Understanding and encouraging the exceptionally gifted' *Roeper Review* vol. 8, no. 1, pp. 24–30.

Kline, B.E. and Short, E.B. 1990 'Gender differences: a research review of social and emotional considerations' in *The challenges of excellence: a vision splendid: selected papers from the 8th world conference on gifted and talented children* eds S. Bailey, E. Braggett and M. Robinson, Australian Association for the Education of the Gifted and Talented, Wagga Wagga, NSW, pp. 151–7.

—— 1991 'Changes in emotional resilience: gifted adolescent females' *Roeper Review* vol. 13, no. 3, pp. 118–21.

Kline, P. 1991 *Intelligence: the psychometric view* Routledge, London.

Kluever, R.C. and Green, K.E. 1990 'Identification of gifted children: a comparison of the scores on the Stanford–Binet 4th edition and Form LM' *Roeper Review* vol. 13, no. 1, pp. 16–20.

Knight, B.A. 1995 'The influence of locus of control on gifted and talented students' *Gifted Education International* vol. 11, no. 1, pp. 31–3.

Knight, B.A., Knight, C. and Brown, T. 1997 'Using computers to develop children's talents' in *Parents as lifelong teachers of the gifted* eds B.A. Knight and S. Bailey, Hawker Brownlow Education, Melbourne, pp. 127–38.

Kohler, F.W. and Strain, P.S. 1993 'The early childhood social skills program' *Teaching Exceptional Children* vol. 25, no. 2, pp. 41–2.

Kohn, A. 1996 *Beyond discipline: from compliance to community* Association for Supervision and Curriculum Development, Alexandria, VA.

—— 1999 *Punished by rewards: the trouble with gold stars, incentive plans, A's, praise and other bribes* 2nd edn, Houghton Mifflin, Boston, MA.

Kokot, S.J. 2003 'Diagnosing and treating learning disabilities in gifted children: a neurodevelopmental perspective' *Gifted Education International* vol. 17, no. 1, pp. 42–54.

Kolb, K.J. and Jussim, L. 1994 'Teacher expectations and underachieving gifted children' *Roeper Review* vol. 17, no. 1, pp. 26–30.

Kolloff, P.B. and Moore, A.D. 1989 'Effects of summer programs on the self-concepts of gifted children' *Journal for the Education of the Gifted* vol. 12, no. 4, pp. 268–76.

Konza, D. 1997 'Developing an affective curriculum: programming for the social/emotional needs of gifted students' *The Australasian Journal of Gifted Education* vol. 6, no. 1, pp. 5–10.

Kostelnick, M.J., Stein, L.C., Whiren, A.P. and Soderman, A.K. 2002 *Guiding children's social development: theory to practice* 4th edn, Thomson, New York.

Kulik, J.A. and Kulik, C-L.C. 1982 'Research synthesis on ability grouping' *Educational Leadership* vol. 39, no. 8, pp. 619–21.

—— 1984 'Synthesis of research on effects of accelerated instruction' *Educational Leadership* vol. 42, no. 2, pp. 84–9.

—— 1992 'Meta-analytic findings on grouping programs' *Gifted Child Quarterly* vol. 36, no. 2, pp. 73–7.

—— 1997 'Ability grouping' in *Handbook of gifted education* 2nd edn, eds N. Colangelo and G.A. Davis, Allyn & Bacon, Boston, MA, pp. 230–42.

Kunkel, M.A., Chapa, B., Patterson, G. and Walling, D.D. 1995 'The experience of giftedness: a concept map' *Gifted Child Quarterly* vol. 39, no. 3, pp. 126–34.

Lajoie, S.P. and Shore, B.M. 1981 'Three myths? the over-representation of the gifted among dropouts, delinquents and suicides' *Gifted Child Quarterly* vol. 25, no. 3, pp. 138–43.

Lambert, E.B. and Clyde, M. 2000 *Re-thinking early childhood theory and practice* Social Science Press, Katoomba, NSW.

Lando, B.Z. and Schneider, B.H. 1997 'Intellectual contributions and mutual support among developmentally advanced children in homogeneous and heterogeneous work/discussion groups' *Gifted Child Quarterly* vol. 41, no. 2, pp. 44–57.

Laycock, F. 1979 *Gifted children* Scott, Foresman & Co, Glenview, IL.

Lea-Wood, S.S. and Clunies-Ross, G. 1995 'Self-esteem of gifted adolescent girls in Australian schools' *Roeper Review* vol. 17, no. 3, pp. 195–7.

Lee, L. 2000 'Teachers' conceptions of giftedness: what does it mean for young girls and boys?' *The Australasian Journal of Gifted Education* vol. 9, no. 2, pp. 24–32.

Lehman, E.B. and Erdwins, C.J. 1981 'The social and emotional adjustment of young, intellectually-gifted children' *Gifted Child Quarterly* vol. 25, no. 3, pp. 134–7.

Leroux, J.A. 1988 'Voices from the classroom: academic and social self-concepts of gifted adolescents' *Journal for the Education of the Gifted* vol. 11, no. 3, pp. 3–18.

Leroux, J.A. and Levitt-Perlman, M. 2000 'The gifted child with attention deficit disorder: an identification and intervention challenge' *Roeper Review* vol. 22, no. 3, pp. 171–6.

LeVine, E.S. and Kitano, M.K. 1998 'Helping young gifted children reclaim their strengths' in *The young gifted child: potential and promise, an anthology* ed. J.F. Smutny, Hampton Press, Cresskill, NJ, pp. 282–94.

LeVine, E.S. and Tucker, S. 1986 'Emotional needs of gifted children: a preliminary, phenomenological view' *The Creative Child and Adult Quarterly* vol. 11, no. 3, pp. 156–65.

Lewis, J.D. and Knight, H.V. 2000 'Self-concept in gifted youth: an investigation employing the Piers–Harris subscales' *Gifted Child Quarterly* vol. 44. no. 1, pp. 45–53.

Lewis, M. and Louis, B. 1991 'Young gifted children' in *Handbook of gifted education* eds N. Colangelo and G.A. Davis, Allyn & Bacon, Boston, MA, pp. 365–81.

Lewis, R.B., Kitano, M.K. and Lynch, E.W. 1992 'Psychological intensities in gifted adults' *Roeper Review* vol. 15, no. 1, pp. 25–31.

Li, A.K.F. and Adamson, G. 1992 'Gifted secondary students' preferred learning style: cooperative, competitive, or individualistic?' *Journal for the Education of the Gifted* vol. 16, no. 1, pp. 46–54.

Lloyd, L. 1997 'Multi-age classes: an option for all students?' *The Australasian Journal of Gifted Education* vol. 6, no. 1, pp. 11–20.

LoCicero, K.A. and Ashby, J.S. 2000 'Multidimensional perfectionism in middle school age gifted students: a comparison to peers from the general cohort' *Roeper Review* vol. 22, no. 3, pp. 182–5.

Loeb, R.C. and Jay, G. 1987 'Self-concept in gifted children: differential impact in boys and girls' *Gifted Child Quarterly* vol. 31, no. 1, pp. 9–14.

Loehlin, J.C. 2000 'Group differences in intelligence' in *Handbook of intelligence* ed. R.J. Sternberg, Cambridge University Press, Cambridge, pp. 176–93.

Louis, B. and Lewis, M. 1992 'Parental beliefs about giftedness in young children and their relation to actual ability level' *Gifted Child Quarterly* vol. 36, no. 1, pp. 27–31.

Lovecky, D.V. 1992 'Exploring social and emotional aspects of giftedness in children' *Roeper Review* vol. 15, no. 1, pp. 18–25.

—— 1994a 'Exceptionally gifted children: different minds' *Roeper Review* vol. 17, no. 2, pp. 116–20.

—— 1994b 'The moral gifted child in a violent world' *Understanding Our Gifted* vol. 6, no. 3, p. 3.

—— 1998 'Spiritual sensitivity in gifted children' *Roeper Review* vol. 20, no. 3, pp. 178–83.

Lowrie, T. 1998 'Developing metacognitive thinking in young children: a case study' *Gifted Education International* vol. 13, no. 1, pp. 23–7.

Lubinski, D. 2003 'Exceptional spatial abilities' in *Handbook of gifted education* 3rd edn, eds N. Colangelo and G.A. Davis, Allyn & Bacon, Boston, MA, pp. 521–32.

Lubinski, D., Benbow, C.P. and Sanders, C.E. 1993 'Reconceptualizing gender differences in achievement among the gifted' in *Interna-tional handbook of research and development of giftedness and talent* eds K.A. Heller, F.J. Mönks and A.H. Passow, Pergamon, Oxford, pp. 693–708.

Luftig, R.L. and Nichols, M.L. 1991 'An assessment of the social status and perceived personality and school traits of gifted students by non-gifted peers' *Roeper Review* vol. 13, no. 3, pp. 148–53.

Lupowski, A.E. 1984 'Gifted students in rural school do not *have* to move to the city' *Roeper Review* vol. 7, no. 1, pp. 13–16.

Luscombe, A. and Riley, T.L. 2001 'An examination of self-concept in academically gifted adolescents: do gender differences occur?' *Roeper Review* vol. 24, no. 1, pp. 20–2.

Lynd-Stevenson, R.M. and Herne, C.M. 1999 'Perfectionism and depressive affect: the pros and cons of being a perfectionist' *Personality and Individual Differences* vol. 26, no. 3, pp. 549–62.

Macleod, R. 2004 'Gifted girls: so much to do, so little time' in *Gifted and talented: New Zealand perspectives* 2nd end, eds D. McAlpine and R. Moltzen, Kanuka Grove Press, Palmerston North, pp. 483–99.

MacNaughton, G. 2003 *Shaping early childhood learners, curriculum and contexts* Open University Press, Berkshire.

MacNaughton, G. and Williams, G. 1998 *Techniques for teaching young children: choices in theory and practice* Longman, Sydney.

Maker, C.J. 1996 'Identification of gifted minority students: a national problem, needed changes and a promising solution' *Gifted Child Quarterly* vol. 40, no. 1, pp. 41–50.

Maker, C.J. and Nielson, A.B. 1995 *Teaching models in education of the gifted* 2nd edn, Pro-Ed, Austin, TX.

Maker, C.J. and Schiever, S.W. 1989 'Purpose and organization of the volume' in *Critical issues in gifted education: defensible programs for cultural and ethnic minorities* eds C.J. Maker and S. W. Schiever, Pro-Ed, Austin, TX, pp. xv–xix.

Maddux, C.D., Scheiber, L.M. and Bass, J.E. 1982 'Self-concept and social distance in gifted children' *Gifted Child Quarterly* vol. 26, no. 2, pp. 77–81.

Manaster, G.J., Chan, J.C., Watt, C. and Wiehe, J. 1994 'Gifted adolescents' attitudes toward their giftedness: a partial replication' *Gifted Child Quarterly* vol. 38, no. 4, pp. 176–8.

Manaster, G.J. and Powell, P.M. 1988 'A framework for understanding gifted adolescents' psychological maladjustment' *Roeper Review* vol. 6, no. 1, pp 70–3.

Maree, J.G. and Ebersöhn, L. 2002 'Emotional intelligence and achievement: redefining giftedness?' *Roeper Review* vol. 16, no. 3, pp. 261–73.

Mares, L. 1991 *Young gifted children* Hawker Brownlow Education, Melbourne.

—— 1997 'Personality characteristics and achievement: how parents can help' in *Parents as lifelong teachers of the gifted* eds B.A. Knight and S. Bailey, Hawker Brownlow Education, Melbourne, pp. 49–61.

Mares, L. and Byles, J. 1994 *One step ahead: early admission of, and school provisions for, gifted infants* Hawker Brownlow Education, Melbourne.

Marsh, H.W. 1990 'The structure of academic self-concept: the Marsh/Shavelson model' *Journal of Educational Psychology* vol. 82, no. 4, pp. 623–36.

Marsh, H.W., Byrne, B.M. and Shavelson, R.J. 1988 'A multifaceted academic self-concept: its hierarchical structure and its relation to academic achievement' *Journal of Educational Psychology* vol. 80, no. 3, pp. 366–80.

Marsh, H.W., Chessor, D., Craven, R. and Roche, L. 1995 'The effects of gifted and talented programs on academic self-concept: the big fish strikes again' *American Educational Research Journal* vol. 32, no. 2, pp. 285–319.

Marsh, H.W. and Craven, R.G. 1998 'The big fish little pond effect, optimal illusions, and misinterpretations: a response to Gross (1997)' *The Australasian Journal of Gifted Education* vol. 7, no. 1, pp. 6–15.

Martin, A.J. 2002 'Motivating the gifted and talented: lessons from research and practice' *The Australasian Journal of Gifted Education* vol. 11, no. 2, pp. 26–34.

Maslow, A.H. 1968 *Toward a psychology of being* 2nd edn, Van Nostrand, Princeton, NJ.

Matthews, M. 1992 'Gifted students talk about cooperative learning' *Educational Leadership* vol. 50, no. 2, pp. 48–50.

Mauk, J.E., Reber, M. and Batshaw, M.L. 1997 'Autism and other pervasive developmental disorders' in *Children with disabilities* 4th edn, ed. M.L. Batshaw, MacLennan & Petty, Sydney, pp. 425–47.

Maxwell, E. 1998 ' "I can do it myself!": reflections on early self-efficacy' *Roeper Review* vol. 20, no. 3, pp. 183–7.

Mayer, J.D., Perkins, D.M., Caruso, D.R. and Salovey, P. 2001 'Emotional intelligence and giftedness' *Roeper Review* vol. 23, no. 3, pp. 131–7.

McAlpine, D. and Moltzen, R. eds 2004 *Gifted and talented: New Zealand perspectives* 2nd edn, Kanuka Grove Press, Palmerston North.

McBride, N. 1992 'Early identification of the gifted and talented students: where do teachers stand?' *Gifted Education International* vol. 8, no. 1, pp. 19–22.

McClelland, R., Yewchuk, C. and Mulcahy, R. 1991 'Locus of control in underachieving and achieving gifted students' *Journal for the Education of the Gifted* vol. 14, no. 4, pp. 380–92.

McCluskey, K.W., Baker, P.A. and Massey, K.J. 1996 'A twenty-four year longitudinal look at early entrance to kindergarten' *Gifted and Talented International* vol. 11, no. 2, pp. 72–5.

McCoach, D.B. and Siegle, D. 2003 'The structure and function of academic self-concept in gifted and general education students' *Roeper Review* vol. 25, no. 2, pp. 61–5.

McCord, J. 1993 'Conduct disorder and antisocial behaviour: some thoughts about processes' *Development and Psychopathology* vol. 5, pp. 321–9.

McKenzie, J.A. 1986 'The influence of identification practices, race and SES on the identification of gifted students' *Gifted Child Quarterly* vol. 30, no. 2, pp. 93–5.

McLoughlin, J.A. and Lewis, R.B. 2001 *Assessing special students* 5th edn, Merrill Prentice Hall, Upper Saddle River, NJ.

McNemar, Q. 1964 'Lost: our intelligence? Why?' *American Psychologist* vol. 19, no. 12, pp. 871–82.

Meador, K. 1996 'Meeting the needs of young gifted students' *Childhood Education* vol. 72, no. 5, pp. 6–9.

Melson, G.F., Ladd, G.W. and Hsu, H-C. 1993 'Maternal support networks, maternal cognitions, and young children's social and cognitive development' *Child Development* vol. 64, no. 5, pp. 1401–17.

Mendaglio, S. 1994 'Gifted sensitivity to criticism' *Gifted Child Today* vol. 17, no. 3, pp. 24–5.

—— 1995a 'Children who are gifted/ADHD' *Gifted Child Today* vol. 18, no. 4, pp. 37–40.

—— 1995b 'Sensitivity among gifted persons: a multi-faceted perspective' *Roeper Review* vol. 17, no. 3, pp. 169–73.

Milgram, R.M. and Hong, E. 1999 'Multipotential abilities and vocational interests in gifted adolescents: fact or fiction?' *International Journal of Psychology* vol. 34, no. 2, pp. 81–93.

Miller, M. 1991 'Self-assessment as a specific strategy for teaching the gifted learning disabled' *Journal for the Education of the Gifted* vol. 14, no. 2, pp. 178–88.

Miller, N.B., Silverman, L.K. and Falk, R.F. 1994 'Emotional development, intellectual ability, and gender' *Journal for the Education of the Gifted* vol. 18, no. 1, pp. 20–38.

Moltzen, R. 2004a 'Characteristics of gifted children' in *Gifted and talented: New Zealand perspectives* 2nd edn, eds D. McAlpine and R. Moltzen, Kanuka Grove Press, Palmerston North, pp. 67–92.

—— 2004b 'Underachievement' in *Gifted and talented: New Zealand perspectives* 2nd edn, eds D. McAlpine and R. Moltzen, Kanuka Grove Press, Palmerston North, pp. 371–400.

Montgomery, D. 1996 *Educating the able* Cassell, London.

—— 2001 'Teaching the more able: an update' *Gifted Education International* vol. 15, no. 3, pp. 262–80.

Moon, S.M. 2003 'Counseling families' in *Handbook of gifted education* 3rd edn, eds N. Colangelo and G.A. Davis, Allyn & Bacon, Boston, MA, pp. 388–402.

Moon, S.M., Kelly, K.R. and Feldhusen, J.F. 1997 'Specialized counseling services for gifted youth and their families: a needs assessment' *Gifted Child Quarterly* vol. 41, no. 1, pp. 16–25.

Moon, S.M., Swift, M. and Shallenberger, A. 2002 'Perceptions of a self-contained class for fourth- and fifth-grade students with high to extreme levels of intellectual giftedness' *Gifted Child Quarterly* vol. 46, no. 1, pp. 64–79.

Moore, L.C. and Sawyers, J.K. 1987 'The stability of original thinking in young children' *Gifted Child Quarterly* vol. 31, no. 3, pp. 126–9.

Morelock, M.J. 1996 'Perspectives of giftedness: on the nature of giftedness and talent: imposing order on chaos' *Roeper Review* vol. 19, no. 1, pp. 4–12.

Morelock, M.J. and Morrison, K. 1996 *Gifted children have talents too: multi-dimensional programmes for the gifted in early childhood* Hawker Brownlow Education, Melbourne.

Morgan, H. 1996 'An analysis of Gardner's theory of multiple intelligences' *Roeper Review* vol. 18, no. 4, pp. 263–9.

Moss, E. 1990 'Social interaction and metacognitive development in gifted preschoolers' *Gifted Child Quarterly* vol. 34, no. 1, pp. 16–20.

—— 1992 'Early interactions and metacognitive development of gifted preschoolers' in *To be young and gifted* eds P.S. Klein and A.J. Tannenbaum, Ablex, Norwood, NJ, pp. 278–318.

Mosteller, F., Light, R.J. and Sachs, J.A. 1996 'Sustained inquiry in education: lessons from skill grouping and class size' *Harvard Educational Review* vol. 66, no. 4, 797–842.

Mruk, C.J. 1999 *Self-esteem: research, theory and practice* 2nd edn, Free Association Books, London.

Naglieri, J.A. and Kaufman, J.C. 2001 'Understanding intelligence, giftedness and creativity using the PASS theory' *Roeper Review* vol. 23, no. 3, pp. 151–6.

Nail, J.M. and Evans, J.G. 1997 'The emotional adjustment of gifted adolescents: a view of global functioning' *Roeper Review* vol. 20, no. 1, pp. 18–21.

National Association for the Education of Young Children (NAEYC) 1988 'NAEYC position statement on standardized testing of young children 3 through 8 years of age' *Young Children* vol. 43, no. 3, pp. 42–7.

National Association for the Education of Young Children (NAEYC) and the National Association of Early Childhood Specialists in State Departments of Education (NAECS/SDE) 1991 'Guidelines for appropriate curriculum content and assessment in programs serving children ages 3 through 8' *Young Children* vol. 46, no. 3, pp. 21–38.

Neihart, M. 1999 'The impact of giftedness on psychological well-being: what does the empirical literature say?' *Roeper Review* vol. 22, no. 1, pp. 10–17.

—— 2000 'Gifted children with Asperger's syndrome' *Gifted Child Quarterly* vol. 44, no. 4, pp. 222–30.

—— 2002a 'Gifted children and depression' in *Social and emotional development of gifted children: what do we know?* eds M. Neihart, S.M. Reis, N.M. Robinson and S.M. Moon, National Association for Gifted Children, Washington, DC, pp. 93–101.

—— 2002b 'Delinquency and gifted children' in *Social and emotional development of gifted children: what do we know?* eds M. Neihart, S.M. Reis, N.M. Robinson and S.M. Moon, National Association for Gifted Children, Washington, DC, pp. 103–12.

—— 2002c 'Risk and resilience in gifted children: a conceptual frame-work' in *Social and emotional development of gifted children: what do we know?* eds M. Neihart, S.M. Reis, N.M. Robinson and S.M. Moon, National Association for Gifted Children, Washington, DC, pp. 113–122.

Neihart, M., Reis, S.M., Robinson, N.M. and Moon, S.M. eds 2002 *Social and emotional development of gifted children: what do we know?* National Association for Gifted Children, Washington, DC.

Neisworth, J.T. and Bagnato, S.J. 1992 'The case against intelligence testing in early intervention' *Topics in Early Childhood Special Education* vol. 12, no. 1, pp. 1–20.

Nevo, B. 1994 'Definitions, ideologies, and hypotheses in gifted education' *Gifted Child Quarterly* vol. 38, no. 4, pp. 184–6.

Nidiffer, L.G. and Moon, S.M. 1994 'Serving the gifted dyslexic and gifted at risk: using differentiated-integrated curricula and enrichment' *Our Gifted Children* vol. 2, no. 8, pp. 39–43.

Niebrzydowski, L. 1997 'Influences which promote high-level attainment in children of pre-school age' *High Ability Studies* vol. 8, no. 2, pp. 179–88.

Nielsen, M.E. and Mortorff-Albert, S. 1989 'The effects of special education service on the self-concept and school attitude of learning disabled/gifted students' *Roeper Review* vol. 12, no. 1, pp. 29–36.

Noble, K.D., Subotnik, R.F. and Arnold, K.D. 1999 'To thine own self be true: a new model of female talent development' *Gifted Child Quarterly* vol. 43, no. 4, pp. 140–9.

Norman, A.D., Ramsay, S.G., Roberts, J.L. and Martray, C.R. 2000 'Effect of social setting, self-concept, and relative age on the social status of moderately and highly gifted students' *Roeper Review* vol. 23, no. 1, pp. 34–9.

Olszewski, P., Kulieke, M.J. and Willis, G. 1987 'Changes in the self-perceptions of gifted students who participate in rigorous academic programs' *Journal for the Education of the Gifted* vol. 10, no. 4, pp. 287–303.

Olszewski-Kubilius, P. 2002 'A summary of research regarding early entrance to college' *Roeper Review* vol. 24, no. 3, pp. 152–7.

Olszewski-Kubilius, P., Kulieke, M.J. and Krasny, N. 1988 'Personality dimensions of gifted adolescents: a review of the empirical literature' *Gifted Child Quarterly* vol. 32, no. 4, pp. 347–52.

Oram, G.D., Cornell, D.G. and Rutemiller, L.A. 1995 'Relations between academic aptitude and psychosocial adjustment in gifted program students' *Gifted Child Quarterly* vol. 39, no. 4, pp. 236–44.

Orange, C. 1997 'Gifted students and perfectionism' *Roeper Review* vol. 20, no. 1, pp. 39–41.

Orlick, T. 1982 *The second cooperative sports and games book* Pantheon, New York.

Parker, W. 1996 'Psychological adjustment in mathematically gifted students' *Gifted Child Quarterly* vol. 40, no. 3, pp. 154–61.

Parker, W. and Adkins, K.K. 1995 'Perfectionism and the gifted' *Roeper Review* vol. 17, no. 3, pp. 173–6.

Parker, W. and Mills, C.J. 1996 'The incidence of perfectionism in gifted students' *Gifted Child Quarterly* vol. 40, no. 4, pp. 194–9.

Passow, A.H. and Frasier, M.M. 1996 'Toward improving identification of talent potential among minority and disadvantaged students' *Roeper Review* vol. 18, no. 3, pp. 198–202.

Patrick, C.L. 1990 'Motivating the gifted under-achiever: unleashing potential' in *The challenges of excellence: a vision splendid: selected papers from the 8th world conference on gifted and talented children* eds S. Bailey, E. Braggett and M. Robinson, Australian Association for the Education of the Gifted and Talented, Wagga Wagga, NSW, pp. 170–5.

—— 2000 'Genetic and environmental influences on the development of cognitive abilities: evidence from the field of developmental behavior genetics' *Journal of School Psychology* vol. 38, no. 1, pp. 79–108.

Patton, J.M. 1992 'Assessment and identification of African-American learners with gifts and talents' *Exceptional Children* vol. 59, no. 2, pp. 150–9.

Patton, M.M. and Kokoski, T.M. 1996 'How good is your early childhood science, mathematics, and technology program?: strategies for extending your curriculum' *Young Children* vol. 51, no. 5, pp. 38–44.

Paulson, F.L., Paulson, P.R. and Meyer, C.A. 1991 'What makes a portfolio a portfolio?' *Educational Leadership* vol. 48, no. 5, pp. 60–3.

Paulus, P. 1984 'Acceleration: more than grade skipping' *Roeper Review* vol. 7, no. 2, pp. 98–100.

Pendarvis, E. and Howley, A. 1996 'Playing fair: the possibilities of gifted education' *Journal for the Education of the Gifted* vol. 19, no. 2, pp. 215–33.

Penney, S. and Wilgosh, L. 2000 'Fostering parent–teacher relationships when children are gifted' *Gifted Education International* vol. 14, no. 3, pp. 217–29.

Perkins, D.N., Jay, E. and Tishman, S. 1993 'Beyond abilities: a dispositional theory of thinking' *Merrill Palmer Quarterly* vol. 39, no. 1, pp. 1–21.

Perleth, C., Lehwald, G. and Browder, C.S. 1993 'Indicators of high ability in young children' in *International handbook of research and development of giftedness and talent* eds K.A. Heller, F.J. Mönks and A.H. Passow, Pergamon, Oxford, pp. 283–310.

Perry, D. and Bussey, K. 1984 *Social development* Prentice Hall, Englewood Cliffs, NJ.

Peters, W.A.M., Grager-Loidl, H. and Supplee, P. 2000 'Underachievement in gifted children and adolescents: theory and practice' in *International handbook of giftedness and talent* 2nd edn, eds K.A. Heller, F.J. Mönks, R.J. Sternberg and R.F. Subotnik, Pergamon, Oxford, pp. 609–20.

Peterson, J. 1993 'Peeling off the elitist label: smart politics' *Gifted Child Today* vol. 16, no. 2, pp. 31–3.

Peterson, J.S. and Rischar, H. 2000 'Gifted and gay: a study of the adolescent experience' *Gifted Child Quarterly* vol. 44, no. 4, pp. 231–46.

Pfeiffer, S.I. 2001 'Emotional intelligence: popular but elusive construct' *Roeper Review* vol. 23, no. 3, pp. 138–42.

Phillips, D.A. 1984 'The illusion of incompetence among academically competent children' *Child Development* vol. 55, no. 6, pp. 2000–16.

—— 1987 'Socialization of perceived academic competence among highly competent children' *Child Development* vol. 58, no. 5, pp. 1308–20.

Phillips, D.A. and Howes, C. 1987 'Indicators of quality child care: review of research' in *Quality in child care: what does research tell us?* ed. D. Phillips, National Association for the Education of Young Children, Washington, DC, pp. 1–19.

Piechowski, M.M. 2003 'Emotional and spiritual giftedness' in *Handbook of gifted education* 3rd edn, eds N. Colangelo and G.A. Davis, Allyn & Bacon, Boston, MA, pp. 403–16.

Piirto, J. 1999 *Talented children and adults* 2nd edn, Merrill, Upper Saddle River, NJ.

Plomin, R. and Price, T.S. 2003 'The relationship between genetics and intelligence' in *Handbook of gifted education*, 3rd edn, eds N. Colangelo and G.A. Davis, Allyn & Bacon, Boston, MA, pp. 113–23.

Plucker, J.A. and McIntire, J. 1996 'Academic survivability in high-potential, middle school students' *Gifted Child Quarterly* vol. 40, no. 1, pp. 7–14.

Plucker, J.A. and Stocking, V.B. 2001 'Looking outside and inside: self-concept development of gifted adolescents' *Exceptional Children* vol. 67, no. 4, pp. 535–48.

Plunkett, M. 2000 'Impacting on teacher attitudes toward gifted students' *The Australasian Journal of Gifted Education* vol. 9, no. 2, pp. 33–42.

Pohl, M. 1997 *Teaching thinking skills in the primary years: a whole school approach* Hawker Brownlow Education, Melbourne.

Pope, A.W., McHale, S.M. and Craighead, E.W. 1988 *Self-esteem enhancement with children and adolescents* Pergamon, New York.

Porath, M. 1996 'Affective and motivational considerations in the assessment of gifted learners' *Roeper Review* vol. 19, no. 1, pp. 13–17.

Porteous, M.A. 1979 'A survey of the problems of normal 15-year-olds' *Journal of Adolescence* vol. 2, no. 4, pp. 307–23.

Porter, L. 1997 'A proposed model describing the realisation of gifted potential' *The Australasian Journal of Gifted Education* vol. 6, no. 2, pp. 33–43.

—— 1999 'Behaviour management practices in child care centres', unpublished doctoral dissertation, University of South Australia, Adelaide.

—— ed. 2002a *Educating young children with additional needs* Allen & Unwin, Sydney.

—— ed. 2002b *Educating young children with special needs* Paul Chapman, London/Sage, Thousand Oaks, CA.

—— 2002c 'A proposed model describing the realisation of gifted potential' in *The gifted enigma: a collection of articles* eds W. Vialle and J. Geake, Hawker Brownlow, Melbourne, pp. 326–45.

—— 2003 *Young children's behaviour: practical approaches for caregivers and teachers* 2nd edn, Elsevier, Sydney/Paul Chapman, London/Brookes, Baltimore, MD.

—— 2005 *Children are people too: a guide for parents to children's behaviour* 4th edn, East Street Publications, Adelaide.

Porter, L. and McKenzie, S. 2000 *Professional collaboration with parents of children with disabilities* Whurr, London.

Prichard, B. 1985 'Parenting gifted children—the fun, the frustration' *Gifted Child Today* no. 41, pp. 10–13.

Proctor, T.B., Black, K.N. and Feldhusen, J.F. 1986 'Early admission of selected children to elementary school: a review of the research literature' *Journal of Educational Research* vol. 80, no. 2, pp. 70–6.

Proctor, T.B., Feldhusen, J.F. and Black, K.N. 1988 'Guidelines for early admission to elementary school' *Psychology in the Schools* vol. 25, no. 1, pp. 41–3.

Pugach, M. 1988 'Special education as a constraint on teacher education reform' *Journal of Teacher Education* vol. 49, no. 3, pp. 52–9.

Pugh, G. and Selleck, D.R. 1996 'Listening to and communicating with young children' in *The voice of the child: a handbook for professionals* eds R. Davie, G. Upton and V. Varma, Falmer Press, London, pp. 120–36.

Putallaz, M. and Gottman, J.M. 1981 'An interactional model of children's entry into peer groups' *Child Development* vol. 52, no. 3, pp. 986–94.

Putallaz, M. and Wasserman, A. 1990 'Children's entry behavior' in *Peer rejection in childhood* eds S.R. Asher and J.D. Coie, Cambridge University Press, Cambridge, pp. 60–89.

Pyryt, M.C. 1996 'IQ: easy to bash, hard to replace' *Roeper Review* vol. 18, no. 4, pp. 255–8.

Pyryt, M.C. and Mendaglio, S. 1994 'The multidimensional self-concept: a comparison of gifted and average-ability adolescents' *Journal for the Education of the Gifted* vol. 17, no. 3, pp. 299–305.

Rabinowitz, M. and Glaser, R. 1985 'Cognitive structure and process in highly competent performance' in *The gifted and talented: developmental perspectives* eds F.D. Horowitz and M. O'Brien, American Psychological Association, Washington, DC, pp. 75–98.

Randall, V. 1997 'Gifted girls: what challenges do they face: a summary of the research' *Gifted Child Today* vol. 20, no. 4, pp. 42–4, 46–9.

Rea, D.W. 2000 'Optimal motivation for talent development' *Journal for the Education of the Gifted* vol. 23, no. 2, pp. 187–216.

Reid, N.A. 2004 'Evaluation of programmes' in *Gifted and talented: New Zealand perspectives* 2nd edn, eds D. McAlpine and R. Moltzen, Kanuka Grove Press, Palmerston North, pp. 425–39.

Reis, S.M. 1987 'We can't change what we don't recognize: understanding the special needs of gifted females' *Gifted Child Quarterly* vol. 31, no. 2, pp. 83–9.

—— 2002 'Gifted females in elementary and secondary school' in *Social and emotional development of gifted children: what do we know?* eds M. Neihart, S.M. Reis, N.M. Robinson and S.M. Moon, National Association for Gifted Children, Washington, DC, pp. 125–35.

Reis, S.M. and Callahan, C.M. 1989 'Gifted females: they've come a long way—or have they?' *Journal for the Education of the Gifted* vol. 12, no. 2, pp. 99–117.

Reis, S.M. and McCoach, D.B. 2000 'The underachievement of gifted students: what do we know and where do we go?' *Gifted Child Quarterly* vol. 44, no. 3, pp. 152–70.

Reis, S.M. and Moon, S.M. 2002 'Models and strategies for counseling, guidance, and social and emotional support of gifted and talented students' in *Social and emotional development of gifted children: what do we know?* eds M. Neihart, S.M. Reis, N.M. Robinson and S.M. Moon, National Association for Gifted Children, Washington, DC, pp. 251–66.

Reis, S.M. and Purcell, J.H. 1993 'An analysis of content elimination and strategies used by elementary classroom teachers in the curriculum compacting process' *Journal for the Education of the Gifted* vol. 16, no. 2, pp. 147–70.

Reis, S.M. and Renzulli, J.S. 1982 'A case for a broadened conception of giftedness' *Phi Delta Kappan* vol. 63, no. 9, pp. 619–20.

—— 1992 'Using curriculum compacting to challenge the above-average' *Educational Leadership* vol. 50, no. 2, pp. 51–7.

Reis, S.M. and Westberg, K.L. 1994 'The impact of staff development on teachers' ability to modify curriculum for gifted and talented students' *Gifted Child Quarterly* vol. 38, no. 3, pp. 127–35.

Renzulli, J.S. 1973 'Talent potential in minority group students' *Exceptional Children* vol. 39, no. 6, pp. 437–44.

—— 1982 'Dear Mr, and Mrs. Copernicus: we regret to inform you ...' *Gifted Child Quarterly* vol. 26, no. 1, pp. 11–14.

—— 1986 'The three-ring conception of giftedness: a developmental model for creative productivity' in *Conceptions of giftedness* eds R.J. Sternberg and J.E. Davidson, Cambridge University Press, Cambridge, pp. 53–92.

Renzulli, J.S. and Park, S. 2000 'Gifted dropouts: the who and the why' *Gifted Child Quarterly* vol. 44, no. 4, pp. 261–71.

Richert, E.S. 1987 'Rampant problems and promising practices in the identification of disadvantaged gifted students' *Gifted Child Quarterly* vol. 31, no. 4, pp. 149–54.

—— 1997 'Excellence with equity in identification and programming' in *Handbook of gifted education* 2nd edn, eds N. Colangelo and G.A. Davis, Allyn & Bacon, Boston, MA, pp. 75–88.

Riley, T.L. 1997 'Talking about "being gifted" with your child' *Tall Poppies* August, pp. 10–12.

Rimm, S.B. 1984 'The characteristics approach: identification and beyond' *Gifted Child Quarterly* vol. 28, no. 4, pp. 181–7.

—— 1986 *Underachievement syndrome: causes and cures* Apple Publishing, Watertown, WI.

—— 1987 'Why do bright children underachieve' *Gifted Child Today* vol. 10, no. 6, pp. 30–6.

—— 2002 'Peer pressures and social acceptance of gifted students' in *Social and emotional development of gifted children: what do we know?* eds M. Neihart, S.M. Reis, N.M. Robinson and S.M. Moon, National Association for Gifted Children, Washington, DC, pp. 13–18.

—— 2003a 'Underachievement: a national epidemic' in *Handbook of gifted education* 3rd edn, eds N. Colangelo and G.A. Davis, Allyn & Bacon, Boston, MA, pp. 424–43.

—— 2003b See *Jane win for girls: a smart girl's guide to success* Free Spirit Press, Minneapolis, MN.

Rimm, S.B. and Lovance, K.J. 1992a 'How acceleration may prevent underachievement syndrome' *Gifted Child Today* vol. 15, no. 2, pp. 9–14.

—— 1992b 'The use of subject and grade skipping for the prevention and reversal of underachievement' *Gifted Child Quarterly* vol. 36, no. 2, pp. 100–5.

Ring, B. and Shaughnessy, M.F. 1993 'The gifted label, gifted children and the aftermath' *Gifted Education International* vol. 9, no. 1, pp. 33–5.

Risemberg, R. and Zimmerman, B.J. 1992 'Self-regulated learning in gifted students' *Roeper Review* vol. 15, no. 2, pp. 98–101.

Rist, R.C. 1970 'Student social class and teacher expectations: the self-fulfilling prophecy in ghetto education' *Harvard Educational Review* vol. 40, no. 3, pp. 411–51.

Ritchhart, R. 2001 'From IQ to IC: a dispositional view of intelligence' *Roeper Review* vol. 23, no. 3, pp. 143–50.

Rivera, D.B., Murdock, J. and Sexton, D. 1995 'Serving the gifted/learning disabled' *Gifted Child Today* vol. 18, no. 6, pp. 34–7.

Robinson, A. 1990a 'Cooperation or exploitation? The argument against cooperative learning for talented students' *Journal for the Education of the Gifted* vol. 14, no. 1, pp. 9–27.

—— 2003 'Cooperative learning and high ability students' in *Handbook of gifted education* 3rd edn, eds N. Colangelo and G.A. Davis, Allyn & Bacon, Boston, MA, pp. 282–92.

Robinson, N.M. 1987 'The early development of precocity' *Gifted Child Quarterly* vol. 31, no. 4, pp. 161–4.

—— 1993 'Identifying and nurturing gifted, very young children' in *International handbook of research and development of giftedness and talent* eds K.A. Heller, F.J. Mönks and A.H. Passow, Pergamon, Oxford, pp. 507–24.

—— 1996 'Counseling agendas for gifted young people: a commentary' *Journal for the Education of the Gifted* vol. 20, no. 2, pp. 128–37.

Robinson, N.M., Lanzi, R.G., Weinberg, R.A., Ramey, S.L. and Ramey, C.T. 2002 'Family factors associated with high academic competence in former Head Start children at third grade' *Gifted Child Quarterly* vol. 46, no. 4, pp. 278–90.

Robinson, N.M. and Noble, K.D. 1991 'Social-emotional development and adjustment of gifted children' in *Handbook of special education: research and practice* eds M.C. Wang, M.C. Reynolds and H.J. Walberg, Pergamon Press, Oxford, pp. 57–76.

Robinson, N.M. and Robinson, H. 1992 'The use of standardized tests with young gifted children' in *To be young and gifted* eds P.S. Klein and A.J. Tannenbaum, Ablex, Norwood, NJ, pp. 141–70.

Robisheaux, J.A. and Banbury, M.M. 1994 'Students who don't fit the mold: identifying and educating gifted ESL students' *Gifted Child Today* vol. 17, no. 5, pp. 28; 31.

Roedell, W.C., Jackson, N.E. and Robinson, H.B. 1980 *Gifted young children* Teachers College, Columbia University, New York.

Roeper, A. 1977 'The young gifted child' *The Gifted Child Quarterly* vol. 21, no. 3, pp. 388–96.

—— 1995a 'How to help the underachieving gifted child' in *Annemarie Roeper: selected writings and speeches*, Free Spirit, Minneapolis, MN, pp. 53–7.

—— 1995b 'Parenting the gifted' in *Annemarie Roeper: selected writings and speeches*, Free Spirit, Minneapolis, MN, pp. 144–51.

Rogers, K.B. 1989 'Teachers of gifted children' *Roeper Review* vol. 11, no. 3, pp.145–50.

—— 2001 'Grouping the gifted: myths and realities' *Gifted Education Communicator* vol. 32, no. 1, pp. 20–36.

—— 2002 *Re-forming gifted education: matching the program to the child* Great Potential Press, Scottsdale, AZ.

Rogers, K.B. and Kimpston, R.D. 1992 'Acceleration: what we do vs what we do not know' *Educational Leadership* vol. 50, no. 2, pp. 58–61.

Rogers, K.B. and Span, P. 1993 'Ability grouping with gifted and talented students: research and guidelines' in *International handbook of research and development of giftedness and talent* eds K.A. Heller, F.J. Mönks and A.H. Passow, Pergamon, Oxford, pp. 585–92.

Rost, D.H. and Czeschlik, T. 1994 'The psycho-social adjustment of gifted children in middle childhood' *European Journal of the Psychology of Education* vol. 9, no. 1, pp. 15–25.

Rothman, G.R. 1992 'Moral reasoning, moral behavior, and moral giftedness: A developmental perspective' in *To be young and gifted* eds P.S. Klein and A.J. Tannenbaum, Ablex: Norwood, NJ, pp. 321–47.

Rowe, H. 1990 'Testing and evaluation of persons with handicap' in *The exceptional child: an introduction to special education* ed. S. Butler, Harcourt Brace Jovanovich, Sydney, pp. 543–68.

Rubin, Z. 1980 *Children's friendships* Harvard University Press, Boston, MA.

Runco, M.A. 1993 'Divergent thinking, creativity, and giftedness' *Gifted Child Quarterly* vol. 37, no. 1, pp. 16–22.

—— 1997 'Is every child gifted?' *Roeper Review* vol. 19, no. 4, pp. 220–4.

Rutter, M. 1985 'Resilience in the face of adversity: protective factors and resistance to psychiatric disorder' *British Journal of Psychiatry* vol. 147, pp. 598–611.

Ryan, R.M. and Deci, E.L. 1996 'When paradigms clash: comments on Cameron and Pierce's claim that rewards do not undermine intrinsic motivation' *Review of Educational Research* vol. 66, no. 1, pp. 33–8.

Sainato, D.M. and Carta, J.J. 1992 'Classroom influences on the development of social competence in young children with disabilities' in *Social competence of young children with disabilities: issues and strategies for intervention* eds S.L. Odom, S.R. McConnell and M.A. McEvoy, Paul H. Brookes, Baltimore, MD, pp. 93–109.

Sameroff, A.J. 1990 'Neo-environmental perspectives on developmental theory' in *Issues in the developmental approach to mental retardation* eds R.M. Hodapp, J.A. Burack and E. Zigler, Cambridge University Press, Cambridge, pp. 93–113.

Sankar-DeLeeuw, N. 2002 'Gifted preschoolers: parent and teacher views on identification, early admission, and programming' *Roeper Review* vol. 24, no. 3, pp. 172–7.

Sapon-Shevin, M. 1986 'Teaching cooperation' in *Teaching social skills to children: innovative approaches* 2nd edn, eds G. Cartledge and J.F. Milburn, Pergamon, New York, pp. 270–302.

—— 1987 'Explaining giftedness to parents: why it matters what professionals say' *Roeper Review* vol. 9, no. 3, pp. 180–4.

—— 1990 'Gifted education and the deskilling of classroom teachers' *Journal of Teacher Education* vol. 41, no. 1, pp. 39–48.

—— 1994 *Playing favorites: gifted education and the disruption of community* State University of New York, Albany, NY.

—— 1996a 'Beyond gifted education: building a shared agenda for school reform' *Journal for the Education of the Gifted* vol. 19, no. 2, pp. 194–214.

—— 1996b 'Including all children and their gifts within regular classrooms' in *Controversial issues confronting special education: divergent perspectives* 2nd edn, eds W. Stainback and S. Stainback, Allyn & Bacon, Boston, MA, pp. 69–80.

Sattler, J.M. 2001 *Assessment of children* 4th edn, Sattler, San Diego, CA.

Sawyer, R.N. 1988 'In defense of academic rigor' *Journal for the Education of the Gifted* vol. 11, no. 2, pp. 5–19.

Sayler, M.F. and Brookshire, W.K. 1993 'Social, emotional, and behavioral adjustment of accelerated students, students in gifted classes, and regular students in eighth grade' *Gifted Child Quarterly* vol. 37, no. 4, pp. 150–4.

Schaffer, H.R. 1998 *Making decisions about children: psychological questions and answers* 2nd edn, Blackwell, Oxford.

Schauer, G.H. 1976 'Emotional disturbance and giftedness' *Gifted Child Quarterly* vol. 20, no. 4, pp. 470–8.

Schiever, S.W. and Maker, C.J. 1997 'Enrichment and acceleration: an overview and new directions' in *Handbook of gifted education* 2nd edn, eds N. Colangelo and G.A. Davis, Allyn & Bacon, Boston, MA, pp. 113–25.

Schneider, B.H., Clegg, M.R., Byrne, B.M., Ledingham, J.E. and Crombie, G. 1989 'Social relations of gifted children as a function of age and school program' *Journal of Educational Psychology* vol. 81, no. 1, pp. 48–56.

Schraw, G. and Graham. T. 1997 'Helping gifted students develop metacognitive awareness' *Roeper Review* vol. 20, no. 1, pp. 4–8.

Schultz, R.A. 2002a 'Understanding giftedness and underachievement: at the edge of possibility' *Gifted Child Quarterly* vol. 46, no. 3, pp. 193–208.

—— 2002b 'Illuminating realities: a phenomenological view from two underachieving gifted learners' *Roeper Review* vol. 24, no. 4, pp. 203–12.

Schunk, D.H. 1987 'Peer models and children's behavioral change' *Review of Educational Research* vol. 57, no. 2, pp. 149–74.

Schwanenflugel, P.J., Stevens, T.P.M. and Carr, M. 1997 'Metacognitive knowledge of gifted children and nonidentified children in early elementary school' *Gifted Child Quarterly* vol. 41, no. 2, pp. 25–35.

Scott, M.S., Deuel, L.S., Jean-Francois, B. and Urbano, R.C. 1996 'Identifying cognitive gifted ethnic minority children' *Gifted Child Quarterly* vol. 40, no. 3, pp. 147–53.

Sears, R.R. 1977 'Sources of life satisfactions of the Terman gifted men' *American Psychologist* vol. 32, pp. 119–28.

Seeley, K. 1993 'Gifted students at risk' in *Counseling the gifted and talented* ed. L.K. Silverman, Love Publishing, Denver, CO, pp. 263–75.

Seely, A.E. 1996 *Portfolio assessment* Hawker Brownlow Education, Melbourne.

Segal, N.L. 2000 'Virtual twins: new findings on within-family environmental influences on intelligence' *Journal of Educational Psychology* vol. 92, no. 3, pp. 442–8.

Sekowski, A. 1995 'Self-esteem and achievements of gifted students' *Gifted Education International* vol. 10, no. 2, pp. 65–70.

Seligman, M.E.P. 1975 *Helplessness: on depression, development and death* W.H. Freeman & Co, San Francisco, CA.

—— 1995 *The optimistic child* Random House, Sydney.

Shaklee, B.D. 1992 'Identification of young gifted students' *Journal for the Education of the Gifted* vol. 15, no. 2, pp. 134–44.

—— 1993 'Preliminary findings of the Early Assessment for Exceptional Potential project' *Roeper Review* vol. 16, no. 2, pp. 105–9.

—— 1998 'Educationally dynamic environments for young gifted children' in *The young gifted child: potential and promise, an anthology* ed. J.F. Smutny, Hampton Press, Cresskill, NJ, pp. 358–68.

Shaklee, B.D. and Viechnicki, K.J. 1995 'A qualitative approach to portfolios: the early assessment for exceptional potential model' *Journal for the Education of the Gifted* vol. 18, no. 2, pp. 156–70.

Sharma, R. 2001 *A study of teachers' perceptions of gifted and talented children in early childhood settings* unpublished Masters thesis, The University of Western Sydney, Sydney.

Shaywitz, S.E., Holahan, J.M., Freudenheim, D.A., Fletcher, J.M., Makuch, R.W. and Shaywitz, B.A. 2001 'Heterogeneity within the gifted: higher IQ boys exhibit behaviors resembling boys with learning disabilities' *Gifted Child Quarterly* vol. 45. no. 1, pp. 16–23.

Shore, B.M. and Delcourt, M.A.B. 1996 'Effective curricular and program practices in gifted education and the interface with general education' *Journal for the Education of the Gifted* vol. 20, no. 2, pp. 138–54.

Shore, B.M. and Dover, A.C. 1987 'Metacognition, intelligence and giftedness' *Gifted Child Quarterly* vol. 31, no. 1, pp. 37–9.

Shore, B.M. and Kanevsky, L.S. 1993 'Thinking processes: being and becoming gifted' in *International handbook of research and development of giftedness and talent* eds K.A. Heller, F.J. Mönks and A.H. Passow, Pergamon, Oxford, pp. 133–48.

Siegle, D. and McCoach, D.B. 2002 'Promoting a positive achievement attitude with gifted and talented students' in *Social and emotional development of gifted children: what do we know?* eds M. Neihart, S.M. Reis, N.M. Robinson and S.M. Moon, National Association for Gifted Children, Washington, DC, pp. 237–49.

Siegle, D. and Schuler, P.A. 2000 'Perfectionism differences in gifted middle school students' *Roeper Review* vol. 23, no. 1, pp. 39–44.

Silverman, L.K. 1989a 'Invisible gifts, invisible handicaps' *Roeper Review* vol. 12, no. 1, pp. 37–42.

—— 1989b 'Personality plus: perfectionism' *Understanding Our Gifted* January, p. 11.

—— ed. 1993a *Counseling the gifted and talented* Love Publishing, Denver, CO.

—— 1993b 'The gifted individual' in *Counseling the gifted and talented* ed. L.K. Silverman, Love Publishing, Denver, CO, pp. 3–28.

—— 1994 'Perfectionism' *Gifted and Talented Children's Association Newsletter* no. 96, p. 8.

—— 1997 'Family counseling' in *Handbook of gifted education* 2nd edn, eds N. Colangelo and G.A. Davis, Allyn & Bacon, Boston, MA, pp. 382–97.

—— 1998 'Through the lens of giftedness' *Roeper Review* vol. 20, no. 3, pp. 204–10.

—— 2002 *Upside-down brilliance: the visual-spatial learner* DeLeon, Denver, CO.

—— 2003 'Gifted children with learning disabilities' in *Handbook of gifted education* 3rd edn, eds N. Colangelo and G.A. Davis, Allyn & Bacon, Boston, MA, pp. 533–43.

Silverman, L.K., Chitwood, D.G. and Waters, J.L. 1986 'Young gifted children: can parents identify giftedness?' *Topics in Early Childhood Special Education* vol. 6, no. 1, pp. 23–38.

Silverman, L.K. and Maxwell, E. 1996 *Characteristics of giftedness scale* Gifted Development Center, Denver, CO.

Sisk, D. 2002 'Spiritual intelligence: the tenth intelligence that integrates all other intelligences' *Gifted Education International* vol. 16, no. 3, pp. 208–13.

Slater, A. 1995 'Individual difference in infancy and later IQ' *Journal of Child Psychology and Psychiatry and Related Disciplines* vol. 36, no. 1, pp. 69–112.

Slavin, R.E. 1987a 'Ability grouping and student achievement in elementary schools: a best-evidence synthesis' *Review of Educational Research* vol. 57, no. 3, pp. 293–336.

—— 1987b 'Cooperative learning and the cooperative school' *Educational Leadership* vol. 45, no. 3, pp. 7–13.

—— 1990a 'Achievement effects of ability grouping in secondary schools: a best-evidence synthesis' *Review of Educational Research* vol. 60, no. 3, pp. 471–99.

—— 1991 'Are cooperative learning and 'untracking' harmful to the gifted? Response to Allan' *Educational Leadership* vol. 48, no. 6, pp. 68–71.

Smerechansky-Metzger, J.A. 1995 'The quest for multiple intelligences: using MI theory to create exciting teaching and learning experiences' *Gifted Child Quarterly* vol. 18, no. 3, pp. 12–15.

Smidt, S. 1998 *Guide to early years practice* Routledge, London.

Smith, M.D., Coleman, M., Dokecki, P.R. and Davis, E.E. 1977 'Recategorized WISC-R scores of learning disabled children' *Journal of Learning Disabilities* vol. 10, no. 7, pp. 48–54.

Smutny, J.F. 1998 *Gifted girls* Phi Delta Kappa Educational Foundation, Bloomington, IN.

—— 2001 *Stand up for your gifted child: how to make the most of kids' strengths at school and at home* Free Spirit, Minneapolis, MN.

Smutny, J.F., Veenker, K., and Veenker, S. 1989 *Your gifted child: how to recognize and develop the special talents in your child from birth to age seven* Ballantine, New York.

Smutny, J.F., Walker, S.Y. and Meckstroth, E.A. 1997 *Teaching young gifted children in the regular classroom: identifying, nurturing, and challenging ages 4–9* Free Spirit Publishing, Minneapolis, MN.

Snowden, P.L. 1995 'Educating young gifted children' *Gifted Child Today* vol. 18, no. 6, pp. 16–25, 41.

Soden, Z. 2002a 'Daily living skills' in *Educating young children with additional needs* ed. L. Porter, Allen & Unwin, Sydney, pp. 117–39.

—— 2002b 'Daily living skills' in *Educating young children with special needs* ed. L. Porter, Paul Chapman, London/ SAGE, Thousand Oaks, CA, pp. 117–39.

Solow, R. 2001 'Parents' conceptions of giftedness' *Gifted Child Today* vol. 24, no. 2, pp. 14–22.

Southern, W.T. and Jones, E.D. 1992 'The real problems with academic acceleration' *Gifted Child Today* vol. 15, no. 2, pp. 34–8.

Southern, W.T., Jones, E.D. and Fiscus, E.D. 1989 'Practitioner objections to the academic acceleration of gifted children' *Gifted Child Quarterly* vol. 33, no. 1, pp. 29–35.

Southern, W.T., Jones, E.D. and Stanley, J.C. 1993 'Acceleration and enrichment: the context and development of program options' in *International handbook of research and development of giftedness and talent* eds K.A. Heller, F.J. Mönks and A.H. Passow, Pergamon, Oxford, pp. 387–410.

Sowa, C.J. and May, K.M. 1997 'Expanding Lazarus and Folkman's paradigm to the social and emotional adjustment of gifted children and adolescents (SEAM)' *Gifted Child Quarterly* vol. 41, no. 2, pp. 36–43.

Sowa, C.J., McIntire, J., May, K.M. and Bland, L. 1994 'Social and emotional adjustment themes across gifted children' *Roeper Review* vol. 17, no. 2, pp. 95–8.

Spangler, R.S. and Sabatino, D.A. 1995 'Temporal stability of gifted children's intelligence' *Roeper Review* vol. 17, no. 3, pp. 207–10.

Spearman, C. 1927 *The abilities of man* Macmillan, New York.

Spicker, H.H. and Southern, W.T. 1998 'Early childhood giftedness among the rural poor' in *The young gifted child: potential and promise, an anthology* ed. J.F. Smutny, Hampton Press, Cresskill, NJ, pp. 147–64.

Spicker, H.H., Southern, W.T. and Davis, B.I. 1987 'The rural gifted child' *Gifted Child Quarterly* vol. 31, no. 4, pp. 155–7.

Spirito, A., Stark, L.J., Grace, N. and Stamoulis, D. 1991 'Common problems and coping strategies reported in childhood and early adolescence' *Journal of Youth and Adolescence* vol. 20, no. 5, pp. 531–44.

Stanley, G.K. and Baines, L. 2002 'Celebrating mediocrity? How schools shortchange gifted students' *Roeper Review* vol. 25, no. 1, pp. 11–13.

Stedtnitz, U. 1995 'Psychosocial dimensions of talent: some major issues' *Actualizing talent: a lifelong challenge* eds J. Freeman, P. Span and H. Wagner, Cassell, London, pp. 42–55.

Stephens, T.M. 1988 'Eliminating special education: is this the solution?' *Journal of Teacher Education* vol. 49, no. 3, pp. 60–4.

Sternberg, R.J. 1986 'Identifying the gifted through IQ: why a little bit of knowledge is a dangerous thing' *Roeper Review* vol. 8, no. 3, pp. 143–7.

—— 1988 'A three-facet model of creativity' in *The nature of creativity* ed. R.J. Sternberg, Cambridge University Press, Cambridge, pp. 125–47.

—— 1996 'Neither elitism nor egalitarianism: gifted education as a third force in American education' *Roeper Review* vol. 18, no. 4, pp. 261–3.

—— ed. 2000 *Handbook of intelligence* Cambridge University Press, Cambridge.

—— 2003 'Giftedness according to the theory of successful intelligence' in *Handbook of gifted education* eds N. Colangelo and G.A. Davis, Allyn & Bacon, Boston, MA, pp. 88–99.

Sternberg, R.J. and Davidson, J.E. 1986 'Conceptions of giftedness: a map of the terrain' in *Conceptions of giftedness* eds R.J. Sternberg and J.E. Davidson, Cambridge University Press, Cambridge, pp. 3–18.

Sternberg, R.J., Ferrari, M., Clinkenbeard, P. and Grigorenki, E.L. 1996 'Identification, instruction, and assessment of gifted children: a construct validation of a triarchic model' *Gifted Child Quarterly* vol. 40, no. 3, pp. 129–37.

Sternberg, R.J. and Grigorenko, E.L. 1993 'Thinking styles and the gifted' *Roeper Review* vol. 16, no. 2, pp. 122–30.

—— 2003 'The theory of successful intelligence as a basis for gifted education' *Gifted Child Quarterly* vol. 46, no. 4, pp. 265–77.

Sternberg, R.J. and Lubart, T.I. 1991 'An investment theory of creativity and its development' *Human Development* vol. 34, pp. 1–31.

—— 1992 'Creative giftedness in children' in *To be young and gifted* eds P.S. Klein and A.J. Tannenbaum, Ablex, Norwood, NJ, pp. 33–51.

Sternberg, R.J. and Zhang, L. 1995 'What do we mean by giftedness? A pentagonal implicit theory' *Gifted Child Quarterly* vol. 39, no. 2, pp. 88–94.

Stewart, E.D. 1981 'Learning styles among gifted/talented students: instructional technique preferences' *Exceptional Children* vol. 48, no. 2, pp. 134–8.

Stonehouse, A. 1991 *Opening the doors: child care in a multi-cultural society* Australian Early Childhood Association, Watson, ACT.

Strike, K.A. 1988 'Fairness and ability grouping' *Educational Theory* vol. 33, nos 3 and 4, pp. 125–34.

Sturgess, A. 2004 'Celebrating the square peg: gifted with specific learning disabilities' in *Gifted and talented: New Zealand perspectives* 2nd edn, eds D. McAlpine and R. Moltzen, Kanuka Grove Press, Palmerston North, pp. 401–24.

Subotnik, R.F., Karp, D.E. and Morgan, E.R. 1989 'High IQ children at midlife: an investigation into the generalizability of Terman's genetic studies of genius' *Roeper Review* vol. 11, no. 3, pp. 139–44.

Swesson, K. 1994 'Helping the gifted/learning disabled: understanding the special needs of the "twice exceptional"' *Gifted Child Today* vol. 17, no. 5, pp. 24–6.

Swiatek, M.A. 1995 'An empirical investigation of the social coping strategies used by gifted adolescents' *Gifted Child Quarterly* vol. 39, no. 3, pp. 154–61.

—— 1998 'Helping gifted adolescents cope with social stigma' *Gifted Child Today* vol. 21, no. 3, pp. 42–6.

Swiatek, M.A. and Benbow, C.P. 1991 'Ten-year longitudinal follow-up of ability-matched accelerated and unaccelerated gifted students' *Journal of Educational Psychology* vol. 83, no. 4, pp. 528–38.

Sylva, K. 1994 'School influences of children's development' *Journal of Child Psychology and Psychiatry and Related Disciplines* vol. 35, no. 1, pp. 135–70.

Tannenbaum, A.J. 1983 *Gifted children: psychological and educational perspectives* Macmillan, New York.

—— 1991 'The meaning and making of giftedness' in *Handbook of gifted education* eds N. Colangelo and G.A. Davis, Allyn & Bacon, Boston, MA, pp. 27–44.

—— 1992 'Early signs of giftedness: research and commentary' in *To be young and gifted* eds P.S. Klein and A.J. Tannenbaum, Ablex, Norwood, NJ, pp. 3–32.

—— 2003 'The meaning and making of giftedness' in *Handbook of gifted education* eds N. Colangelo and G.A. Davis, 3rd edn, Allyn & Bacon, Boston, MA, pp. 45–59.

Taplin, M. and White, M. 1998 'Parents' and teachers' perception of gifted provision' *The Australasian Journal of Gifted Education* vol. 7, no. 1, pp. 42–9.

Tardif, T.Z. and Sternberg, R.J. 1988 'What do we know about creativity?' in *The nature of creativity* ed. R.J. Sternberg, Cambridge University Press, Cambridge, pp. 429–40.

Taylor, R.L. 2000 *Assessment of exceptional students: educational and psychological procedures* 5th edn, Allyn & Bacon, Boston, MA.

Taylor, S. 2004 'Social and emotional development' in *Gifted and talented: New Zealand perspectives* 2nd edn, eds D. McAlpine and R. Moltzen, Kanuka Grove Press, Palmerston North, pp. 441–66.

Terman, L.M., Oden, M.H., Bayley, N., Marshall, H., McNemar, Q. and Sullivan, E.B. 1947 *The gifted child grows up* Stanford University Press, Stanford, CT.

Thompson, L.A. and Plomin, R. 2000 'Genetic tools for exploring individual differences in intelligence' in *International handbook of giftedness and talent* 2nd edn, eds K.A. Heller, F.J. Mönks, R.J. Sternberg and R.F. Subotnik Pergamon, Oxford, pp. 157–64.

Thurstone, L.L. 1938 'Primary mental abilities' *Psychometric Monograph No. 1* University of Chicago Press, Chicago, IL.

Tidwell, R. 1980 'A psycho-educational profile of 1,593 gifted high school students' *Gifted Child Quarterly* vol. 24, no. 2, pp. 63–8.

Tomlinson, C.A. 1996 'Good teaching for one and all: does gifted education have an instructional identity?' *Journal for the Education of the Gifted* vol. 20, no. 2, pp. 155–74.

Toll, M.F. 1993 'Gifted learning disabled: a kaleidoscope of needs' *Gifted Child Today* vol. 16, no. 1, pp. 34–5.

Tong, J. and Yewchuk, C. 1996 'Self-concept and sex-role orientation in gifted high school students' *Gifted Child Quarterly* vol. 40, no. 1, pp. 15–23.

Torrance, E.P. 1998 'Economically disadvantaged children' in *The young gifted child: potential and promise, an anthology* ed. J.F. Smutny, Hampton Press, Cresskill, NJ, pp. 95–118.

Townsend, M. 2004 'Acceleration and enrichment: a union rather than a choice' in *Gifted and talented: New Zealand perspectives* 2nd edn, eds D. McAlpine and R. Moltzen, Kanuka Grove Press, Palmerston North, pp. 289–308.

Trawick-Smith, J. 1988 '"Let's say you're the baby, OK?": play leadership and following behavior of young children' *Young Children* vol. 43, no. 5, pp. 51–9.

Tremblay, R.E., Masse, B., Perron, D., LeBlanc, M., Schwartzman, A.E. and Ledingham, J.E. 1992 'Early disruptive behavior, poor school achievement, delinquent behavior, and delinquent personality: longitudinal analyses' *Journal of Consulting and Clinical Psychology* vol. 60, no. 1, pp. 64–72.

Tucker, B. and Hafenstein N.L. 1997 'Psychological intensities in young gifted children' *Gifted Child Quarterly* vol. 41, no. 3, pp. 66–75.

Tyler-Wood, T. and Carri, L. 1993 'Verbal measures of cognitive ability: the gifted low SES student's albatross' *Roeper Review* vol. 16, no. 2, pp. 102–5.

Udvari, S.J. and Schneider, B.H. 2000 'Competition and the adjustment of gifted children: a matter of motivation' *Roeper Review* vol. 22, no. 4, pp. 212–6.

Vallerand, R.J., Gagné, F., Senécal, C. and Pelletier, L.G. 1994 'A comparison of the school intrinsic motivation and perceived competence of gifted and regular students' *Gifted Child Quarterly* vol. 38, no. 4, pp. 172–5.

van Boxtel, H.W. and Mönks, F.J. 1992 'General, social, and academic self-concepts of gifted adolescents' *Journal of Youth and Adolescence* vol. 21, no. 2, pp. 169–86.

Van Tassel-Baska, J. 1992 'Educational decision making on acceleration and grouping' *Gifted Child Quarterly* vol. 36, no. 2, pp. 68–72.

—— 1995 'The development of talent through curriculum' *Roeper Review* vol. 18, no. 2, pp. 98–102.

—— 2003 'What matters in curriculum for gifted learners: reflections on theory, research and practice' in *Handbook of gifted education* 3rd edn, eds N. Colangelo and G.A. Davis, Allyn & Bacon, Boston, MA, pp. 174–183.

Van Tassel-Baska, J., Olszewski-Kubilius, P. and Kulieke, M. 1994 'A study of self-concept and social support in advantaged and disadvantaged seventh and eighth grade gifted students' *Roeper Review* vol. 16, no. 3, pp. 186–91.

Vaughn, V.L., Feldhusen, J.F. and Asher, J.W. 1991 'Meta-analyses and review of research on pull-out programs in gifted education' *Gifted Child Quarterly* vol. 35, no. 2, pp. 92–8.

Veenman, S. 1995 'Cognitive and noncognitive effects of multigrade and multi-age classes: a best-evidence synthesis' *Review of Educational Research* vol. 65, no. 4, pp. 319–81.

—— 1996 'Effects of multigrade and multi-age classes reconsidered' *Review of Educational Research* vol. 66. no. 3, pp. 323–40.

Vespi, L. and Yewchuk, C. 1992 'A phenomenological study of the social-emotional characteristics of gifted learning disabled children' *Journal for the Education of the Gifted* vol. 16, no. 1, pp. 55–72.

Vestal, J.C. 1993 'Parental advocacy for the gifted' *Gifted Child Today* vol. 16, no. 2, pp. 8–13.

Vialle, W. 1997 'Giftedness from a multiple intelligence perspective' in *Parents as lifelong teachers of the gifted* eds B.A. Knight and S. Bailey, Hawker Brownlow Education, Melbourne, pp. 31–42.

Vialle, W., Ashton, T., Carlon, G. and Rankin, F. 2001 'Acceleration: a coat of many colours' *Roeper Review* vol. 24, no. 1, pp. 14–19.

Vialle, W. and Geake, J. eds 2002 *The gifted enigma: a collection of articles* Hawker Brownlow, Melbourne.

Vialle, W. and Konza, D. 1997 'Testing times: problems arising from misdiagnosis' *Gifted Education International* vol. 12, no. 1, pp. 4–8.

Wallace, B. 1983 'Meeting the needs of exceptionally able children' *Gifted Education International* vol. 2, no. 1, pp. 4–7.

—— 1986a 'Curriculum enrichment then curriculum extension: differentiated educational development in the context of equal opportunities for all children' *Gifted Education International* vol. 4, no. 1, pp. 4–9.

—— 1986b 'Creativity: some definitions: the creative personality; the creative process; the creative classroom' *Gifted Education International* vol. 4, no. 2, pp. 68–73.

Ward, C.D. 1996 'Adult intervention: appropriate strategies for enriching the quality of children's play' *Young Children* vol. 51, no. 3, pp. 20–5.

Webb, J.T. 1993 'Nurturing social-emotional development of gifted children' in *International handbook of research and development of giftedness and talent* eds K.A. Heller, F.J. Mönks and A.H. Passow, Pergamon, Oxford, pp. 525–38.

Webb, J. and Latimer, D. 1997 'ADHD and children who are gifted' *Gifted* April 1997, pp. 21–2.

Webb, J.T., Meckstroth, E.A. and Tolan, S.S. 1991 *Guiding the gifted child: a practical source for parents and teachers* Hawker Brownlow Education, Melbourne.

Wechsler, D. 1958 *The measurement and appraisal of adult intelligence* 4th edn, Williams & Wilkins, Baltimore, MD.

—— 2002 *WPPSI-III: technical and interpretive manual* The Psychological Corporation, San Antonio, TX.

—— 2003 WISC-IV: *administration and scoring manual* The Psychological Corporation, San Antonio, TX.

Weill, M.P. 1987 'Gifted/learning disabled students: their potential may be buried treasure' *The Clearing House* vol. 60, no. 8, pp. 341–3.

Weinfeld, R., Barnes-Robinson, L., Jeweler, S. and Shevitz, B. 2002 'Academic programs for gifted and talented/learning disabled students' *Roeper Review* vol. 24, no. 4, pp. 226–33.

Westberg, K.L., Archambault, F.X. Jr. and Brown, S.W. 1997 'A survey of classroom practices with third and fourth grade students in the United States' *Gifted Education International* vol. 12, no. 1, pp. 29–33.

Westberg, K.L., Archambault, F.X Jr., Dobyns, S.M. and Salvin, T.J. 1993 'The classroom practices observation study' *Journal for the Education of the Gifted* vol. 16, no. 2, pp. 120–46.

Westby, E. 1997 'Do teachers value creativity?' *Gifted and Talented International* vol. 12, no. 1, pp. 15–17.

White, C.S. 1985 'Alternatives for assessing the presence of advanced intellectual abilities in young children' *Roeper Review* vol. 8, no. 2, pp. 73–5.

White, K.R. 1982 'The relation between socioeconomic status and academic achievement' *Psychological Bulletin* vol. 91, no. 3, pp. 461–81.

White, L. 2000 'Underachievement of gifted girls: causes and solutions' *Gifted Education International* vol. 14, no. 2, pp. 125–32.

Whitmore, J.R. 1980 *Giftedness, conflict, and underachievement* Allyn & Bacon, Boston, MA.

—— 1981 'Gifted children with handicapping conditions: a new frontier' *Exceptional Children* vol. 48, no. 2, pp. 106–14.

—— 1986 'Understanding a lack of motivation to excel' *Gifted Child Quarterly* vol. 30, no. 2, pp. 66–9.

Whitmore, J.R. and Maker, C.J. 1985 *Intellectual giftedness in disabled persons* Pro-ed, Austin, TX.

Willard-Holt, C. 1994 'Strategies for individualising instruction in regular classrooms' *Roeper Review* vol. 17, no. 1, pp. 43–5.

Wilson, P. 1996 *Challenges and changes in policy and thinking in gifted education in Australia* Hawker Brownlow Education, Melbourne.

Winebrenner, S. 2001 *Teaching gifted kids in the regular classroom* 2nd edn, Free Spirit Press, Minneapolis, MN.

Wingenbach, N. 1998 'The gifted-learning-disabled child: in need of an integrative education' in *The young gifted child: potential and promise, an anthology* ed. J.F. Smutny, Hampton Press, Cresskill, NJ, pp. 190–8.

Winner, E. 1996 *Gifted children: myths and realities* Basic Books, New York.

Winner, E. and Martino, G. 2000 'Giftedness in non-academic domains: the case of the visual arts and music' in *International handbook of giftedness and talent* 2nd edn, eds K.A. Heller, F.J. Mönks, R.J. Sternberg and R.F. Subotnik, Pergamon, Oxford, pp. 95–110.

—— 2003 'Artistic giftedness' in *Handbook of gifted education* 3rd edn, eds N. Colangelo and G.A. Davis, Allyn & Bacon, Boston, MA, pp. 335–49.

Wood, K.J. and Care, E. 2002 'The relationship between perfectionism and intelligence in a group of adolescents' *The Australasian Journal of Gifted Education* vol. 11, no. 1, pp. 22–9.

Wolery, M. 1996 'Using assessment information to plan intervention programs' in *Assessing infants and preschoolers with special needs* 2nd edn, eds M. McLean, D.B. Bailey Jr and M. Wolery, Merrill, Englewood Cliffs, NJ, pp. 491–518.

Wolfle, J. 1989 'The gifted preschooler: developmentally different, but still 3 or 4 years old' *Young Children* vol. 44, no. 3, pp. 41–8.

—— 1990 'Gifted preschoolers within the classroom' *Early Child Development and Care* vol. 63, pp. 83–93.

—— 1991 'Underachieving gifted males: are we missing the boat?' *Roeper Review* vol. 13, no. 4, pp. 181–4.

Worrell, F.C. 2002 'Global and domain-specific self-concepts in academically talented Asian American and White adolescents' *Gifted Child Quarterly* vol. 46, no. 2, pp. 90–7.

Worthen, B.R. and Spandel, V. 1991 'Putting the standardized test debate in perspective' *Educational Leadership* vol. 48, no. 5, pp. 65–9.

Wright, L. and Borland, J.H. 1993 'Using early childhood developmental portfolios in the identification and education of young, economically disadvantaged, potentially gifted students' *Roeper Review* vol. 15, no. 4, pp. 205–10.

Wright, L. and Coulianos, C. 1991 'A model program for precocious children: Hollingworth preschool' *Gifted Child Today* vol. 14, no. 5, pp. 24–9.

Wright, P.B. and Leroux, J.A. 1997 'The self-concept of gifted adolescents in a congregated program' *Gifted Child Quarterly* vol. 41, no. 3, pp. 83–94.

Yarborough, B.H. and Johnson, R.A. 1983 'Identifying the gifted: a theory–practice gap' *Gifted Child Quarterly* vol. 27, no. 3, pp. 135–8.

Yewchuk, C.R. 1995a 'The "mad genius" controversy: implications for gifted education' *Journal for the Education of the Gifted* vol. 19, no. 1, pp. 3–29.

—— 1995b 'Eminence and emotional stability: historical and contemporary views' *Gifted and Talented International* vol. 10, no. 2, pp. 52–5.

Yewchuk, C.R. and Lupart, J.L. 2000 'Inclusive education for gifted students with disabilites' in *International handbook of giftedness and talent* 2nd edn, eds K.A. Heller, F.J. Mönks, R.J. Sternberg and R.F. Subotnik, Pergamon, Oxford, pp. 659–70.

Zentall, S.S. 1989 'Self-control training with hyperactive and impulsive children' in *Cognitive-behavioral psychology in the schools* eds J.N. Hughes and R.J. Hall, Guilford, New York, pp. 305–46.

Zentall, S.S., Moon, S.M., Hall, A.M. and Grskovic, J.A. 2001 'Learning and motivational characteristics of boys with AD/HD and/or giftedness' *Exceptional Children* vol. 67, no. 4, pp. 499–519.

Zohar, D. and Marshall, I. 2000 *SQ – spiritual intelligence: the ultimate intelligence* Bloomsbury, London.

Zorman, R 1997 'Eureka: the cross-cultural model for identification of hidden talent through enrichment' *Roeper Review* vol. 20, no. 1, pp. 54–61.

INDEX

ability grouping 88
– *see also* grouping
Aborigines 37, 172, 175
abuse of children 100
academic
   giftedness 8, 12, 138, 190, 214, 215
   self-esteem **69–70**, 86
acceleration 70–1, 146, 148, 151, 153–4,
   168, 171, 196, 202, 215
acceptance 61, **67–8**, 78
accidents 17
acclaim 31, 43
accountability 162, 200
accuracy of tests 125
acknowledgment 74–5, 101
ADHD 14, **186–9**
adjustment, emotional **55–60**, 129, 152,
   154–5, 209–10
   sibling 210–12
adoption 81
adult business 16, 93, **95–6**, 212
advocacy
   by parents 67–8, 133, 161, **217–19**
   by teachers 203, 204
   role of assessment 123
affection 79–80
age 56, 71, 85
   of entry to school 168
   – *see also* early entry

aggression 79, 83, 88, 89, 184, 188, 193,
   194
aims of programs 142–3
alertness 13–14, 185
altruism 43
anti-bias curriculum 174–5
anti-intellectualism 109, 171, 213
anxiety 48, 50–1, 184, 186, 210, 212
arousal 13
   – *see also* alertness
artistic skills 4, 11, **18**, 35
Asperger syndrome 180, 186
assertiveness 90, 101
assessment **121–40**, 202, 203, 215
   authentic/naturalistic 118, 134
   defined 122
   of dual exceptionalities 194–5
assimilationism 172
asynchronous development 51, 94, 208
attachment 19, 26
attention
   deficit disorders 14, **186–9**
   skills 13–14, 35, 133, 144–5, 181, 186,
   187
   – *see also* concentration
attitudes
   to giftedness 107–19, 177
   to learning 114, 115, 148, 218
   – *see also* dispositions

attributions 92, **99,** 160, 166, 171, 210
auditory sequential learning 9, 15, 183, 213
authentic assessment 118, 131, 134
authoritarian discipline 91, 101, 102, 212
authority of parents 52, 208
  – *see also* leadership
autonomy 58, 61–2, 73, 91
  issues for gifted 92–5
  ways to promote
  – *see also* independence
average 30, 110, 136

Bayley Mental Scales 132
behavioural difficulties 52, 93–4, 133, 145,
  152, **212**
  and ADHD 189
  of disadvantaged children 176
  of children with disabilities 181, 184,
  190, 192–3
behaviourism 99–100
belonging 61, 78, 81
bias
  cultural 174
  of assessment 126
  of parental assessment 128–9
  of research samples 5–6, 55–6
big-fish-little-pond effect 72
boredom 52, 78, 144, 152
  – *see also* challenge
bossing children 93, 102, 212
bottom-up programming 142
boy code 167, 170
boys 4, 85–6, **165–9,** 203, 213, 215, 221
  – *see also* gender
bubble, teaching 147
bullying 171, 210

career counselling 152, 171, **221–2**
ceilings, test 139, 190
central auditory processing disorder 184
central nervous system 41–2
challenge 47, 66
  and emotional giftedness 21
  and stress 51
  behavioural 52, 68
  cultural 175

intellectual 4, 13, 16, 40, 69, 72, 140,
  144, 145, 160
  for children with disabilities 187, 192,
  193, 194, 195
  social 53, 54, 79, 80, 97
checklists 131–2
choice 73, 95 102, 160, 196
classification 123
  – *see also* labelling
climate 160, 171, 174, 192, 195, 213
coaching 64, 73, 76
  social skills 87, **89–90**
collaboration with parents 108–9, 140,
  161–3, 175, 193, 200, 202, 203
Columbus group 36
common sense 207, 211
community 117, 143
compacting, curriculum 151
companionship 80
competence 73, 91, 142
competition 24, 74, 81, 84, 88, 170, 171,
  194, 210, 214
  – *see also* rivalry
compliance 100, 167
  – *see also* conformity, nonconformity
comprehension – *see* language skills
comprehensive assessment 122, 133
computers 161, 178, 196, 212
concentration skills 4, 14, 26, 58, 94, 124,
  144–5
  – *see also* attention
conformity 170, 191, 220
  – *see also* nonconformity
conservative definitions 23, 28–9, 38, 136,
  201
considerate behaviour 100–1, 102
consultants 202–3
contract 101–2
convergent thinking 33, 35, 133
cooperation 101, 143
cooperative
  activities 87–8, 171, 174–5
  learning 88, 194
coping 8, 51, 57, 63, **97,** 102, 152, 219
counselling 152, 171
  for parents 172

creative adults 170
  mental health of 54
creativity 9, 15, **31–2**, 35, 142, 146, 215
  and culture 174
  and gender 168, 170
  and recognition of giftedness 130, 138
critical thinking 143, 159, 196
culture 55, 65, 78
  and definition of giftedness 36–8, 125
  and programming 141, 147, 148, 165
  effects on identification 125–6, 129,
    130, 133, 173
culture-fair assessment 126, 135, 173–4
culture of romance 167
curvilinear model 59

Dabrowski, K. 48–9
daydreaming 16, 186
defensibility of assessment 123–4
definition
  assessment 122
  giftedness 4, 23, 28–38, 125,136,
    200–1
  intelligence 30, 34
  health 37
  talent 4, 28
  testing 122
delinquency 53, 170
democracy 112
dependency 92
  – *see also* independence
depression 50, 193
developmental appropriateness 218
  of assessment 122
  of placement 152
diabetes 188
differentiation of curriculum 134–161,
    195–7, 202
  content 145, 148–56, 195–6
  environment 145, 146–8
  process 145, 156–60, 196–7
  product 146, 161, 198
disabilities 4, 69, 115, 128, 133, 167, 176,
    180–9, 208, 215
  characteristics of giftedness and
    disabilities 183–4

disadvantage, educational 116, 123, 126,
    133, **165–79**, 201, 203
  – *see also* dual exceptionalities
discipline 93–4
  – *see also* guidance
discrepancy of assessment 134–5, 138–9
discrimination 172
disengagement of teachers 145
dispositions 35, 42, 73, **142–3**, 159, 201, 204
divergent thinking 32, 33, 34
diversity 146, 171, 174, 195, 201
drawing skills 3, 18
dressing 3, 15, 26
drop out 48, 52–3
drug use 51
dual exceptionalities 69, 189, 208, 214
  – *see also* disabilities
dysfunctional thinking 97–9
dyslexia 180
dysgraphia 180

ear infections 128, 184
early entry 27, 118, 147, **151–3, 154–5**,
    171, 203, 216
early exit 152
eating disorders 48
educational fraud 118
effort 75, 92, 160, 182, 191, 220
egalitarianism 112
egocentricity 11, **18–19**, 20
elitism 110, 112, 175, 207
emotional
  adjustment **55–60**, 129, 152, 154–5,
    209–10
  characteristics 12, **20–23**, 36
  disturbance 51, 54–5
  intelligence/giftedness 21, 41, 207, 214,
    215
  needs model 60–2
empathy 11, **18–19**, 20, 58, 81, 101
engagement 3, 143, 193, 196, 201, 204
English 4, 126, 175
enrichment 148, 202
entity view of giftedness 43, 92, 219–20
environmental stimulation 6, 8, 27, 38, **40**,
    42

equity 116, 179
  of assessment 125–6
  – *see also* elitism
escape 100
ethics 145, 202, 203
evaluation 43, 200, **203–4**
excellence 76
exceptional giftedness **23–5**, 36, 57, 83,
  134, 139–40, 156
  – *see also* extreme, highly gifted
existential awareness 12
expectations
  of children 4, 50, 68, 70, 72, **76–7**, 94,
    144, 146, 167, 180, 184, 190, 194,
    195, 209, 222
  of minority cultural children 173, 174
  of others 82–3
  of teachers 218
experimentation 60, 100
exploration 40
extension 151, 217
extracurricular activities 175, 192, 196,
  218
extreme giftedness 85
  – *see also* exceptional giftedness
extroverts 86–7

failure 70, 72, 75–6, 88, 99, 146, 171, 184,
  191, 195
false negatives/positives 125
family functioning 51, 53, 71, 191
fatigue 7, 8, 58, 182, 195
favouritism 207, 211
fears 12, 21
feedback 42, 64, **73–7**, 157, 159, 160, 175,
  204, 209–10
fetal alcohol syndrome 41
fine motor skills 17, 22, 138, 154 161
  – *see also* handwriting
flitting 3
food intolerances 189
fraud, educational 118
friendships 11
  benefits of 78–9
  degrees of 88–9
  – *see also* social skills

frustration 22, 58, 145, 184, 194, 212
fulfilment 4, 43, 62, 192
fun 62, 79, 160

games 11, 19, 67, 80–1
  cooperative 87–8
gap year 152–3
Gardner, H. 33–4, 40–1, 111
general ability 30, 34, 35
genetics 27, 41–2, 62, 169, 207
gender **165–9**, 213
  and learning disabilities 166, 182
  and recognition of giftedness 166
  and self-esteem 71–2
  and social adjustment 85–6
giftedness, definition 4, **28–38**
girls 4, 70, 83, 85–6, 92, **165–9**, 191, 203,
  213, 221
  – *see also* gender
goal orientation 93
goals – *see* aims, mission
grade skipping 152, 153–6, 171, 211, 215
grammar 17
group size 146
grouping 147–8, 178, 202
growing down 96
guidance of behaviour 93, **99–102**, 212
Guilford, J.P. 32–3, 34

habituation 14
handwriting 12, 138, 161, 183, 187, 190,
  195, 197, 222
helicopter parents 207
helplessness 51, 58, 92, 93
  – *see also* locus of control
high-IQ definition 29–31
high maintenance children 67, 78, 80, 208
highly gifted 130
  – *see also* exceptional giftedness
hobbies 222
holistic learning 10, 35, 37, 185, 213
Hollingworth, L. 47
home schooling 25, 214, 215
homophobia 167, 221
homosexuality 221
hothousing 28, 43, 115, 135

humour 10, 17, 58, 183
hyperactivity 14, **186–9**
  – *see also* overactivity

ideal self 64, 65, 68, 75
identification by provision model 126–8
identification of giftedness 110
  cultural influences on 125–6
  difficulty of 4–5, 115
  effects of 84, 115, 129, 209
  teacher accuracy 129–30
imaginary playmates 19
imposter syndrome 69
impulsivity 9, 13, 51, 52, 184, 186, 188,
  194
incremental view of giftedness 43, 220
inclusive education 118–9
independence 9, 15, 58, 91, 92, 178, 194,
  215
information processing skills 30, 35, 38,
  42
injustice 172, 175, 179
integrated content 148, 217
intelligence, defined 30, 34
intellectual disability 186
intellectual giftedness
  compared with academic 8, 12, 138
  signs of 6–10, 12–16
intellectual peers 19, 26, 52, 67, 82, **84–5**,
  86, 115, 152, 155, 168, 177, 188
intensity 12, 21, 36, 47
interdisciplinary content 148
interests of children 11, 148–9, 152, 157,
  167, 183, 189, 196, 221
interpersonal skills 33–4, 41
intimacy 79, 80, 81, 89, 168, 172, 221
intrapersonal skills 33–4
introversion
  of children 80, **81–2**, 86–7
  of parents 68
involuntary minorities 169, 172
IQ tests 132–4
  advantages of 133–4, 135
  and learning disabilities 181
  limitations of 111, 133, 135
isolation 80, 85, 168, 186

justice 12, 20, 58, 172, 175, 179
  – *see also* moral reasoning

Kaufman Assessment Battery 132
kinaesthetic intelligence 33
  – *see also* motor, physical skills

label, gifted 4, 110, 123, 180
  effects of 84, 115, 129, 209, 210
  underachievement 190
language skills 10, **16–17**, 33, 35, 41
leadership 11, 20, 43, 58, 79, **83–4**, 90,
  169, 170, 171, 215
  by parents 93, 102, 212
learning difficulties 63, 69, 110, 191, 203,
  205
  – *see also* disabilities
learning disabilities – *see* disabilities
learning style 8–10, **13–16**, 75
  of gifted children with disabilities 183,
  191, 194, 196
  of exceptionally gifted 24–5
  of minority children 175
levels of abilities 23, 24, 29
  and self-esteem 59
  and social adjustment 84–5
liberal definitions 28–9, 38, 136, 201
lies 20, 221
limbic system 47
listening to children 76, 93, 95
locus of control 9, 14, 49, 51, 57, 58, 91,
  92, 95, 97, 99, 210, 213
  and minority children 174
  and underachievement 191
loneliness 78, 79, **81**

macho culture 168, 169
mandate 200
Maori 37, 172, 173
Maslow, A. 60
mastery orientation 92
  – *see also* locus of control
mathematics 12, 33, 35, 59, 70, 85, 138,
  151, 181, 183, 190
  – *see also* numeracy
McCarthy scales 132

mean 136
 – *see also* average
mediated learning/play 156–8
memory 7, 32, 33, 35, 42, 183, 196
mental age 137
mental illness 53–4, 176
mental retardation 186
mentors 168, 171, 213
metacognitive skills 7, 9, 17, 35, 48, 69,
   143, 144, **159**
   and attention deficit disorders 186
   and autonomy 94–5
   and identification 130–1
minimal brain dysfunction 186
minority cultures 169, 172–5, 178, 204
   and underachievement 169–70, 190
   – *see also* culture
mission 201
mistakes 40, 58, 68, **75–7**, 95, 99, 146,
   210
mode 30
Montessori schooling 215
mood disturbances 48
moral reasoning 12, 20, 49, 70, 209, 217
motivation 13, 74, 131, 143, 152, **159–60**,
   193
   and learning disabilities 182, 196
   and underachievement 192
motor skills 10, **17**, 138
multi-age grouping 147–8
multicultural curricula 174–5
multipotentiality 222
multisensory experiences 174
multiple capacities/intelligences 29, **33–4**,
   111
musical skills 11, **18**, 33

national resources rationale 112, 201
naturalistic intelligence 33
neurosis 48
nomination by teachers 129–31, 174
nonconformity 9, 12, 15, 23, 25, 53, 58,
   170, 190, 195, 208, 217
normality 30, 136, 217, 220
normed tests 132
   – *see also* IQ tests

numeracy skills 8, 12, 24, 32
 – *see also* mathematics

observation
   by parents 128–9, 162
   by teachers 129–31, 134
obstacles to achievement 38, 43
occupational therapy 185
open-ended activities 118, 150–1
outcomes 201, 203–4
overactivity 181
   – *see also* ADHD, hyperactivity
overexcitability 48–9

pace 146, 148, 151
parent, collaboration with 108–9, 140,
   161–3, 175, 193, 200, 202, 203
parent observation 128–9
parenting gifted children 206–23
parents'
   educational history 162, 208
   role 56, 108–9
   values 206–7
   wishes 154
partial acceleration 153–4
peer
   pressure 71, 82, 166–7, 191
   tutoring 24–5, 82
percentile ranks 136–7
perfectionism 12, 22, 48, 50, 51, 58, **68–9**,
   76, 99, 166, 191, 209
performance IQ 154, 181
perseverance 9, 42, 144, 171, 191, 196
persistence 212
   – *see also* perseverance
philosophy 201
phonics 16, 183, 187
physical
   self-esteem 70
   skills 35
   – *see also* motor skills
placement 50, 55, 67, 72, 147
pluralism 172
policy 141, **199–204**, 216
popularity 70, 81, 90, 168, 170
portfolios 131

potency 91, 95, 96–7, 101
potential 33, 62, 112, **113**, 201, 209, 222
  of women 166
  and underachievement 190, 192
poverty 4, 116, 125, 168, **175–8**, 191, 203
pragmatism 122
praise 64, **74–5**
preferential treatment 211
  – *see also* favouritism
prefrontal lobes 47, 188
prejudice
  about giftedness 107, **108–9**, 129
  cultural 174
priorities 111–2
procedures 200
prodigies 25, 129
products 73–4
professionalism 109, 162
provisions for gifted 115–9
psychiatric disturbances 48, 53–4
pull-out programs 117, 147, 175, 214
punishment 100, 102, 212

qualitative debate 35–6

Raven's matrices 174
reading 12, 13, 16, 41, 154, 190
  and exceptional giftedness 24, 25
  difficulties 180–1
rebellion 100
recall 7
  – *see also* memory
reflectiveness 13
reflexes 17
reformist programming 141–2, 165
rehearsal 9, 16, 94
reliability, test 123–4, 133
reliance on adults 143–4
  – *see also* independence
remedial assistance 196
  – *see also* special education
repetition 16, 26, 150
resilience 63, **96–7**, 102, 176
resistance 93, 100
resources
  for children 146

  for teachers 203
  – *see also* support
responsibility 93, **95–6**, 102, 200, 212
responsiveness 12, 21, 36, 47
retaliation 100
rewards 14, 74, 100, 212
rigour 143, 145
rivalry 160, 211
  – *see also* competition
role of parents 56, 200, 208–9
Robin Hood effect 88
romance, culture of 167
romantic relationships 220–1
rural children 85, 177–8

sample bias 5–6, 55–6
savants 25
schooling options 214–17
screening 125
segregated gifted programs 116–7
self-actualisation 43, 62
  – *see also* fulfilment
self-concept 12, 21, 64, 65, 67, 75, 82
  multifaceted 69–70
self-efficacy 91, 96–7, 144, 169
  – *see also* locus of control
self-esteem 21–2, 61, **66–72**, 79, 91,
    133
  and gender 70, 71–2, 167
  and underachievement 191
  causes of low 72–3
  comparison of low and healthy 66
  definition of 65–6
  effects of grouping on 147
  evidence about 49–50
  of children with disabilities 182, 184,
    193
  of parents 208
  routes to healthy 73–7
self-confidence 70, 73, 79
self-perception 65
sensitivity 12, 13, 21, 22, 36, 47, 51, 58
  of boys 71, 168
  sensory 185
sensory integration difficulties 185,
    186

separation from parents 3, 26, 168, 215
sequential skills 9, 15, 128, 181, 183, 184, 213
sexual
  abuse 100
  identity 221
  knowledge 220–21
  maturity 153
siblings 84, 94, 191, 207
  adjustment 210–12
signs of advanced development 5–23
single-sex schooling 215
size
  of groups/class 146, 178
  of schools 215
sleeping 14
social
  adjustment methods 86–90
  confidence 86
  difficulties 48, 53
  issues for gifted 79–84, 153
  play 87
  self-esteem 70–1
  skills 18–20, **89–90**, 194
solitary play 11, 81, 87
solitude 86–7, 102
spatial learning 10, **15–16**, 32, 33, 35, 138–9, 171, 181, 183, 213
special education 110, **113–4**, 116–7, 201, 215
Spearman, C. 30
speech and language skills 10, **16–17**
  – *see also* verbal giftedness
spelling 24, 183, 197, 222
spiritual intelligence 22, 170, 175
  – *see also* existential awareness
sport 20, 24, 55, 70, 109, 155, 170
stamina 155
standard deviations 136, 181
Stanford-Binet 132, 136, 138
status 93, 94, 171, 221
Steiner schools 215
stereotypes
  about giftedness 56, 129–30
  cultural 173, 174
  gender 20, 166, 167, 168, 169, 171

socioeconomic 176
stigma 72, 83, 165, 214
streaming 147
stress 50, 55, 57, 58, 93, 94, 95–6, 102, 176, 194
style, learning 8–10, **13–16**, 75
  of gifted children with disabilities 183, 191, 194, 196
  of exceptionally gifted 24–5
  of minority children 175
subject acceleration 153–4
submission 100
suicide 48, 51–2
support for teachers 107, 119, 177
syllogistic reasoning 57

tact 83, 90, 135
tailored activities 149–50
talent, definition 4, 28
teacher-directed programming 141
teacher identification/nomination 25,
Terman, L. 47, 112
testing, defined 112
  – *see also* IQ testing
themes of play 146, **148–9**
theory 201–2
thinking skills 152, 158–9
  – *see also* metacognitive skills
Thurstone, L.L. 32, 34
tiered
  activities 151
  products 161
time allowances 146, 197
top-down programming 141
tourist curriculum 174
tracking 147
training
  of assessors 126
  of teachers 107, 109, 119, 162, 201, 202, 203
transitions 203, 217
transformist programming 141–2
trophy wives 221

underachievement 52, 53, 114–5, 190–3, 203

causes 191–2
and ADHD 189
and gender 169
and self-esteem 71
understanding giftedness, children 52, 219–20
utility of assessment 123

validity, tests 123–4
values 42, 53, 171, 172, 204, 206–7, 217, 221
verbal giftedness 16–17, 57, 82–3, 85, 93, 139, 183, 221
verbal IQ 154, 181
visual-spatial learning 10, **15–16**, 32, 35, 138–9, 183, 196, 213

vocabulary 16, 24, 25
voluntary minorities 169

Waldorf schooling 215
wait and hover technique 89
Wechsler, D. 30, 132
Wechsler IQs 136, 138
WISC-IV 132–3
wisdom 30
workaholics 68
working memory 7, 188
worries 50
WPPSI-III 132, 133
writing 12, 138, 161, 183, 187, 190, 195, 197, 222